WRITING CREATIVE NONFICTION

Theodore A. Rees Cheney

WRITING CREATIVE NONFICTION

*How to Use Fiction Techniques
to Make Your Nonfiction
More Interesting, Dramatic – and Vivid*

TEN SPEED PRESS
Berkeley, California

1☉
TEN SPEED PRESS
P.O. Box 7123
Berkeley, California 94707

Text design by Nancy Austin
Composition by Hal Hershey
Cover design by Fifth Street Design Associates

Library of Congress Cataloging-in-Publication Data
Cheney, Theodore A. Rees (Theodore Albert Rees), 1928 -
 Writing creative nonfiction / Theodore Rees Cheney.
  p. cm.
 Includes bibliographical references and index.
 ISBN 0-89815-411-1
 1. Reportage literature—Technique. 2. Nonfiction novel—Technique. 3. Narration
 (Rhetoric) I. Title.
PN3377.5.R45C46 1990
808'.02—dc20

First Printing, 1991

Manufactured in the United States of America

1   2   3   4   5   -   95   94   93   92   91

DEDICATED TO
CAPOTE, TALESE, & WOLFE

*They had the early courage to break away
and report the world to us in words more vivid,
more dramatic, more accurate.*

ACKNOWLEDGMENTS

I acknowledge here the women who helped, each in her own way, with the production of this book: The woman who made my life possible and creative, Ruth Rees Cheney, my mother; Dorothy Bates Cheney, the woman who has allowed me the necessary freedom to write, my wife; Carol Cartaino, who saw the potential for this book when others wondered and worried; and Nancy Dibble, who edited the original book with so much dedication, patience, and understanding.

CONTENTS

Apply the ideas from the previous chapter to descriptions of how people live in groups and do what the groups do. Report on the realities of their lives after observing: the games they play, their fads of fashion and food, the specific prices they pay for items they can't possibly live without, and bits of captured conversations.

Zoom in on the individual's life, either to give us insight into its essence, or to provide us insight into the larger group of which the individual seems typical. Give us specific concrete details: gestures, clothes, favorite drinks, hobbies; characteristic behavior patterns; even his or her dialect, jargon, specialized knowledge.

Creative nonfiction writers recognize that no technique so quickly nor so thoroughly "involves" the reader as does captured conversation (the nonfiction equivalent of dialog). Their writing abounds in either direct or indirect quotes of conversations—whether from interviewing or eavesdropping. People also reveal themselves through their monologs (speeches, lectures, long answers, etc.) and through other "logs" of their lives: journals, diaries, memoirs, letters, telegrams, and even through their graffiti. These sources are earnestly sought by writers.

The writer must decide just which angle of approach to use, and then what point of view (or multiple points) to adopt for a particular piece written for a particular purpose aimed at a specific audience. Should the writer adopt the first or third person point of view? When is it all right to switch points of view? What is "voice" in this context and how do you let it enter your creative nonfiction?

ONE

CREATIVE
NONFICTION

The lead in my proposal to write this book read: "Some of the most exciting and creative writing today is happening within what has begun to be called "the literature of fact." Today's readers want quality nonfiction even more than they want quality fiction—witness the prominence of nonfiction books on the best-seller lists and in book club selections over the past twenty years, and the predominance of nonfiction articles in magazines. People may want facts, but they want those facts presented interestingly, i.e., creatively."

Since that time, William Zinsser has added to the third edition of his best-selling book, *On Writing Well*, a new chapter, "Nonfiction As the New American Literature." In that chapter he points out (as general editor of the Book-of-the-Month Club) how the emphasis in that first of the great book clubs has changed over the years. When it began in the 1920s, it provided most readers their easiest access to American literature, which was primarily fiction. After World War II, he reports, we turned overnight into a "fact-minded nation." The club's members demanded more and more nonfiction, and the club provided it.

Quality Paperback Book Club (a subsidiary of BOMC) has come on the scene more recently, and it, too, emphasizes nonfiction. Looking for another indicator, I reviewed the *New York Times Book Review* for a three-Sunday period. In those three issues, they reviewed sixteen books under "Fiction and Poetry." Under "Nonfiction," they reviewed sixty-one books. I knew intuitively that the number of nonfiction titles would be higher, but I was surprised by the numbers. Nonfiction is, indeed, the new American literature.

1

Ronald Weber, professor of American Studies at Notre Dame, has done a great service for all of us interested in creative nonfiction through his research and books on the subject (*The Reporter As Artist: A Look at the New Journalism Controversy* and *The Literature of Fact*). In the latter book, he had this to say about the popularity of this genre:

> Another way of thinking about the popularity of nonfiction writing was to see it as a literary response to the emergence of a new kind of mass audience. In his review of Tom Wolfe's first book, Dwight Macdonald, taking note of the book's broad sales, suggested that it was not so much addressed to the nonreading young, as the title (*The Kandy-Kolored Tangerine-Flake Streamline Baby*) might have indicated, but to a large and growing public that feels it really should take an interest and is looking for guidance as to what is, currently, "The Real Thing." This was not the old middlebrow public but a liberally educated public that had been through the required surveys of literature yet was caught up in a contemporary fascination with the new and topical.
>
> With the new nonfiction, the audience received information but received it entertainingly, with familiar literary trimmings. It received an up-to-date factual fiction that abandoned the dreariness of day-to-day journalism yet did not fly off in the strange and complex ways of Barth, Borges, Barthelme, and other fabulists. What the audience was offered, in other words, had both the authority of literature and the authority of fact, and so had broad appeal for a new mass audience with college-trained tastes that sought "culture" yet wanted to be in on what was happening now. From this perspective, it was suggested that nonfiction had begun to function in something of the same way for an educated middle class as the realistic novel had for an emerging economic middle class—it brought the news and brought it engagingly.

What is this genre of writing labeled variously as *personal journalism, literary journalism, dramatic nonfiction, the new journalism, parajournalism, the new nonfiction, the nonfiction novel, the literature of fact*, etc.? My feeling is that since it *is* nonfiction, and since everyone agrees that it is written *creatively*, it can best be labeled *creative nonfiction*.

Creative nonfiction requires the skill of the storyteller and the research ability of the reporter. Creative nonfiction writing doesn't just report the facts—it delivers the facts in ways that move people toward a deeper understanding of the topic. Creative nonfiction writers must become authorities on the subject of their articles or books. They must not only understand all the facts, but also see beyond them to discover their underlying meaning. And then they must dramatize that meaning in an interesting, evocative, informative way.

Conventional nonfiction writers have usually presumed that nonfiction's purpose was not to entertain but to inform, to teach, to lecture. The latest research into how we learn, however, has found that we learn best when we are at the same time entertained, when there is joy and pleasure in the learning. The strongest, most lasting memories are those embedded in emotion. Creative nonfiction writers inform their readers better by making the reading experience vivid and enjoyable.

Short of a valid definition of creative nonfiction, let's listen to several comments by knowledgeable writers as they circle the field trying to home in on just what is this more-or-less-new, more-or-less-old, method of writing nonfiction.

Dan Wakefield said in an early book about the new journalism (*Between the Lines*):

> I am writing now for those readers—including myself—who have grown increasingly mistrustful of and bored with anonymous reports about the world, whether signed or unsigned, for those who have begun to suspect what we reporters of current events and problems so often try to conceal: that we are really individuals after all, not all-knowing, all-seeing Eyes but separate, complex, limited, particular "I"s.

Gay Talese, one of the first and best practitioners of creative nonfiction, wrote in his book (*Fame and Obscurity*) that collected many of his early articles:

> The new journalism, though often reading like fiction, is not fiction. It is, or should be, as reliable as the most reliable reportage, although it seeks a larger truth than is possible through the mere compilation of verifiable facts, the use of direct quotations, and adherence to the rigid organizational style of the older form. The new journalism allows, demands in fact, a more imaginative approach to reporting, and it permits the writer to inject himself into the narrative if he wishes, as many writers do, or to assume the role of a detached observer, as other writers do, including myself.

Tom Wolfe reports in his book (*The New Journalism*) that he entered that strange arena with an article in *Esquire*: "There Goes (Varoom! Varoom!) That Kandy-Kolored (Thphhhhhh!) Tangerine-Flake Streamline Baby (Rahghhh!) Around the Bend (Brummmmmmmmmm)..." Some people said that it was sort of a short story, but Mr. Wolfe says in *The New Journalism*:

> This article was by no means like a short story, despite the use of scenes and dialogue. I wasn't thinking about that at all. It is hard to say what it was like. It was a garage sale, that piece ... vignettes, odds and ends of scholarship, bits of memoir, short bursts of sociology, apostrophes, epithets, moans, cackles, anything that came into my head, much of it thrown together in a rough and awkward way. That was its virtue. It showed me the possibility of there being something "new" in journalism. What interested me was not simply the discovery that it was possible to write accurate non-fiction with techniques usually associated with novels and short stories. It was that—plus. It was the discovery that it was possible in non-fiction, in journalism, to use any literary device, from the traditional dialogisms of the essay to stream-of-consciousness, and to use many different kinds simultaneously, or within a relatively short space ... to excite the reader both intellectually and emotionally. I am not laying all those gladiolas on that rather curious first article of mine, you understand. I'm only talking about what it suggested to me.

Seymour Krim, in his article collected in *Reporter As Artist*, said: "The American realistic short story from Stephen Crane to post—John O'Hara has now been inherited by the imaginative newspaperman, like [Jimmy] Breslin, and all the independent probing of reality that the best native literary artists of the past have achieved can now be tried by a creative reporter without undue sweat."

Mr. Krim went on later in that article to say:

> ... there is a definite advantage to the newspaperman in recreating reality if he uses every conceivable literary avenue open to him; for his job, depending on the intensity of his sense of mission, is to penetrate ever more deeply into the truth of every story—and this can only be done if he has the instruments of language, narrative know-how, character-development, etc., that until now have always been associated with fiction.

Ronald Weber, in his introduction to *Reporter As Artist*, wrote:

So the New Journalism, on both its literary and journalistic sides, comes down to personal writing, with wide variations in how personal the writer chooses to get and how deeply an artistically distorting mechanism his individual consciousness becomes. And therein, in its essential "I" quality, is a good part of the explanation for the attention that has greeted the New Journalism—as well as for much of the criticism it has drawn.

One way of thinking about the popularity of the New Journalism is to say that it's "I" writing for an "I" time, personal writing for an age of personalism. . . . The New Journalism, one might suggest, Wolfe's and everyone else's, is merely a symptom of the times—the journalist unmasking his shadow and often unburdening his soul in a period when everyone else is doing the same.

Ken Metzler, professor of journalism at the University of Oregon, wrote in an article ("Show, Don't Tell: How to Write Dramatic Nonfiction") for the *Ragan Report*:

It was the novelist E. M. Forster who said a story can have only one virtue: that of making its audience want to know what happens next. Conversely, he said a story can have but one fault: that of making the audience *not* want to know what happens next. He was talking of fiction, of course. But of late journalists have begun to pay more heed to the theories and techniques of the creative writer. The result has been the infusion of the drama and tension of fiction into the veracity of fact. . . . The point is that you can give your own writing extraordinary power by applying some of the fundamentals of dramatic literature to writing factual articles . . . . The advantages of writing nonfiction in "story" form are many. You get the reader involved. You make the reader want to know what happens next. You get the reader closer to the action or the personalities that you portray. And, perhaps, you even come a little closer to "truth."

Professor Metzler doesn't know it, but that very article triggered in my mind the idea to write this book. Many of us are indebted to him for his excellent books, including *Creative Interviewing*, and now I'm in his debt for such an inspiring article in the *Ragan Report* (a weekly survey of ideas and methods for communication executives). His survey was certainly of an idea whose time had come—and it came to me from him.

In his book *The Literary Journalists*, Dr. Norman Sims wrote:

Literary journalists bring themselves into their stories to greater or lesser degrees and confess to human failings and emotions. Through their eyes, we watch ordinary people in crucial contexts.... These authors understand and convey feeling and emotion, the inner dynamics of cultures. Like anthropologists and sociologists, literary reporters view cultural understanding as an end. But, unlike such academics, they are free to let dramatic action speak for itself.... Whatever we name it, the form is indeed both literary and journalistic and it is more than the sum of its parts.

I don't think it worth worrying too much about, but many people like to spend time arguing over whether this kind of writing is "new" or "old." It's been practiced more and more frequently since the 1960s, but that was not the very beginning. Before that, people had written nonfiction with occasional forays into the world of fiction to enliven their writing, but they didn't usually adapt more than one or two so-called fiction techniques. Tom Wolfe says that it probably got its start back in the eighteenth and nineteenth centuries with the travel writers who gave personal accounts of their travels, particularly as they went around visiting various countries within the empires of the day. Later, Wolfe says, some people deliberately set off on adventurous travels in order to come home and write about them in their autobiographies.

In our own country, journalist Jack London was applying many fiction techniques to enliven his reporting. Donald McQuade and Robert Atwan, in *Popular Writing in America*, reprinted an article in London wrote for *Collier's Weekly* in May 1906, "The Story of an Eye Witness" (an account of the San Francisco earthquake):

...By Wednesday afternoon, inside of twelve hours, half the heart of the city was gone. At that time I watched the vast conflagration from out on the bay. It was dead calm. Not a flicker of wind stirred. Yet from every side wind was pouring in upon the city. East, west, north, and south, strong winds were blowing upon the doomed city. The heated air rising made an enormous suck. Thus did the fire of itself build its own colossal chimney through the atmosphere. Day and night, this dead calm continued, and yet, near to the flames, the wind was often half a gale, so mighty was the suck.

Shelley Fisher Fishkin, in her excellent study of imaginative writers who began as reporters of fact (*From Fact to Fiction*), wrote about Ernest

Hemingway: "What continued to interest Hemingway throughout his writing career, in fiction as well as journalism, was the search for the precisely correct concrete image that would evoke a specific scene vividly and economically. His reports on the Spanish civil war as a correspondent for the North American Newspaper Alliance (NANA), for example, were filled with highly evocative images that helped the reader sense the experience of a city under siege, of a people plunged into battle. Fishkin quotes from Hemingway's "On the Shelling of Madrid" as an example:

> MADRID—At the front, a mile and a quarter away, the noise came as a heavy coughing grunt from the green pine-studded hillside opposite. There was only a gray wisp of smoke to mark the insurgent battery position. Then came the high inrushing sound, like ripping of a bale of silk. It was all going well over into the town, so, out there, nobody cared. But in town, where all the streets were full of Sunday crowds, the shells came with the sudden flash that a short circuit makes and then the roaring crash of granite-dust. During the morning, twenty-two shells came into Madrid.
>
> They killed an old woman returning home from the market, dropping her in a huddled black heap of clothing, with one leg, suddenly detached, whirling against the wall of an adjoining house.
>
> They killed three people in another square, who lay like so many torn bundles of old clothing in the dust and rubble when the fragments of the "155" had burst against the curbing...

Hemingway was writing his dispatches with these fictional techniques back in 1937. That NANA dispatch was reprinted in Hemingway's *By-Line*.

Fishkin's book also reports on Theodore Dreiser: "Looking back on his experience as a 'feature man' in Pittsburgh, Dreiser recalled that his 'mood or word pictures about a summer storm, a spring day, a visit to the hospital, the death of an old switchman's dog, the arrival of the first mosquito...gave me my first taste of what it means to be a creative writer....'"

Obviously, creative nonfiction writing is not brand new, but changes come slowly. It is now pretty much accepted as legitimate, provided it stays within ethical limits applied to journalism (see the chapter on Ethics). Just how old, or how new, is of interest to academic people studying such evolutions and revolutions within literature, but this book concerns itself more with how to write in this interesting way to make our modern readers more receptive.

If it's true that creative nonfiction gains every day in its popularity with the average, reasonably well-educated public, why might this be? In addition to the fact that most people today want to read factual material presented in a vivid, interesting way, they also turn to nonfiction because it's not only truer than fiction, it's often stranger than fiction. Seymour Krim wrote in 1966:

> Reality itself has become so extravagant, in its contradictions, absurdities, violence, speed of change, science-fictional technology, weirdness, and constant unfamiliarity, that just to match what is with accuracy takes the conscientious reporter into the realms of the Unknown—into what used to be called "the world of the imagination."
>
> And yet *that* is the wild world we all live in today when we just try to play it straight.
>
> If living itself often seems more and more like a nonstop LSD trip... what fertile truths can most fiction writers tell us about a reality that has far outraced them at their own game? How can they compete with the absurd and startling authorship of each new hour?

Barbara La Fontaine, a senior editor at *Sports Illustrated*, wrote an article in *Harper's* magazine (December 1986) germane to this point. After giving her readers a number of illustrations about how truth is stranger than fiction, she quotes an article found in the London *Daily Express*: "Kitchen Cuddlers Floored—Human Catapult Ends Wife's Kissing Session."

> Lonely husband Graham Street called on his wife to kiss and make up, but when he saw her cuddling a man in the kitchen, he flew off the handle... literally.
>
> He went into the garden and knocked up a makeshift springboard from a plank and two car tyres. Then he launched himself head-first through the window.
>
> He touched down in the sink, and slid gently to the floor. Then he took a knife from the table drawer and held it to his throat....

She ended the article saying: "What I mean to say is, I'm not going one-on-one with reality, no." Her article was headlined: "Truer Than Strange: Why I Am Not a Short-Story Writer." Who needs fiction in a world so strange? asks the creative nonfiction writer.

TWO

OPENINGS: DRAMATIC AND SUMMARY METHODS

This book will discuss several techniques for telling a story, whether fiction or nonfiction, but the techniques all grow out of two basic, fundamental methods: the Dramatic (or scenic) Method and the Summary (or narrative) Method. Like so many great truths, the methods may sound too pat, too simple; they're simple only in that they are so fundamental, so important.

I had never heard about them until I read Leon Surmelian's excellent book, *Techniques of Fiction Writing*. I am forever in his debt—and you will soon be. Surmelian wrote about these methods as applied to fiction, but I've since found that they may be the missing link that binds fiction to nonfiction, the link that makes some nonfiction more creative than some other nonfiction—and thus increases the potential of journalistic nonfiction to aspire to art.

A creative nonfiction writer will typically conceive of his or her story as a series of scenes connected by a series of summaries—drama connected by narrative. He or she will plan an article or book around a series of scenes, selecting those events that seem to have the greatest dramatic potential, and then organizing them in what seems the best sequence (not always chronological). The writer will then accomplish other of his or her purposes in between with what we'll call "summaries." We'll

9

use "summaries" here to mean the typical narrative journalists write, summaries of what happened, as distinct from a running account of what is happening at the moment. If it were a running account, we'd use the dramatic method.

One writer might tell a story largely by scenes, while another might approach the same events using the summary method. The latter might have an occasional scene, but summary predominates. The former almost certainly has some summary material between scenes, but the method remains predominantly dramatic. Most creative nonfiction writers today blend the two methods, but with more scenes than the more traditional journalist. As we'll see in a later chapter, this business of writing scene by scene is one of the many techniques borrowed by the nonfiction writer from the fiction writer.

Writing by the dramatic method (in scenes) appeals to creative nonfiction writers because they see, as fiction writers see, that scenes give vitality, movement, action—life—to a story. Scenes have people doing things, saying things, moving right along in life's ongoing stream. Even when reporting about the past, writers may place scenes in present tense, thus making the past the present. The reader enjoys the feeling of being eyewitness to the action. Traditional journalists usually have to rely on reporting what's already happened, secondhand witnesses who lack the credibility of the eyewitness.

The creative nonfiction writer tries to be an eyewitness on the scene. If that's impossible, he or she researches a past event in much greater depth than the daily reporter has time to do. The creative nonfiction writer may then write a credible scene in the present tense, making the past seem present. Of course, this places a great responsibility on the creative non-fiction writer: The reader must not be deliberately duped into thinking the writer was actually at the scene if he or she hadn't been.

The dramatic (scenic) method is the cinematographer's close-up shot; the summary (narrative) method, the long shot. We believe the close-up shot because that's how we see most of life (close up), particularly when dealing with people. Not that we totally distrust the long shot, but as in life, we take what we haven't seen or heard for ourselves with a grain of salt—we await corroborating evidence from other sources before believing what we're told. We don't like being told—we like to find out for ourselves.

You've probably heard (and perhaps even heeded) the advice given so often: SHOW, don't TELL. Well, dramatic method is *show;* summary method is *tell.*

For purposes of easy discussion, I've probably made it sound as though a scene is written complete, then a summary written complete to tie it to the next scene, then some more summary, etc. In practice, it may work out that way, but normally the two methods merge. A scene may well have some short narrative summary interspersed through it. Even in the midst of a long summary passage, one or two lines of quoted conversation may occur in a kind of tiny scene. A single paragraph may use several techniques of both scene and summary. No tight rules exist—only the general rule that it must serve to accomplish part of the writer's purpose.

More will be said throughout this book about the several techniques used to carry out these two basic methods, but let's start off by demonstrating how some of our best writers use these methods for their article or book openings. The reader should not leave this chapter thinking that these two methods exist only to serve openings; they are used throughout an article, throughout a book. I've simply decided to illustrate this important truth by showing their use in openings.

Let's look first at the dramatic method as applied to openings; then we'll discuss in more detail the summary method and several techniques to apply it to openings.

DRAMA IN MODERN NONFICTION

When nonfiction writers advise beginners to SHOW rather than TELL their stories as much as possible, they're saying: *Put more drama into your nonfiction writing*—show us what's happening. We believe what we SEE; we distrust what we're TOLD. That's the secret to modern writing, whether fiction or nonfiction: We believe our eyes and ears—our senses.

We all know that for most people the most used sense is the visual one, yet we forget to put that knowledge into action when we write. Professional writers don't forget.

When writers talk about "showing," they mean more than visualizing for the reader's inner eye. They mean that you can also "show" us something about a person by letting us "hear" him or her speak. You may show us one thing when we hear a man speaking before the Rotary Club; you may "show" us something quite different when you let us hear him talk with a waitress when he's out of town on business. Unless you have also described him for us, we can't "see" him, but your words have certainly "shown" him to us. We've had several views of him just through his conversations. (Our language is built so much around the visual sense that it's difficult to write about this business of "showing" without reverting to visual words like "views," "perspectives," "see," and even "show" itself.)

Dramatic writing has a key ingredient that distinguishes life from non-life, the snake from the stick—*motion, action*. Good, dramatic nonfiction openings tend to move; they have life within them, life that moves, that gets somewhere.

In a good piece of nonfiction, if life doesn't get somewhere in the opening lines, the reader must at least sense movement or the promise of movement—we must sense that the freeze-frame will soon leap into action. The good nonfiction writer knows, however, that readers will not wait long. The playgoer may not walk back up the aisle if he or she doesn't like the first few words of the play on stage, but the article reader can simply flip to another article if the movement of life is neither present nor promised.

Years ago, readers would stay with the writer, sometimes for many pages, while the writer warmed up to tell the actual story. That was the style of the day; it fit the slow pace of life in that time. Today sees readers beset on all sides by the rapidity of transportation, the rapid pace of television, and the pace of life in general. The reader today also faces many conflicting, overlapping demands for his or her limited time. This is all complicated by what is seen as an ever-shortening attention span in adults as well as in children.

At first glance, a shortened attention span would seem to spell nothing but negatives about the future of reading—and, closer to our hearts, writing. Fortunately, there exists another side to the coin. As the result of television and the increasing pace of life in general, most people today are quicker on the uptake. They're ready to receive and process in their brains concentrated bursts of information much more rapidly than readers several generations ago could.

This two-sided coin (or is it a two-edged sword?) influences our writing—at least our thinking about our writing. On the one hand, readers generally can accept high loads of information because of increased abilities, but on the other hand, they're quicker to put aside a piece of writing that doesn't seem sufficiently interesting, entertaining, or informative. This means that modern writers can be more direct, creating an impression with a few bold strokes, a single exemplary, vivid incident, and some carefully selected concrete details. In the past century, we'd have been expected to labor over pages of detail and background before ever getting to the point.

If the writer intends to have readers, he or she must grab them and do everything possible to stretch that short attention span. The first 250 words must do it, or the attention shifts to other words more urgently persuasive. Professional writers know that and act on that knowledge. The beginning writer knows it, too, but fails to act on it. His or her openings resemble more a professional baseball pitcher's motions: a long, involved, often self-conscious wind-up, punctuated partway by a furtive look to check first base, another squeeze of the rosin bag, and then finally, another tug at the visor, followed by another hitch at the pants, and then the pitch itself—sometimes three pages too late to catch the reader. The modern nonfiction writer steps to the mound, checks out the batter, and hurls the word directly at the reader. It may end up a curve, but the game's begun—and we're hooked, we're grabbed, we're involved in a game, not in some long, fancy wind-up. *Involved*—that's it. Good openings make us feel we're there, in the infield, and involved in the action.

Like much good fiction today, nonfiction articles often begin *in medias res*, in the middle of things, of some action, some event. An opening can begin in the midst of some very dramatic action with people talking about things we may not at first understand (but are intrigued by) or it can begin with very little or no conversation. Although no one would want rules on this, many nonfiction pieces today start out in conversation.

In nonfiction, as in fiction, when people appear, and particularly when they begin to converse, everything comes to life. Until then, it's largely promise. Knowing this about fiction leads many creative nonfiction writers to open in conversation. The reader comes down the aisle looking for his seat while taking in the dialog progressing on stage—and is immediately engrossed, even before flipping down the upholstered seat. A good article opening in dialog (conversation) can engage its readers before they slip off their scarves and take a seat.

DRAMATIC OPENINGS

With the following dramatic scene, George Orwell opened a book about his early years, *Down and Out in Paris and London*. It puts us immediately into the environment he's about to discuss. Not content with "telling" us about his street, Rue du Coq d'Or, he "shows" us the street by letting us hear some of the inhabitants speak. He doesn't have them speak just so we can hear their speech patterns; he has them speak of things that show us what life was like on the street of the golden rooster.

> The Rue du Coq d'Or, seven in the morning. A succession of furious, choking yells from the street. Madame Monce, who kept the little hotel opposite mine, had come out onto the pavement to address a lodger on the third floor. Her bare feet were stuck into sabots and her grey hair was streaming down.
>
> *Madame Monce: "Salope! Salope!* How many times have I told you not to squash bugs on the wallpaper? Do you think you've bought the hotel, eh? Why can't you throw them out of the window like everyone else? *Putaine! Salope!"*
>
> Thereupon a whole variegated chorus of yells, as windows were flung open on every side and half the street joined in the quarrel. They shut up abruptly ten minutes later, when a squadron of cavalry rode past and people stopped shouting to look at them.

Although this chapter is about openings, the ending of Orwell's opening is what a journalist might call a "natural close"; all action in the opening scene stops when the people stop to watch the cavalry ride past. This gives the writer a perfectly natural opportunity to step back and launch into a summary section that tells us more about life there on that cobblestone street.

All writers of good nonfiction know the value of conversation throughout a piece. They are particularly aware of its power to grab the reader right from the beginning. Nonfiction which doesn't let us hear the human interaction tends soon to lose readers.

In his justly famous book on paleontology, *In Patagonia*, Bruce Chatwin opened Chapter 20, "An Old Log Cabin," with some very simple but vivid conversation. Although we don't hear his side of the conversation, we feel his presence, partly by the way he sticks his hand into the scene in line 2:

> "Feel it," she said. "Feel the wind coming through."
> I put my hand to the wall. The draught blew through the chinks where the mortar had fallen out. The log cabin was the North American kind. In Patagonia they made cabins differently and did not chink them with mortar.
> The owner of the cabin was a Chilean Indian woman called Sepulveda.
> "In winter it's terrible," she said. "I covered the wall with *materia plastica* but it blew away. The house is rotten, Señor, old and rotten. I would sell it tomorrow. I would have a concrete house which the wind cannot enter."
> Señor Sepulveda was grogged out of his mind, half-sitting, half-lying by the kitchen stove.
> "Would you buy the house?" she asked.
> "No," I said, "but don't sell it for nothing. There are North American gentlemen who would pay good money to take it away piece by piece."

Chatwin shows the cabin partly by letting us hear the inhabitant (the way Orwell did earlier) and he uses those parts of the conversation that tell (show) us something about the subject (cabin), not just something about the old woman. A valuable part of this technique is that the writer (and his reader) get two-for-one. Through the person's words we learn something of the person while learning simultaneously something of the subject.

Chatwin uses an interesting device when he has the woman speak in Spanish, referring to *materia plastica*. The author could have had any other words in Spanish to give us the "flavor" of the Spanish conversation, but he chose *materia plastica*, presumably because he felt that even a Norte Americano gentleman with no flair whatever for foreign languages could hardly miss the point. Again, we get a two-for-one: we learn that she's tried in vain to use some plastic stuff to keep out the wind; that the Patagonian winds of winter could lead to one's discontent; and we're reminded that the entire conversation is probably in Spanish.

Hunter S. Thompson is particularly adept at capturing the nuances of conversations and often uses them to establish in the opening the overall tone, as he did in the following piece about the Kentucky Derby, "The Kentucky Derby is Decadent and Depraved." Whether these conversations are verbatim reports may be moot in your mind, but we do know right away that they sound reasonably true to what we would expect to hear in that situation with those particular types of people. Notice how easily, efficiently, and effectively conversation gets us into a scene, dragging us along deeper and deeper into the article—the purpose, after all, of a dramatic, scenic, involving opening.

> I got off the plane around midnight and no one spoke as I crossed the dark runway to the terminal. The air was thick and hot, like wandering into a steam bath. Inside, people hugged each other and shook hands … big grins and a whoop here and there: "By God! You old bastard! Good to see you, boy! *Damn* good … and I *mean* it!"
>
> In the air-conditioned lounge I met a man from Houston who said his name was something or other—"But just call me Jimbo"—and he was here to get it on. "I'm ready for *anything*, by God! Anything at all. Yeah, what are you drinking?" I ordered a Margarita with ice, but he wouldn't hear of it: "Naw, naw … what the hell kind of drink is that for Kentucky Derby Time? What's *wrong* with you, boy?" He grinned and winked at the bartender. "Goddam, we gotta educate this boy. Get him some good *whiskey* … "
>
> I shrugged. "Okay, a double Old Fitz on ice." Jimbo nodded his approval.
>
> "Look." He tapped me on the arm to make sure I was listening. "I know this Derby crowd, I come here every year, and let me tell you one thing I've learned—this is no town to be giving people the impression you're some kind of faggot. Not in public, anyway. Shit, they'll roll you in a minute, knock you in the head and take every goddam cent you have."
>
> I thanked him and fitted a Marlboro into my cigarette holder…

Nothing need be said about his use of conversation to open his article. It sounds to me absolutely, totally, right-on-the-money true to life. We might note here, even though this chapter does not deal with the technique, how Thompson has also appealed to our senses: visual (how dark it was); tactile (that the air was thick and hot like a steam bath; that people hugged and shook hands); and aural (his use of "whoop"); perhaps our sense of taste (his reference to several iced drinks). He tapped our tactile sense again when the man tapped him on the arm, and although I may be exaggerating, he appealed both to my sense of vision and to my tactile sense when he said that he "fitted" the cigarette into the holder—I could feel that fitting action. It's worth noting, too, that he did not "tell" us all about these matters in one "descriptive" paragraph. Each sense was tapped in context—when it came up in the story. That's the modern way to do it—weave, weave, weave.

Richard Selzer's *The Discus Thrower* begins the way a short story might. We see a person immediately, the author describing the man physically, in very vivid language, language that gives us unexpected images, unexpected metaphors.

> I spy on my patients. Ought not a doctor to observe his patients by any means and from any stance, that he might the more fully assemble evidence? So I stand in the doorways of hospital rooms and gaze. Oh, it is not all that furtive an act. Those in bed need only look up to discover me. But they never do.
>
> From the doorway of Room 542 the man in the bed seems deeply tanned. Blue eyes and close-cropped white hair give him the appearance of vigor and good health. But I know that his skin is not brown from the sun. It is rusted, rather, in the last stage of containing the vile repose within. And the blue eyes are frosted, looking inward like the windows of a snowbound cottage. This man is blind. This man is also legless—the right leg missing from midthigh down, the left from just below the knee. It gives him the look of a bonsai, roots and branches pruned into the dwarfed facsimile of a great tree.

Dr. Selzer arrests us right away by his descriptions, particularly the simile that shows us what the man's eyes look like by saying they're frosted like the windows of a snowbound cottage—they look inward. Then he shows us through another striking simile that this legless man looks like a bonsai tree, the dwarfed facsimile of a great tree. That "shows" us more about this once great man than it "tells" us what he looks like—a fine example of how "showing" differs from "telling."

Let's look now at author George Plimpton in *Paper Lion* as he puts us on the football field when he goes out for the first time to learn (the hard way) what it feels like to face a line of professional football players. He involves us not by conversation but by vivid description of himself in action—a scene. His use of vivid, concrete words involves us immediately.

> I came up off the bench slowly, working my fingers up into my helmet to get at my ears. As I crossed the sidelines I was conscious then

only of moving into the massive attention of the crowd, but seeing ahead out of the opening of my helmet the two teams waiting. Some of the defense were already kneeling at the line of scrimmage, their heads turned so that helmeted, silver, with the cages protruding, they were made to seem animal and impersonal—wildlife of some large species disturbed at a waterhole—watching me come toward them. Close to, suddenly there was nothing familiar about them. With the arc lights high up on the standards, the interiors of their helmets were shadowed—perhaps with the shine of a cheekbone, the glint of an eye—no one recognizable, nor a word from them. I trotted by the ball. Its trade name "Duke" was face up. The referee was waiting, astride it, a whistle at the end of a black cord dangling from his neck. The offensive team in their blue jerseys, about ten yards back, on their own twenty-yard line, moved and collected in the huddle formation as I came up, and I slowed, and walked toward them, trying to be calm about it, almost lazying up to them to see what could be done.

As another example of an opening that does not depend on dialog for its strength, read this paragraph that opens Chapter 3, "An August Day's Sail," in *Spring Tides* by Samuel Eliot Morison:

A light, caressing southerly breeze is blowing; just enough to heel the yawl and give her momentum. The boy and I get under way from the mooring by the usual ritual. I take in the ensign, hoist the mizzen, cast off the main sheet and slack the backstays; he helps me hoist the mainsail, sway the halyards and neatly coil them. I take the wheel and the main sheet in hand, the boy casts off the mooring rope and hoists the jib, and she goes like a lively dog let off the leash.

Now that's what this chapter is all about—letting a lively article off the leash. The longer it's held under leash by nondramatic, nonvivid, noninvolving language, the less likely the reader will be excited—everyone's more excited by a dog that's unleashed and hurtling forward off the page.

SUMMARY OPENINGS

The summary method, essential to most creative nonfiction, requires a teller, whereas the dramatic method requires the people to live out the story right before our eyes. The summary method has its values and strengths, of course, but its weakness lies in the teller. No matter who tells the story, the reader knows a story is being told—he or she is not watching it unfold. As in life, we tend to believe more what we overhear than what we're told. Therein lies the explanation of why the teller method is a weakness—it relies on hearing. The dramatic method relies more on seeing, and that's the sense we're more used to relying on. Summary lacks imagery, except in the hands of our finest writers. The next few chapters intend to show how our best nonfiction writers make even their summary writing vivid, lively, imagistic, visual. They try to get as close to purely dramatic writing as it's possible to get through summary alone.

The summary method, using various techniques that I'll soon describe, serves extremely important ends. One of its greatest strengths is its ability to telescope time, something the dramatic method can't do without great and sometimes awkward difficulties. A scene operates close to real time, so something that in fact took a long time would take that much time in a scene—or the writer would have to write several scenes to show the passage of time. The time discontinuities between scenes are awkward and obvious, yet modern writers like to achieve the impression of continuous flow in their writing, movement without awkward conjunctions. Cleverly written summaries between scenes can provide smooth transitions through time, even great lengths of time. If scenes are the building blocks of a story, summaries are the cement that binds.

Summaries also serve another time purpose. They slow the pace, allowing suspense to build. Scenes accelerate the pace, not because they're short, but because they're vivid, concrete, and active in their imagery. The clever writer will pace the piece by carefully orchestrating which information he or she will put into rapid scenes, which into slower-paced summary. Most information can be put across by either method, but the pace, suspense, and emotional impact will be different.

Creative nonfiction writers mix both dramatic and summary methods to make nonfiction more interesting for the reader. Straight exposition of facts with no drama, no description, and no interpretation usually makes for dull reading. Journalistic writing traditionally has tended toward that kind of writing—in the interest of "objectivity." Today's creative nonfiction writers believe they can add drama and interpretation without destroying objectivity. They believe they are actually more objective because they're more thorough in their reporting, going to greater depth in their research. This book does not intend to argue that point; it intends only to show how they go about the task of creating nonfiction that reads more interestingly while still respecting the "facts."

Dividing their work arbitrarily into the "dramatic" parts and the "summary" parts is awkward and done here only for the sake of illustration. In the actual writing, of course, the dramatic often blends with the explanatory and the descriptive to make the flow smooth, varied, and interesting.

Since this chapter talks only about typical openings written by creative nonfiction writers, we'll go now to some openings that are more summary than dramatic, not forgetting that they are sometimes part one, part the other, and remembering that it is the author's intent that determines how we might classify a particular opening.

The summary method is carried out by two techniques, description and explanation. I'll discuss first "descriptive summary" because in its appeal to the imagination, it's closer to the dramatic method than is "explanatory summary," which will be taken up later.

Descriptive vs. Explanatory Summary

Descriptive summary is distinguished from explanatory by its presenting us with the *quality* of an action. While explanatory summary would capture the sequence, the logic, and the meaning of the action, moving us through *time*, descriptive summary concerns itself with giving us an overall sensory impression, moving us through *space*.

If, for example, we were writing about a battle going on, descriptive summary would give us interesting snapshots of the action, details of the uniforms, the weapons, the sounds and smells of battle. Explanatory summary, on the other hand, would be apt to tell us about the tactics of both sides, the progress of the battle and even of the war. Descriptive summary could never give us the war; it would give us pictures of specific engagements, particular ships, individual soldiers and sailors. Explanatory summary would give us national strategies, information about the movement of huge armies, about the economics of war, the results of war. Descriptive summary would have us learn about war by having us hear the scream of one shell, the whimper of one man. Depending on the writer and the work, some of this descriptive work might be shifted to the dramatic method, letting us hear two wounded men in a foxhole talking about what it'll be like if they ever get home. The usual method would combine some drama, some description, some explanation.

Descriptive summary, in turn, is carried out by two descriptive techniques: informative description and suggestive description (shortened here to *informative* and *suggestive*).

Informative and Suggestive Description

Informative description tends toward analysis, lists, numbers, categories; and it intends completeness. It allows no interpretation; it presents just the facts. *Informative* (sometimes called *technical*) tells us how the new machine works, never how marvelous an invention it is, nor anything about its probable effects upon the future of mankind—certainly nothing about the beauty of the beast. Beauty lies in *suggestive* description.

Suggestive does not pretend to completeness; it prefers incompleteness, impressionism. Suggestive looks to our imagination for its power. Informative builds its power upon rock solid facts, data, logic. Suggestive does not trust facts (it says, "Don't confuse me with facts"); it prefers the truths of metaphor. Informative distrusts the inaccuracy, the incompleteness, the vagueness of metaphor. Suggestive will not hesitate to interpret the meaning of that described; informative considers interpretation pretentious and beyond its ken. Suggestive says that nothing lies beyond its ken.

The word "suggestive" is used because this kind of description suggests (and only suggests) something to the reader's imagination, enabling it to bring to the description its own previous similar experiences in order to understand. Informative would not trust the limitations of the reader's memory; it wants understanding, comprehension—and it wants it *now*.

As a final attempt to distinguish these two forms of descriptive summary, consider the difference between two descriptions of the same thing. One is an ad in the paper listing a cabin to buy:

> *Cabin for sale. 20 x 20 log. 1 Bdrm.*
> *Sm. kitch. FP. 5 ac. Stream. Shed.*

Rewriting that informative description into a suggestive description for a letter home to his parents, a young man might write something like this:

Dear folks,

I'm thinking of buying a terrific log cabin up on the Deerkill River—you know, up near where you used to go back in the old days, Dad. It's got plenty of room downstairs with a bedroom loft up under the slanting log roof. I'll love lying there and looking up at those rough hewn timbers thinking about Abe Lincoln and all the other greats (like me) who lived in log cabins. I understand that logs have the highest insulation value of any materials—and they look so great, outside and in. And what a fireplace! I could fit a six-foot Yule log in there next Christmas. And it's got all the fire tools and hooks for hanging pots over the fire and everything. There's this great shed attached to the back, sort of a lean-to, that I can convert into a place for writing. Do you think you could lend me …

Not too many creative nonfiction pieces fall into the informative category, because it is ordinarily too informational, too technical to be "creative," thus falling outside the purview of this book. There follows only one example of informative description, one by Jan Morris from "The Best of Everything," in *Journeys*. You might argue that it is not purely "informative," and I'd have to agree. It certainly has a lot about its description that's "suggestive," but I think it's more informative than suggestive.

On Sunday evening in summer the week-end sailors of Stockholm come streaming home from their sailing grounds in the Baltic peninsula—from Vaxholm and Grinda, from Gallno and Djuro and Moja, where the island-jumbled waters of the Swedish coast debouch into the open sea. The sun is glinting then on the golden baubles that ornament the towers and steeples of their city; flags fly bravely from masts and rooftops; and the small boats hasten sun-bleached and purposeful through the harbor, bronzed fathers at the helm, tousled children flat on the deck, like ships of a light flotilla returning from distant action.

Into the Slussen lock the boats jam themselves, watched by the lockkeeper in his glass cabin (TV monitor flickering in its shadows), and with a ponderous movement of steel gates, a swoosh and dripping of water, they are raised from the level of the sea to the level of the lake that lies beyond; and so they disperse into the gathering dusk, away among the myriad creeks of the city, to nose their way into unsuspected canals between apartment blocks, to tie up at private jetties among the trees, or to disappear into the numberless marinas that lie concealed, like so many little naval bases, all over the watery capital.

The technical information she's put in there about Stockholm (the locks, steel gates, TV monitor, numberless marinas, etc.) is made more interesting because she's mixed it in attractively with all the more suggestive description. She has mixed her "informative" words with her "descriptive" words very artistically so that we come away not only with an excellent image in our minds of a Sunday evening in Stockholm as the weekend sailors come streaming home to harbor, we also learn many "facts" (information) about Stockholm as a watery capital.

Although that opening does give us factual information, it can't be considered informative description, or technical writing. Straight informational writing is not often used for openings by creative nonfiction writers because it naturally lacks in its details, its information, and its data, that which is human, scenic, dramatic, vivid. Jan Morris has here found a way, however, to provide us information buoyantly afloat on a sea of imagery.

Taking a cue from Jan Morris and her enjoyment of Stockholm, I've selected the following opening that's also about Stockholm, from Cynthia Ozick's "Enchantments at First Encounter" ("The Sophisticated Traveler," *New York Times* supplement). Ozick is better known, of course, for her fine fiction, and we can see that influence on the way she presents Stockholm to us. With this excerpt we leave informative description and turn to suggestive description, another technique for applying the descriptive summary method.

> One morning in Stockholm, after rain and just before November, a mysteriously translucent shadow began to paint itself across the top of the city. It skimmed high over people's heads, a gauzy brass net, keeping well above the streets, skirting everything fabricated by human arts—though one or two steeples were allowed to dip up into it, like pens filling their nibs with palest ink. It made a sort of watermark over Stockholm, as if a faintly luminous river ran overhead; yet with no more weight or gravity than a vapor.

Since this is an example of "suggestive description," we have to accept the mysteriously translucent shadow that paints itself high above Stockholm's streets. We may not be sure just what it is, but we're reasonably sure it's a cloud formation of some kind. We allow the creative nonfiction writer, as we would a poet, to bathe us in beauty. If the intent of the piece were to educate us about meteorological phenomena that visit Stockholm, of course, the writer would be obliged to tell us in no uncertain terms what this mysterious overhead stream is, and what its implications are for public health, aircraft safety, etc. It should now be clear, by contrast, that the previous descriptive passage by Jan Morris is more toward the "informative," and this one by Cynthia Ozick more toward the "suggestive" side of the description scales.

Had Michael Herr written the following excerpt from *Dispatches* about just one night in one Vietnam battle, or about just one location, it could have been called a "dramatic opening," but since it deals with Vietnam scenes in general, it falls into what I've labeled the summary method, using the technique of suggestive description.

> You could watch mortar bursts, orange and gray-smoking, over the tops of trees three and four kilometers away, and the heavier shelling from support bases further east along the DMZ, from Camp Carrol and the Rockpile, directed against suspected troop movements or NVA rocket and mortar positions. Once in a while—I guess I saw it happen three or four times in all—there would be a secondary explosion, a direct hit on a supply of NVA ammunition. And at night it was beautiful. Even the incoming was beautiful at night, beautiful and deeply dreadful.
>
> I remembered the way a Phantom pilot had talked about how beautiful the surface-to-air missiles looked as they drifted up toward his plane to kill him, and remembered myself how lovely .50-calibre tracers could be, coming at you as you flew at night in a helicopter, how slow and graceful, arching up easily, a dream so remote from anything that could harm you. It could make you feel a total serenity, an elevation that put you above death, but that never lasted very long. One hit anywhere in the chopper would bring you back, bitten lips, white knuckles and all, and then you knew where you were.

Certain words and phrases give away the fact that a piece of writing is summary rather than dramatic in form. In the particular example from *Dispatches* above, we see phrases like: you *could* see; *once in a while—I guess I saw*; *there would be* a secondary explosion; *I remembered the way* a Phantom pilot...; coming at you *as you* flew...; one hit... *would bring* you back.

Although many of these italicized expressions are in past tense, that's not what makes the form summary rather than dramatic. Herr could have written something very dramatic in form and yet have had all the verbs in past tense. The difference is that the dramatic form requires that all the action be in a scene that occurs once and once only—as life's scenes naturally occur. As soon as the writer begins using phrases like "*we used to always*, there *would be, as you flew*," we see that the action was actually a series of actions spread over time. The way to write "dramatically" is to write about one continuous action in essentially one place by essentially the same people. This point will be elaborated in the chapter about how creative nonfiction writers tend to write scene by scene, i.e., dramatically.

The following exemplary writing opens Joan Didion's "Los Angeles Notebook" from her collection of essays, *Slouching Towards Bethlehem*. Of all the better-known creative nonfiction writers today, Ms. Didion writes some of the best suggestive description (summary in method). This essay about the Santa Ana wind of southern California does more than leave us with an image, it creates deep within us a mood.

> There is something uneasy in the Los Angeles air this afternoon, some unnatural stillness, some tension. What it means is that tonight a Santa Ana will begin to blow, a hot wind from the northeast whining down through the Cajon Pass, blowing up sandstorms out along Route 66, drying the hills and the nerves to the flash point. For a few days now we will see smoke back in the canyons, and hear sirens in the night. I have neither heard nor read that a Santa Ana is due, but I know it, and almost everyone I have seen today knows it too. We know it because we feel it. The baby frets. The maid sulks. I rekindle a waning argument with the telephone company, then cut my losses and lie down, given over to whatever is in the air. To live with the Santa Ana is to accept, consciously or unconsciously, a deeply mechanistic view of human behavior.

For fear that I've not yet made crystal clear the distinction between the dramatic (scenic) and summary methods, I've taken Joan Didion's excellent summary opening to "Los Angeles Notebook" and written it as though she had decided instead to use the dramatic method. The following are my words, not hers. I hesitate to think how beautifully she would have handled the same task. I should probably slouch off toward Bethlehem, Pa.

> "Juanita," she screamed over the machine, "would you please not run the vacuum in the room where I am. I've told you a thousand times—a hundred times today already. It's hot enough outside without that machine blasting hot air on my feet to remind me."

"Si, señora...about the baby."

"What *about* him."

"He cries in his crib all the time, señora."

"Well, make him stop crying by the time I get back from the airport. That kind of stupid screaming drives his father crazy...and stop sulking. It's bad enough to have one cry-baby around here..."

She helped him tie down the wings and chock the three wheels, both of them working hurriedly to get off the blazing concrete and into the cooler car.

"So, did your writing go well?"

"Are you kidding. What with Juanita sulking around the house, and the baby fretting—and that damned Los Angeles phone company."

"You're still fighting it out with them over that bill? Christ, it was only off by five bucks. You're driving yourself and everybody else nuts over a measly five bucks. Jesus."

"Almost six."

As soon as he got in the car, he turned on *All News Radio*:

Good afternoon folks. Well, this afternoon is livable, but it'll be a different story later today and for the next few days. Yes, folks, that ol' debil Santa Ana is back. She's blowing in from the northeast following her usual track. So, if you can possibly do so, stay off Route 66, and especially out of the Cajon Pass. A listener up that way just called in to warn us that sandstorms are already blasting across the highway—visibility zero. And there's no telling what that'll do to your nice new paint job, or your windshield.

"You know, John, even before I heard the sirens, I knew the Santa Ana was coming. I could feel it deep inside—know what I mean? And then I started behaving stupidly...God, I was so nasty to Juanita—and you know how much I love her...Come on, let's get on home. All I want to do is lie down until dinner's ready. I feel all woolly inside."

I suppose I could have written that better had I used even more words, but I wrote it only to illustrate directly the difference between approaching the same situation as *scene* rather than as *summary*, the method Ms. Didion used. This has not been in any sense a demonstration that one is "better" than the other, but a demonstration that the same information can be put across differently. The two methods are there for you to use—depending on the particular piece and its purpose—and your relative strengths as a writer. In hands less clever than Joan Didion's, the summary method might not have worked out here so well as it did. You can see (despite my writing) the possibilities inherent in the scenic or dramatic method to make the writing involving. In her writing you can see that the same "content" can be put across very efficiently and effectively in far fewer words.

Perhaps if "Los Angeles Notebook" had been the opening chapter of a longer book, Ms. Didion would have used the dramatic method. As it was, she was writing a short essay and would never have squandered so many words (as I did) just to begin establishing character and to set a mood.

Ms. Didion's summary method (through suggestive description) works so well because of her excellent choice of words, of details, of images. Although she's not using the scenic method, she does make her writing concrete and suggestive enough so that we can form our own scenes on our internal screens. That's the optimum—make a passage "visual" without a lot of visualizing adjectives, and without all the words usually necessitated by the dramatic, scenic method. Fiction and nonfiction writers must plan in advance which things might be presented best by scene, which by summary. Since creative nonfiction writers typically write scene by scene, you must sharpen your dramatic facility. And, since scenes are usually joined (or separated) by passages that use one or more techniques of summary, you must also study and perfect these techniques of summary.

As we continue to look at how various professional writers use suggestive description in their openings, let's read "New York," an excellent piece by Gay Talese. Although you'll find many bits of information about the city, the emphasis is certainly on describing New York City (admittedly description not found in the typical tour guide's descriptive prose). This summary opening suggests things to our imagination more than it "explains" what's happening in the city.

> New York City is a city of things unnoticed. It is a city with cats sleeping under parked cars, two stone armadillos crawling up St. Patrick's Cathedral, and thousands of ants creeping on top of the Empire State Building. The ants probably were carried by there by winds or birds, but nobody is sure; nobody in New York knows any more about the ants than they do about the panhandler who takes taxis to the Bowery; or the dapper man who picks trash out of Sixth Avenue trash cans; or the medium in the West Seventies who claims, "I am clairvoyant, clairaudient and clairsensuous."
>
> New York is a city for eccentrics and a center for odd bits of information. New Yorkers blink twenty-eight times a minute, but forty when tense. Most popcorn chewers at Yankee Stadium stop chewing

momentarily just before the pitch. Gum chewers on Macy's escalators stop chewing momentarily before they get off—to concentrate on the last step. Coins, paper clips, ballpoint pens, and little girls' pocket-books are found by workmen when they clean the sea lion's pool at the Bronx Zoo.

As we continue slouching toward the explanatory summary type of opening, we find this one to "Marrakech" by George Orwell. He begins his story here with a great amount of descriptive detail that appeals to our imaginative powers. If he had let us hear some of the conversations going on, this excerpt might have been put under what we've called "dramatic openings," but it stands instead as an excellent example of suggestive description summary. Certainly we learn something (informative) about the culture in Marrakech, but Orwell has woven those pieces of information so well into the description itself, we can't call it "informative" description. The intent of this opening is not to "inform" us but to intrigue us into reading on into the third and subsequent paragraphs where he does inform us about the terrible conditions the local people endure.

> As the corpse went past, the flies left the restaurant table in a cloud and rushed after it, but they came back a few minutes later.
> The little crowd of mourners—all men and boys, no women—threaded their way across the market-place between the piles of pomegranates and the taxis and the camels, wailing a short chant over and over again. What really appeals to the flies is that the corpses here are never put into coffins, they are merely wrapped in a piece of rag and carried on a rough wooden bier on the shoulders of four friends. When the friends get to the burying-ground they hack an oblong hole a foot or two deep, dump the body in it and fling over it a little of the dried-up lumpy earth, which is like broken brick. No gravestone, no name, no identifying mark of any kind. The burying-ground is merely a huge waste of hummocky earth, like a derelict building-lot. After a month or two no one can ever be certain where his own relatives are buried.

As Orwell goes into paragraph three (below) he provides us a good example of how a writer will switch from one basic form (suggestive description) to another basic form (general explanation) when he or she feels that the opening is over.

> When you walk through a town like this—two hundred thousand inhabitants, of whom at least twenty thousand own literally nothing

except the rags they stand up in—when you see how the people live, and still more how easily they die, it is always difficult to believe that you are walking among human beings. All colonial empires are in reality founded upon that fact....

I've included the beginning of the third paragraph to show that after using suggestive descriptive summary to lure us in, he shifts here into general explanatory summary. Orwell could have started right off with the third paragraph as his opening, of course, but he knew that he could not lure us into the article with these rather dry words of straight explanation. He knew, however, that he could make us follow the flies straight into the story where he wanted us. He had an important message to get across to us readers, so he used flies and corpses as bait. Homely? Yes. Ugly? Effective? Definitely.

With paragraph three we leave our discussion of descriptive summary and move into explanatory summary.

General and Expository Explanation

Two major techniques are used in applying the explanatory summary method: general explanatory and expository explanation, the latter being the very end of the dramatic/summary continuum, the least "dramatic" of all writing.

General explanatory (here called *general*) concerns itself with presenting an action for us and does so by appealing largely to our imagination. (The relationship between explanatory and expository writing is analogous to that between suggestive and informative descriptions.)

If, for example, you were to write a book on how to write short stories, you'd have to give broad, *general* instructions that would apply to any short story your reader might someday write—*general explanatory* writing. If, on the other hand, you were writing an article about how you wrote your own award-winning short story, you'd not write in a general way; you'd write in a highly specific way about that one particular story—*expository* writing. You'd be "exposing" for everyone just how you went about writing that terrifically successful story.

Now, just to cinch the distinction. If your article went beyond telling how you wrote that story and drew general advice out of it to show just how the reader might go about writing short stories in general, you'd have crossed back over the line into general explanatory writing.

In "Golden Prague: Travels through a Police State," Manuela Hoelterhoff gets our attention by a descriptive first paragraph, and then moves into a general explanatory summary second paragraph. Recall that I make all these labels and categorizations just to give us a way of talking about the variations that exist within what I've labeled overall as "summary." Writers do not sit down and say to themselves, "I think this calls for an opening that's three-quarters of the way along the summary part of the continuum, somewhere between informative description and general explanatory summary ... "

> We still had a kilometer or so to go, but all the welcoming signs were already there ... the watchtowers; the closely trimmed meadows that couldn't hide a squadron of relapsed field mice. We pulled up the car in front of a roadblock manned by glum, baby-faced guards carrying machine guns.

As we enter the second paragraph in Hoelterhoff's piece, we can see easily that the story has begun. Someone more academic than I might argue that only the first paragraph qualifies as "the opening," but my feeling is that the first two paragraphs work indivisibly together to "open" the article for us:

> We'd driven here from Vienna—less than an hour from the border and some 200 miles from Prague, our destination. Straight ahead was what Neville Chamberlain described as "a faraway little land that few of us know anything about." Chamberlain, to be sure, didn't, and as a result Czechoslovakia became for a few bloody years part of the Nazi empire. Now, of course, thanks to people with similarly informed geopolitical views, the Czechs are tied with cement overshoes to their socialist comrades in the Soviet Union.

The opening to *Landfalls in History* by Hammond Innes lives comfortably, unambiguously, within the labeled walls of general explanatory summary. In these first three paragraphs we find almost no description and little exposition. Almost all the words "tell" us what the article will be about and how it came to be written. Innes does an extremely fine job of luring us into the article by explanatory writing alone, and this requires writing of high calibre. Many nonfiction writers avoid the straight explanatory opening, fearing that it lacks the power to engage us right off.

Some travelers collect country houses; others ecclesiastical buildings, gardens, restaurants. I seem to collect fortresses. And since I have spent quite a slice of my life at sea, mostly with my wife and sailing our own boat, many of these have been sea fortresses on the shores of Europe, vast landmarks that have produced in me a sense of excitement. It is difficult to explain what this means to those who are not sailors. You come across the sea—the Channel, the Mediterranean, even an inland sea like the Marmara—and there is the land. But where is the shelter you are seeking? For many hours perhaps you have been voyaging on the wind, navigating by the speed at which your sails have driven you through the water, by how the wind and tide and breaking seas have moved you, and you are searching, searching through the glasses, hoping to God you have got it right, that the port you have been aiming for will emerge over the bows.

Then, suddenly, there it is, that huge medieval fortress described as "conspic" in the pilot book, standing there solid and reassuring. Then I feel like Cook or Magellan or those distant Vikings who first sighted Vinland, the sense of discovery as strong as if I had crossed an ocean. I have made it, and there to prove it is the fort guarding the entrance to the port.

As we've seen with some of the other openings, other fine writers might have had Mr. Innes and his wife conversing on deck as they approach a new fort to add to their collection of landfalls made. These writers might also have described the state of the sea, the towering of the clouds, and the blowing of the whales as the fort looms on the horizon so pink in the false dawn. If Mr. Innes had written his opening like that, depending on the relative amounts of description and explanation used, of course, we might have had to classify it as a suggestive descriptive form of summary opening. As he did write it, this piece perfectly exemplifies a general explanatory form.

Although we've been talking about dramatic and summary methods in the context of how they're sometimes used in openings, we should not lose sight of the point that almost all nonfiction writing uses these methods throughout, and in different combinations and proportions.

It is mostly the dramatic method that distinguishes what this book calls "creative" nonfiction from "traditional" nonfiction. This is not to say that all traditional nonfiction writing is undramatic. The point is that traditional nonfiction writers, journalists in particular, try *not* to write dramatically, fearing it plays too much on the reader's emotions and tends to distort the "facts," or at least the reader's perception of the facts. The creative nonfiction writer does not want to distort the facts either, but tries, through drama and vivid writing, to get the facts across to readers, especially to readers who might otherwise not even read about the subject. Many readers avoid reading for fear of being bored to death by exposition or explanation that lacks the breath of life, that lacks, despite the numerous facts, realism. If nothing else, creative nonfiction writers worship *realism*. They seek out and treasure specific realistic details, the subject of the next chapter.

THREE

AUTHORITY THROUGH REALISTIC DETAILS

Thinking back a few pages to Joan Didion's essay about the Santa Ana winds, recall how she brought the scene alive partly by including some specifics, some details about the phenomenon. When, for example, she wrote that the Santa Ana is "a hot wind from the northeast whining down through the Cajon Pass," we begin already to understand it. Just telling us that it's a northeast wind helps us imagine it. When it comes "whining down," we can hear it. When we learn then that it's whining down through Cajon Pass, we're there in the pass—whether or not we have any knowledge of that pass. I imagine she could have chosen any number of passes or other ways to tell us where it comes whining down from, but she chose a specific pass—and by selecting Cajon Pass, she did one more little bit of "involving" us in the situation. That Spanish-sounding word, Cajon, put me right there in southern California, or into the southwest deserts, where I'm sure the winds are hot and whining. Being the excellent writer she is, she couldn't stop putting us even deeper into the picture. She has us experience the wind "blowing up sandstorms out along Route 66...."

From the beginnings of writing, authors have known the value of including details in stories and articles, but today's writers go far beyond what used to be done. Charles Dickens was particularly aware of the value of including specific (concrete) details about London's layers of social life, more perhaps than anyone before him. His realistic writing affected novelists for many years, but after a while they forgot the

33

importance of realistic detail and turned to writing that was more intellectual, more abstract. With some exceptions, of course, novelists for
many years after Dickens wrote primarily from within the mind—almost neglecting the way life really was.

Nonfiction writers and journalists of the past, in a sometimes futile attempt to be "objective," did not include great amounts of concrete detail.
They apparently realized that just the mere listing of real life details raised
emotions in the reader—emotions they felt would keep the reader from
reading objectively. Modern nonfiction writers, about whom we're interested in this book, also realize that the mere listing of concrete details,
realistic details, details of real life, will raise emotions within the reader—
and they include the details for that very reason. They feel that the whole
truth has not been put forth unless the emotional context is also there.

Both groups of nonfiction writers, traditional and creative, aim for the
same thing—truth, the accurate portrayal of life. They differ on what
"truth" means and what such accuracy involves: whether a camera lens is
a more accurate reporter of people, things, and events, or whether the
human eye that sees in an emotional context best observes and conveys
the large and small truths of human existence.

TELLING THE "WHOLE TRUTH"

The main point of this chapter is that the mentioning of concrete, realistic details about life raises emotions in the reader—and that that is
not somehow "bad." Emotions inform our understanding all the time.
So, to tell the whole truth about most situations that involve people
(and most situations do) we need to jog the reader's memory, to use
Tom Wolfe's phrase.

The best nonfiction writers today do not tell us how we should think
about something, how we should feel about it, nor what emotions should
be aroused. They simply put the concrete details there in front of us. The
reader's brain, to the extent it has experienced or known something about
an exact or similar situation, will be "jogged" and the old emotion reexpe-
rienced. This squares with what the cognitive scientists are beginning to
believe happens within the brain when an experience is about to be stored
in the memory. Apparently, various details about the experience are
stored along with details of similar, associated, past experiences. When

any detail is experienced in the future, the potential for the entire past experience(s) to be recalled is there—including the emotions surrounding the earlier experience. If this is true, that facts and details are stored along with attendant emotions in a system of cross-files throughout the brain, we writers must recognize that fact—and use it to our advantage.

Even the most conscientious, intelligent reader may soon forget the factual content of a piece if the material entered the brain with little emotion wrapped around it. Cognitive research indicates that humans remember best what enters the brain in an envelope of "emotion."

By "emotion," cognitive scientists mean those feelings we might normally think of as emotions, but they also include expressions that just *imply* emotion—expressions like "terrifyingly hot," rather than "200 degrees Centigrade." Unless the precise figure of 200 degrees Centigrade (as distinct from 199 degrees Centigrade) is significant for the intended reader, "terrifyingly hot" will have more "emotional" meaning—and thus remain longer in the mind.

Too much academic writing ignores this fact, the fact that we humans have not (in our triune brains) evolved very far from our lower animal predecessors, and thus learn (remember) best any emotion-laden images. In the academics' attempts at "objectivity" and precision, some of them think they must avoid, at all costs, any such "interpretive" words like "terrifyingly." After all, they reason: "To whom is it terrifyingly hot?" Not to the scientist, certainly. He or she doesn't think of being terrified by the heat of the autoclave or the molten metal, but is concerned only with recording precisely the temperature observed. If the scientist then writes an article for people unfamiliar with the heat of molten metals, "terrifyingly hot" will make the point more quickly and even more memorably—presumably the twin goals of such writing for the nonscientific audience.

Conversation also provides "emotion" (in the sense I'm using it here) for an article, making the content more human, more understandable, more memorable. George Will, the Pulitzer Prize-winning columnist, knows how to use conversation to put us right into a situation, conversation that pulls us into "On Her Own in the City," a *Washington Post* column about some of the problems growing out of our present welfare system.

When police, responding to her call, arrived at her East Harlem tenement, she was hysterical: "The dog ate my baby." The baby girl had been four days old, twelve hours "home" from the hospital. Home was two rooms and a kitchen on the sixth floor, furnished with a rug, a folding chair, and nothing else, no bed, no crib.

"Is the baby dead?" asked an officer. "Yes," the mother said, "I saw the baby's insides." Her dog, a German shepherd, had not been fed for five days. She explained: "I left the baby on the floor with the dog to protect it." She had bought the dog in July for protection from human menaces.

The writer grabs our attention immediately with the woman's hysterical, barely articulate words: "The dog ate my baby." And later, "I saw the baby's insides." It would require an almost inhuman reader not to read on, even though it's obviously a grisly story unfolding. Will hopes that by repeating for us her actual words he'll make us remember this article for some time to come—perhaps long enough to do something about the problems of poverty.

If we want a reader to understand fully some experience we're writing about, it's necessary to stimulate as many associated memories as possible. Details not only conjure up old memories, they enable us to "understand" the new idea. We've all experienced the difficulty of communicating about a new idea with someone of limited experience. Someone with all kinds of past experiences, however, regardless of their possibly indirect relevance to the one now under discussion, is easy to talk with. Such a person can take a little something from each of a number of experiences and make them relevant to the present one. That, of course, explains the strength of metaphor. The reader says of a metaphor, in effect, "Oh, I understand...this is sort of the same thing I saw (heard, felt, smelled, experienced) back then. It's not exactly the same, but I can understand better now that I've been reminded of what this is like."

As with so much advice about writing, caution and good sense are called for. In an attempt to provide an article with "realism," a writer may load it up with so many details, even excellent details, that the reader gasps under the pressure of so many images. The secret, of course, is to use just enough to do the trick, but how do I know when enough's enough? Since no rules exist, you can best get a feel for how much is enough by reading the various authors quoted in these chapters. The main work is to be selective. Select from all the details you may have collected, in your mind or in a field notebook, those that either singly or in their cumulative strength present what you consider the "essence" of the place, the person, or whatever you're trying to capture. Sometimes a litany of details will be effective in their cumulative power; sometimes, a single one will suffice; and other times, the best method is to weave them into the description or the narrative as they come up logically.

Another possible pitfall in the use of concrete details would be in choosing references that may soon become outdated. In the very attempt to make your subject come alive for readers today, you might use such ephemeral details that, a few years (or even months) from now, they'll have gone out of favor and future readers won't get the point. For example, though today a certain TV actor and his foibles may be known by men and women at all levels of education, even well-educated people in the future may not recall some minor detail about his life. The main piece of advice is to keep your wits about you as you select the details you'll use. If some seem so ephemeral that no one will know about them a year from now, include some details that seem to you more permanent. Even if your reader misses the significance of one or two details, he or she will have enough to work with to figure out your meaning.

One problem difficult to deal with is that of writing for ill-informed readers. What do you do about them? All I can advise is that if they're poorly informed people, they're going to miss much of what you write anyway, so which concrete details you select seems, on the one hand, unimportant. On the other hand, perhaps an ill-informed, marginally literate person will be assisted in his or her understanding by the very concreteness of the details we're discussing here. It seems, then, that we should pay close attention to how we handle the matter of concrete details in attaining realism, because readers of all types and levels seem to need and appreciate them.

That last point raises a question difficult to answer with any certitude: Who will read the creative nonfiction you'll write? The American Society of Journalists and Authors (ASJA) conducted some demographic studies to get a handle on just who their readers are, especially their magazine readers. The study reports that the typical reader of nonfiction magazines, among other characteristics, is about thirty years old; has about a high school education; is probably middle class and holding a blue-collar or white-collar job; is most likely married; and has at least one child.

General readers like the one described above are interested in subjects if they are clearly and vividly expressed, but they're very quick to stop reading an article, or ignore writing that doesn't seem to relate directly to their personal concerns or past experiences. If the writing is on some currently hot topic, or is so extremely lively and well written that it captures their attention, general readers will follow even complex topics outside their usual range of interests.

Most journalists would not include the types of details this young reporter did when he wrote this account of an interview he and a female reporter conducted soon after a young Japanese woman and her mother had lived through an earthquake. Ernest Hemingway was in his early twenties when he wrote this very modern-sounding nonfiction piece for the *Toronto Daily Star* in 1923.

> The door opened one narrow crack. The crack ran from the top of the door to the bottom, and about halfway up it was a very dark, very beautiful face, the hair soft and parted in the middle.
>
> "She is beautiful, after all," thought the reporter. He had been sent on so many assignments in which beautiful girls figured, and so few of the girls had ever turned out to be beautiful.
>
> "Who do you want?" said the girl at the door.
>
> "We're from *The Star*," the reporter said. "This is Miss So and So."
>
> "We don't want to have anything to do with you. You can't come in," the girl said.
>
> "But—" said the reporter and commenced to talk. He had a very strong feeling that if he stopped talking at any time, the door would slam. So he kept on talking. Finally the girl opened the door.
>
> "Well, I'll let you in," she said. "I'll go upstairs and ask my mother."

By putting us right up close to that crack in the door, Hemingway has "involved" us. We are no longer newspaper readers, we're on-the-spot observers, even participants, at the interview. He lures us deeper into the story by giving us a tantalizing glimpse of the girl we expect soon to interview. Not only does he break all journalism rules when he tells us what he "thought," he tells us a bit, a small bit to be sure, but a bit about his life as a reporter—going on other assignments that had promised beautiful girls. Journalists do not usually talk about their lives (particularly not back in 1923). Creative nonfiction writers may, of course, because no one has set down rules or strictures about what the writer may write. Hemingway even quoted himself being interrupted by himself: "But—." This is a very small detail, but we see in it that that's just the way life is. We start out with some sentence, and then shift into something different. In other words, by reporting accurately what happened, instead of following some journalistic "rule," the writer has involved our brains in the scene there on the doorstep. It sounds real.

Here is Hemingway again, this time giving us concrete, realistic details of life in wartime Italy. Nowhere does he "tell" us what to feel about all this business; he simply lays out all these details for us; he "shows" us.

> Sometimes in the dark we heard the troops marching under the windows and guns going past pulled by motor tractors. There was much traffic at night and many mules on the roads with boxes of ammunition on each side of their pack-saddles and gray motor trucks that carried men, and other trucks with loads covered with canvas that moved slower in the traffic. There were big guns too that passed in the day drawn by tractors, the long barrels of the guns covered with green branches and green leafy branches and vines laid over the tractors. To the north we could look across the valley and see a forest of chestnut trees and behind it another mountain on this side of the river.

This quote, although it sounds like nonfiction, is from his novel *A Farewell to Arms*. Most of the strength of this passage comes from the simple listing of details. Some other writer might not have specified, for example, that the forest across the valley was of chestnut trees, but Hemingway knew the value of the realistic detail. Even though we might not know a chestnut tree forest when we look at one from across a valley, we feel confident that the author knows—and that we're in good hands. That's it. The passage sounds *authoritative*. The modern nonfiction writer, too, seeks to sound authoritative, authoritative in the sense that the reader will sense an air of authority about a piece and will give it credence. Interesting, isn't it, that the word *author* is embedded in that word, authority? Anyone with "authority" has the power to persuade; a passage that sounds authoritative persuades us of its validity—so that's what authors try to do, invest their writing with an air of authority. One way to ensure that, of course, is to use words that not only *are* accurate and real, but that *sound* accurate and real. Given enough of them, we believe the message within which they are embedded. Realism has a built-in air of authority, so writers would be prudent to write with realistic details as Hemingway did in this fiction piece and as he did earlier in that nonfiction piece of reporting. I enjoy the irony that Hemingway took this technique of realism from his nonfiction writing and used it when he moved into fiction—and here we are now taking this technique out of fiction and applying it to nonfiction to gain realism when writing about the real.

We can take a leaf, too, from the author Budd Schulberg, as he writes about the famous Stillman's Gym in New York City.

Americans are still an independent and rebellious people—at least in their reactions to signs. Stillman's Gym, up the street from the Garden, offers no exception to our national habit of shrugging off prohibitions. Hung prominently on the gray, nondescript walls facing the two training rings, a poster reads: "No rubbish or spitting on the floor under penalty of the law." If you want to see how the boys handle this one, stick around until everybody has left the joint and see what's left for the janitor to do. The floor is strewn with cigarettes smoked down to their stained ends, cigar butts chewed to soggy pulp, dried spittle, empty match cases, thumbed and trampled copies of the *News*, *Mirror*, and *Journal*, open to the latest crime of passion or the race results, wadded gum, stubs of last night's fight at St. Nick's (manager's comps), a torn-off cover of an Eighth Avenue restaurant menu with the name of a new matchmaker in Cleveland scrawled next to a girl's phone number. Here on the dirty gray floor of Stillman's is the telltale debris of a world as sufficient unto itself as a walled city of the Middle Ages.

That is Budd Schulberg at work writing not nonfiction, but his novel, *The Harder They Fall*. The point is that creative nonfiction writers use this novelistic technique all the time today—a technique that enlivens our nonfiction literature by sounding so realistic. Even though I've never been in such a professional gym, I know from the details he used just what it must be like. Of course my brain informs my emotional reaction by adding to his details bits of my life in high school gyms and in U.S. Navy locker rooms aboard crowded ships. All those details piled on details add to the air of authority, but none so directly as one detail in particular— "manager's comps." That did it for me. Anyone, even I, could probably have invented most of those details just out of a vivid imagination, but who could have invented that marvelously authoritative phrase, Manager's Comps? That has to be TRUTH. I suppose every reader would find one or more details in there that would persuade him or her that this passage has authority. My belief in that one phrase then lent authority to all the other details—I know that I'm inside Stillman's Gym—I'm right there and *involved* in the activities. I'm not looking through the window at the scene inside; I'm at ringside and hearing the leathery thuds and smelling the smells. "Manager's comps" did it for me; "cigar butts chewed to soggy pulp" may have done it for someone else.

That business of manager's comps raises some interesting thoughts about this entire matter of details, authority, and realism. Should Budd Schulberg have interrupted his flow by explaining what manager's comps are? I admit that I didn't know what they are, yet here I am claiming that the phrase "did it for me." How could that be? I'm only using manager's comps as an example to open up the question of how much explanation about jargon or other specialized language a writer is obliged to provide. A writer should give enough details of different kinds that most readers will pick up on one or more—and live with the fact of life that no matter how much he or she explains, someone out there is not going to understand one point or another.

It probably comes down to intent. What's the writer's intention? If it's an educational book or article, then he or she must be reasonably certain that nothing important or significant goes unexplained. If the purpose is to both inform and entertain, as is most often the case with creative nonfiction, then the writer should presume a certain amount of intelligence and experience on the reader's part so that he or she doesn't need to be forever explaining. Naturally, the writer tries every trick in his or her bag to make points clearly, yet make them with flair.

All I've said about how I was persuaded by "manager's comps," even though I didn't understand what they are, should not be interpreted to mean that it doesn't matter whether the writer's words are accurate, provided only that the words "sound" real. Don't invent terms in order to "sound" authoritative. Use specialists' jargon to lend authority, but don't feel obliged to explain it. When perplexed about whether to explain, ask yourself the key question—does the reader really need to know this in order to understand my piece? If not, consider keeping the jargon or special language (for example, the occasional foreign phrase) if your purpose is to develop mood or to give the essence of a place or a person.

Before moving on to a number of examples of how nonfiction writers use concrete details to lend authority to their articles and books, I want to point out an interesting parallelism going on within the writing world. Short story writers, like Raymond Carver, are producing what they call "realistic" writing. Their method is to write in a minimal way, largely the facts of a situation and accurate reporting on what people do. What it all means is left to the reader. The writer does not point out the meaning, nor tell us what emotions to feel, nor what emotions the characters are feeling. All this is left to the reader's brain to add its details of personal experience to what's happening in the story, thereby bringing to the story the emotions felt by the reader in the original experience. Like a *haiku*, this kind of writing requires an intelligent, experienced reader for it to achieve in the reader's brain an emotion as close as possible to what the poet experienced originally.

Carver writes with great attention to realistic details, even a person's smallest moves. The following section is from a short story, "Furious Seasons," from the collection by the same name.

He fumbled in the closet for his insulated boots, his hands tracing the sleeves of each coat until he found the rubber slick waterproof. He went to the drawer for socks and long underwear, then picked up his shirt and pants and carried the armload through the hallway into the kitchen before turning on the light. He dressed and pulled on his boots before starting the coffee. He would have liked to turn on the porch light for Frank but somehow it didn't seem good with Iris out there in bed. While the coffee perked he made sandwiches and when it had finished he filled a thermos, took a cup down from the cupboard, filled it, and sat down near a window where he could watch the street. He smoked and drank the coffee and listened to the clock on the stove, squeaking. The coffee slopped over the cup and the brown drops ran slowly down the side onto the table. He rubbed his fingers through the wet circle across the rough table top.

I've included this short discussion of Raymond Carver's fiction writing because his use of so many realistic details is almost a creative nonfiction writer's style. It's ironic that a few years ago one would have said that this is a fiction writer's style. He has taken realistic details to the ultimate level, one that nonfiction writers should probably not emulate. Nevertheless, creative nonfiction writers could study to their benefit his use of details to create a feeling of *being there*.

As we saw in Hunter Thompson's piece about the Kentucky Derby, he's a master at writing the telling detail, even the detail of a piece of conversation. In his book *Hell's Angels*, he recalls this scene about when the gang he's riding with (for his research work) was confronted by a man working for the local sheriff:

Luckily, my garb was too bastard for definition. I was wearing Levis, Wellington boots from L.L. Bean in Maine, and a Montana sheepherder's jacket over a white tennis shirt. The burr-haired honcho asked me who I was. I gave him my card and asked why he had that big pistol on his belt. "You know why," he said. "The first one of these sonsabitches that gives me any lip I'm gonna shoot right in the belly.

That's the only language they understand." He nodded toward Mohr in the phone booth, and there was nothing in his tone to make me think I was exempted. I could see that his pistol was a short-barreled Smith & Wesson .357 Magnum—powerful enough to blow holes in Mohr's BSA cylinder head, if necessary—but at arm's length it hardly mattered.

Details like Levis and Wellingtons from L.L. Bean help lend authority to the scene, but I could have created those, even though I have no knowledge whatsoever about motorcycle gangs. When the honcho spoke, I saw him. I didn't just hear him; I saw him. Those were the words I'd expect him to say, but it occurred to me that I might have invented those words too. When Hunter Thompson mentioned the .357 Magnum (which I might have come up with, too) he went on to describe it as shortbarreled, and furthermore that it was made by Smith & Wesson. That did it. I was in his power.

Naturally, I'm just speculating *post facto* about what my unconscious was doing, but I know that I ended up seeing that scene, hearing that burr-haired lummox, and seeing the hugeness of the opening in the barrel of that Smith & Wesson. I note, too, that he's absolutely correct—Smith & Wesson *does* have an ampersand in it. It's not Smith AND Wesson. Had the author not done his research (in this case, field research), he would not have had that little ampersand in there, and that would have lessened his credibility in the mind of anyone knowledgeable about pistols. (Someone out there always knows more than the writer about something.) As if he didn't already have me, Thompson threw in that business about a cylinder head—a BSA cylinder head yet. That's writing.

Mastering the Telling Detail

Richard Rhodes, author of *Looking for America* and *Ultimate Powers*, wrote the following in his first book, *The Inland Ground*. In the midst of a section entitled "Death All Day," he wrote this description of one of the men going with him on a hunt for coyotes with his other friend's dogs.

The other third of our party is Ron Nolan, an Ohio boy who overcame New York a few years back to homestead a two-room cabin in the woods outside Kansas City. His cabin contains an Italian racing motorcycle, a KLH-20 plus Stereo, a wall of books, tennis rackets, board games, a hookah, rifles, pistols, a Beretta Golden Snipe .12-gauge over-and-under shotgun, a Pacific shotshell reloader, and outside a golden sand Jaguar XKE convertible and for short hauls an aging Morris Oxford station wagon, likely the only one in the Midwest. Ron is a bachelor.

The quality of these objects that fill Ron's cabin certainly paints a picture for me of a probably young man with more money than anyone needs—and I'd rather adduce it this way than to have Mr. Rhodes "tell" me that this was Ron's economic condition. All the details did their job, but I was pulled in solidly by that hookah, a Pacific shotshell reloader, and by his specifying that the Jaguar was a golden sand color—especially after hearing earlier about a golden snipe. I don't know that the author intended to have these golden references add to the generally affluent scene. I am sure the advertising men knew it when they named the Jaguar and the Beretta. Over-and-undertones of gold never hurt a shotgun sale. As a married man with no hope of a golden sand Jag, I appreciated particularly that short, emphatic sentence—Ron is a bachelor.

John McPhee wrote in the November 26, 1985 issue of the *New Yorker* about the workaday world of a Maine warden-pilot with the unlikely name of John McPhee. As one of the acknowledged masters of the telling detail, the writer McPhee described a flying trip he took with the warden McPhee to check on men who were ice fishing within the warden's jurisdiction.

Brown's Point is actually the delta of a small stream that enters the lake beside the hangar and spews nutrients to crowds of waiting fish. Boats collect in the summer; and as soon as the lake is hard, fishing shacks arrive and remain through the winter. Fishing shacks tend to be heated, furnished, close to civilization, close to paved and numbered roads—shantytowns platted on ice, and clustered where fish are likely to be. In architectural style, at Brown's Point, they range from late-middle Outhaus to the Taj Pelletier, a ten-piece portable cabin with nearly a hundred square feet of floor space, red-curtained windows, cushioned benches, a Coleman stove, a card table, a hi-fi spilling country music, and hinged floorboards that swing upward to reveal eight perfect circles in the ice through which lines can be dangled from cup hooks in the ceiling. If the air outside is twenty below zero, the air inside will be a hundred degrees warmer, while the men in shirtsleeves interrupt their cribbage to lift into the room a wriggling salmon.

McPhee the author, as usual, had me in his thrall after only a few sentences, largely by his creative use of telling details. As I looked back at my experience of reading this paragraph, I found that the details were orchestrated to involve me more and more as I went. I may have been slightly "involved" when I read that the shack came in ten pieces and that it was nearly a hundred square feet, but when I got to the red curtains, I was suddenly there. When I read about those curtains, I had the feeling of seeing the lamp come on in the shack and some rose-colored light coming through those curtains. The cushioned benches (not chairs) made sense to me and added to the realism of my vicarious experience, but when those hinged floorboards swung up, making me step to one side, I was right there in that strange environment.

I was truly hooked, though, by those cup hooks. *Cup hooks*—I would never in a million years have been able to invent that detail. This had the ring of truth—no, not the ring of truth—this was truth. This was real(ism).

The next several examples demonstrate further the versatility of using concrete details as technique. Greta Tilley, a feature writer for the *Greensboro News and Record*, took on what has to be one of the most challenging subjects to write about—teenage suicide. With such an emotion-laden subject, the writer does not want to make an obvious attempt to evoke the reader's emotions, else it becomes a sob story.

Seven weeks have passed, yet the dim lavender room with the striped window curtains has been kept as Tonja left it.

Haphazardly positioned on top of the white French provincial-style dresser are staples of teen-age life: Sure deodorant, Enjoli cologne, an electric curling wand.

A white jewelry box opens to a ballerina dancing before a mirror. Inside, among watches and bracelets, is a gold Dudley High School ring with a softball player etched into one side and a Panther on the other. Also inside was a mimeographed reminder that a $9 balance must be paid in Mrs. Johnson's room for the 1982 yearbook. The deadline was Jan. 15.

There's no need to analyze this, item by pathetic item. It's enough to say that we would all recognize from the listing a teenage girl's dresser, and more important, the interests, the excitements, the life of a teenage person. Even if a reader's experience has been only with a teenage boy's dresser top, there's enough carryover to evoke appropriate emotions.

Leaving this sad story, let's leap across the world to present-day mainland China to note how Annie Dillard, in *Encounters with Chinese Writers*, uses concrete details to put us right beside her on the outskirts of a city. She had made the point earlier on the page that China must depend for most of its food on millions of square miles of terrible soil, soil so dense with clay that China's labor-intensive agricultural system is reflected by actual fingerprints in the soil:

> Driving to this meeting we saw fields on the outskirts of the city, and patches of agriculture. There was a field of eggplant. Separating the rows of eggplants were long stripes of dried mud, five inches high, like thick planks set on edge. These low walls shield shoots and stems from drying winds. We stopped to look. The walls were patted mud; there were fingerprints. There were fingerprints dried into the loess walls around every building in the western city of Xian. There were fingerprints in the cones of drying mud around every tree's roots in large afforestation plots near Hangzhou, and along the Yangtze River. There is good soil in China, too, on which peasants raise three and even four crops a year, and there are 2,000-acre fields, and John Deere tractors—but there is not enough.

In addition to many examples of good writing here, like the alliteration of "walls shield shoots and stems" and the strikingly accurate simile of thick planks on edge, we find author Dillard pulling us down close to the good earth for some close-up views of five-inch high walls—all in preparation for us to see those peasant fingerprints. I could see a master writer at work when she deliberately chose the verb "patted" to set our minds to accept readily the image of fingerprints. I find, too, within that accurate verb, the immediate understanding that this is indeed labor-intensive agriculture, and that the peasant may pat this mud with some care—though perhaps I'm too romantic. In any event, that verb "pat" did what its author probably intended; it prepared the way for fingerprints.

The cones of mud around every tree's roots gave some authority to this paragraph, because that's not agriculture the way we experience it here, but what clinched it for me was the surprising arrival on the scene of that symbol of American agribusiness, the John Deere tractor. Now I knew I was in the hands of not only a capable writer but one with the authority that comes from knowledge, knowledge of the details. John Deere, indeed—wow.

To wrap up for the moment this discussion of realism (although the entire book could be said to deal with it), let's hear a description of the Great Depression written by the man who helped bring this phenomenon to the nation's conscience with his novel *The Grapes of Wrath*. Nothing could have been more "real" for the people who experienced it, but for those who came later, its description needs words that recapture that reality. John Steinbeck did a great service in that regard with his various fictional writings of that era, but what follows comes from a nonfiction article he wrote in the October 1973 *Esquire* for its fortieth birthday issue, "A Primer on the Thirties":

> The Depression was no financial shock to me. I didn't have any money to lose, but in common with millions I did dislike hunger and cold. I had two assets. My father owned a tiny three-room cottage in Pacific Grove in California, and he let me live in it without rent. That was the first safety. Pacific Grove is on the sea. That was the second. People in inland cities or in the closed and shuttered industrial cemeteries had greater problems than I. Given the sea a man must be very stupid to starve. That great reservoir of food is always available. I took a large part of my protein food from the ocean. Firewood to keep warm floated on the beach daily, needing only handsaw and ax. A small garden of black soil came with the cottage. In northern California you can raise vegetables of some kind all year long. I never peeled a potato without planting the skins. Kale, lettuce, chard, turnips, carrots and onions rotated in the little garden. In the tide pools of the bay mussels were available and crabs and abalones and that shiny kelp called sea lettuce. With a line and pole, blue cod, rock cod, perch, sea trout, sculpin could be caught.

I've read other articles about life in the Depression that purported to tell what it was like, but they would typically say something like... "People lived wherever they could find a roof; they'd grow some food if they could; and those near the sea would fish." Somehow, Steinbeck knew it was not enough to say simply that they would burn driftwood to keep warm—he added that all you needed was a handsaw and ax. Those two simple, homely words added reality for me. I could see Steinbeck wandering the beach near Pacific Grove, saw in hand, ax on shoulder. I liked, too, the specificity of black soil—not just soil. It sounded like rich soil that could grow all those vegetables, with several crops a year. I was very young during the Depression, but I do remember chard—and I seem to recall that only near-starvation would take me back to chard. It was the mention of chard here, however, that lent authority to everything else. As a man from Milton, Massachusetts, my brain couldn't make direct contact with those abalones, but it knew chard. Oh, it knew chard.

I've said here and elsewhere in this book that some creative nonfiction writers bend over backward not to tell the reader what "meaning" he or she should take from their words, while some other creative nonfiction writers don't hesitate to editorialize or tell us how to think about something. Even the former group, the group that intends not to editorialize, does so anyway through the realistic details it selects to tell the story. All writing involves selection, choice.

Everything can't be said. Whether the writing involved is an essay, article, or book, some things rather than others are singled out for mention. That they're singled out implies that the author found them more important than what was left out. The overall impression created by this selection constitutes the writer's style, "meaning," stance, his or her own individual truth.

As a writer, you cannot avoid "giving yourself away" in this fashion, and shouldn't try. Rather, you should try to reveal only true things which you indeed feel are important, and to arrange them in relationships that reflect what you believe to be the meaning, the truth of whatever subject you're considering. A laundry-list of landmarks and dates is no less a true picture of New York than a representative slice-of-life description of what one might see at Broadway and 42nd between one and six in the morning. But they're not the same truth, the same vision.

The key word is "representative."

What's representative is what the author presents as representative. The writer's reliability rests in how able he or she is to convince us that the representation is fair—that it is accurate and illuminating to the whole, not distorted or fabricated, but rather, honest in the impression it creates.

If the selection of event and detail is good, it won't need much commentary from the author to show what it means. Just the process of selection and arrangement, if rightly handled, should do that. Excessive commentary is intrusive overkill, like a comic telling you how funny a joke's going to be. You don't want to be told—if it's funny, you'll laugh. If it's not, being told how funny the comic thought it ought to be isn't any help at all. The writer should show, rather than tell, as much as he or she can, and let the selection and combination of details speak for themselves as much as possible.

In addition to all the other ways writers of creative nonfiction use to achieve a high level of realism, they tend also to walk us readers through a story scene by scene.

WRITING SCENE BY SCENE

In traditional journalism, the basic building block was the fact. Reporters rushed around collecting facts from dusty records at City Hall, interviewing experts, and talking with the men and women involved. The more facts the better, facts piled on facts, interview quote stacked on interview quote. All this took place in the name of accuracy, completeness, and objectivity—certainly not in the name of readability or memorability. Creative nonfiction writers remain as respectful of facts. They usually have the time to dig up far more facts about a story than do deadline-haunted reporters, but they don't think of them as the basic building blocks for their stories; they "think scenes" instead.

The scene has now become the fundamental block around which the writer forms the story. Usually a story has a number of scenes involved, so the method is to develop the story scene by scene. The creative nonfiction writer, like the fiction writer, recognizes the power inherent in drama. The scene is the dramatic element both in fiction and creative nonfiction. A scene reproduces the movement of life; life is motion, action.

The writer almost always has the choice of writing in the summary (narrative) form, the scenic (dramatic) form, or in some combination, neither wholly summary nor wholly scenic. The last chapter discussed Scene vs. Summary in greater depth, but a short review here may help.

Because the scenic or dramatic method of writing provides the reader a closer imitation of life than summary ever could, the creative nonfiction writer frequently chooses to write scenically wherever reasonable. He or she wants vivid images to transfer into the mind of the reader, and scenic writing's strength lies in its ability to evoke visual images. A scene is not some anonymous narrator's report about what happened some time in the past; instead, we get the feeling that the action is unfolding before us. A scene makes the past present. We see the characters in action, we see their gestures, we hear their voices in conversation. Our participation, our involvement, is greater in the scene. We can't take part in a summary narrative; we're just students in a room listening to a lecture. As soon as we see the scene, we feel it, smell it, hear it, we believe for the moment that we're in it.

The main point behind writing scene by scene is that since the brain is "involved" in the scenes, it accepts more readily all the other narrative information the writer presents. As in fiction, the writer "uses" scenes for his or her own purposes. He or she has certain narrative work to do, and knows that some of it can be smuggled unobtrusively into scenes. A lot of characterization, for example, can be smuggled into a scene through captured conversation.

By little bits of narrative prose stealthily slipped in around the conversation, the writer can reveal, for example, some of the participants' physical characteristics—hairstyle, beard, snapping eyes, limps, laughs. If the bits remain short and scattered, the reader fails to hear the narrator's voice intruding, and remains involved in the scene. Where narrative summary must be used, the creative nonfiction writer will try, if feasible, to have a main character, or some character, provide the summary statement through a quote, direct or indirect. The reader accepts more readily the words of a character than those of a narrator. Even an indirect quote retains, if the writer's clever, the voice of the character, and thus the reader's sense of participation in the scene—or, at least, the reader has the feeling of observing the scene firsthand, not secondhand, through the eyes of the narrator.

As you plan a story, consider which "events" or "incidents" or "happenings" have the most dramatic potential. Not always, but frequently, this translates into which scenes have the best visual, imagistic potential. These become your inventory of possible scenes—all else must be handled through narrative summary. As in fiction, certain "events" typically have great dramatic potential, so you watch for:

turning points	*showdowns*	*arguments*
flashbacks	*disasters*	*suffering*
successes	*failures*	*life reversals*
beginnings	*births*	*deaths*

Although they are probably major events, don't overlook the potential of small, seemingly insignificant incidents that you can work up into a scene to use for your narrative purposes. In this regard, don't confuse *content* with *method*. The words "drama" and "scene" usually connote a *content* of great significance, but we're using them here in terms of *method*, so the content of a scene may be simple, i.e., not very "dramatic." The following passage from Russell Baker's memoir, *Growing Up*, is an "insignificant" scene, but the scenic method makes it come alive for us. Note that this "scene" has no captured conversation, as scenes more typically do, but the concrete details make it form images tactile, visual, and auditory in our brains.

Before this passage, Russell Baker had pointed out that when he was a child, the outermost edge of his universe was Brunswick, Virginia, *as distant and romantic a place as I ever expected to see.* When his father took him on a trip to Brunswick to see three of Russell's uncles, he discovered that the city had electric light bulbs, telephones, radios. *Rich people lived there. Masons, for heaven's sake. Not just Red Men and Odd Fellows and Moose such as we had around Morrisonville, but Masons. And not just Masons, but Baptists, too....* When they visited his Uncle Tom, the blacksmith, young Russell fell in love with a miracle in a small room.

> At the top of the stairs lay the miracle of plumbing. Shutting the door to be absolutely alone with it, I ran my fingers along the smooth enamel of the bathtub and glistening faucet handles of the sink. The white majesty of the toilet bowl, through which gallons of water could be sent rushing by the slightest touch of a silvery lever, filled me with envy. A roll of delicate paper was placed beside it. Here was luxury almost too rich to be borne by anyone whose idea of fancy toiletry was Uncle Irvey's two-hole privy and a Montgomery Ward catalog.
>
> After gazing upon it as long as I dared without risking interruption by a search party, I pushed the lever and savored the supreme moment when thundering waters emptied into the bowl and vanished with a mighty gurgle. It was the perfect conclusion to a trip to Brunswick.

Imagine that written as narrative summary by someone other than Russell Baker, someone who didn't appreciate the dramatic potential of a boy seeing his first indoor bathroom: *He was impressed to discover that unlike Uncle Irvey's, Uncle Tom's bathroom had running water. He enjoyed listening to the water rushing down into the toilet bowl. The delicate*

*paper next to the bowl was a far cry from the Montgomery Ward catalog in
the two-hole privy he was used to at home.* The words accomplish essentially the same narrative work but miss the potential to involve us in the
experience and to see it through the boy's eyes—no drama. Since no conversation went on in either passage, the difference lies in the concreteness
of the details and the sensory content of Baker's. His writing is vivid, i.e., it
has the stuff of life in it. Mine was merely reporting the facts; his was
drawing a scene, reporting the drama inherent in a minor incident.

The Scene and Its Value

J. Anthony Lukas writes with a clear understanding of the value of
writing scene by scene. His book *Common Ground* has been praised by
Thomas Powers as "a major contribution to American Literature . . . a
compelling narrative of three families caught up in the oldest American
problem—the agony of race. Boston is the scene but the subject is the
burden of history. You may read it for the story—I certainly did—but
you'll remember it as if you had lived it." Most of the chapters center on
one or the other of the three families (Diver, Twymon, or McGoff). Lukas
introduced the families in three short opening chapters, beginning each
chapter with a scene—the scene when a member of the family first hears
about the assassination of the Reverend Martin Luther King, Jr.

CHAPTER 1/DIVER

Sunlight struck the gnarled limbs outside his windows, casting a
thicket of light and shadow on the white clapboards. From his desk
high under the eaves, Colin Diver could watch students strolling the
paths of Cambridge Common or playing softball on the neatly
trimmed diamond. It was one of those brisk afternoons in early
spring, the kind of day which in years past had lured him into the
dappled light, rejoicing in his good fortune. But here he lurked in his
study, walled in by books, overcome by doubt.

CHAPTER 2/TWYMON

An hour after the transistor radios in the project blared the news
of King's death, Snake and Sly (Twymon) were out on Eustis Street
slinging rocks at the police. Around the corner on Dearborn Street,
someone had thrown a brick through a grocery window and every

few minutes a kid would scamper across, grab a juicy grapefruit or a handful of plums, then dash to safety in the jiving black crowd.

But soon the frolic turned serious ...

CHAPTER 3/MCGOFF

It was the moment she liked best, the vegetables spread out before her in voluptuous profusion: squeaky stalks of celery, damp lettuce, succulent tomatoes, chilled radishes. From the sink rose the earthy smells of wet roots and peels, and from all about her the clamor and fracas of a busy kitchen, gearing up for dinner only minutes away.

Mark Patinkin, writing under deadline pressures for the *Providence Journal-Bulletin*, sent back from Africa some of the most touching stories about life in the drought-stricken areas. His articles captured the pathos through dramatic, often scene-by-scene writing. In "They Flee From Hunger But Keep Their Humanity," he writes of life within a refugee camp containing 55,000 men, women, and children at the point of terminal starvation.

We walked on, into one of the hospital units. I paused by a father and son. The son lay in the father's arms. The father called softly to the son.
I turned to the doctor. "That child looks bad," I said.
The doctor bent over for a closer look. "He died during the night," he said.
Back outside, the sun hit the mountains with a beauty that made me stop and stare. We moved toward the more hopeful side of the camp. A hundred fires were going. The day's cooking had begun, with the last of the wood. This was not a secret place. The whole camp knew this was where the limited food supply was prepared. And no one bothered it.
"I still find it hard to understand," said the doctor.
He had long since been able to pull the curtain down on the tragedies of this place. The one thing he still could not get used to was the decency.

Patinkin saw in this small incident (small in terms of all he was witnessing throughout Africa) the potential for drama, drama small enough for the reader to comprehend and become involved in. The overall scene happening to 55,000 people cannot get to our emotions the way a father holding his dead son can. That scene stands, in a sense, for the thousands of similar "minor" incidents happening to these starving refugees. It's meaningful … *representative*. And therefore, *realistic*.

FOUR

THE REALITIES OF GROUP LIFE

W e've been talking about how hard modern nonfiction writers try to invest their articles and books with the feeling of real life, life as it's lived, not as we think it might be, or should be, but as close as possible to the various realities that exist simultaneously in this world. We've seen that one of the more powerful techniques for accomplishing this is the inclusion of details.

I worry about using the word "realistic" because I fear the reader will think of it in one of its present-day connotations—"almost real," e.g., "The wood-grained plastic facade gave the movie set a realistic appearance." I'll use realistic to mean, instead, "real," e.g., "The writer added to the dialog many realistic details"—meaning that to the dialog he or she added many of the details he'd gathered in interviews and during field trips. The details are not merely "realistic," they are details from real life. These details from real life as lived by real people give an article or book (as they do a piece of fiction) a sense of realism.

Since most creative nonfiction deals with men and women, the writers pay particular attention to how these people live, not in the abstract, but in the everyday world. This is difficult to talk about sometimes, because the reader may be thinking, "Don't all nonfiction writers write the truth about the people they're discussing? Do journalists lie?" No, there's no question about that; they all believe they're talking about real people, and would never agree that they speak in the abstract about people—but many do. They've been trained that way in college and on the job.

Until very recently, for example, most newspaper and magazine writers would never quote someone swearing or blaspheming—their words would either be shown with censoring dashes or dots, and only the more "civilized" words would be quoted. If the writer wanted, nevertheless, to write truthfully, he or she would be limited to saying that the man swore and blasphemed outrageously (now, that's writing in the abstract). If the prisoner on his way to the cell raised his middle finger at the reporters, it would likely have been reported that he gestured obscenely at the reporters. This is not being "realistic," because we know that every person from grammar school on probably knows this obscene gesture, and may even have used it.

One of the major points of discussing here the realities of group life is that the writer should report the concrete details, *les petits vrais* (the little truths) of life. So-called concrete details include: gestures and curses, as above; the sports and games people play; their fads of fashion and food; their religious activities; the trappings of their professions; where and how they live; and bits of their captured conversations. In other words, apply the advice given in the last chapter and other chapters to the purpose of establishing for the reader the realities of group life.

Since the last quote was from Mark Patinkin as he described life in Africa, it might be interesting to read now about an economic group that could hardly be more remote from the one he described. In the October 1983 "Sophisticated Traveler" section of the Sunday *New York Times*, William F. Buckley, Jr. wrote about the advantages to cruising the Caribbean in a chartered yacht rather than traveling commercially. All you have to do to make the weekly charter costs is to share the yacht with two other couples—that's all.

> In your own boat. Though, having said that, I confess I have not been aboard a commercial cruising boat during the conventional one or two weeks in the Caribbean. Probably there is much to be said for this way of seeing the islands, in preference to hotel life. But your very own boat is really the way to go, and one might as well quickly confront the proposition, "Isn't this out of the question for the average pocketbook?" The answer is: Yes. But so is a week aboard any of the more luxurious liners or a week at any of the fancier hotels. In round figures—if you include meals, drinks, tips, taxis—you are talking about something over $400 per couple a day, times seven comes to— well, close to $3,000 a week. Last Christmas we chartered a boat that cost $1,000 a day, including food but not drinks, tips or taxis. Throw these in even profusely, and you are still short of $9,000 a week. But

there are three couples sharing the boat, so that the cost, for each couple,—less than $3,000—is comparable to the hotels.

These matter-of-fact words about the cost of yachts, taxis, and tips give us an immediate, realistic impression of life as lived by the wealthy. It's the straightforwardness of the discussion that makes it real for us. Buckley doesn't apologize for, or seem embarrassed by, these high figures. He doesn't compare or contrast that lifestyle with how the rest of us live on vacation. He just says what he wants to say to his audience through accurate and precise details.

When Annie Dillard traveled with the Chinese writers she recorded some vignettes of life in modern China that stay with the reader, first because of her accuracy of observation, and second because of her willingness and ability to put them down just as experienced—not after putting the thoughts first through some kind of ideological pasta machine. My impression is that she writes of the real:

> In the cities, where incomes are five times those in the country, families are saving industrial coupons for years on end to buy a bicycle, or to buy a sewing machine with which to fashion both clothes and bedding from their cotton allotment of six yards per person per year. The family lives in its one or two cement rooms. The wife washes the twigs and stones from the rationed rice and cooks some cabbage on a shared stove. Six days a week the husband and wife put in long hours in their production units; the wife spends two hours a day buying food. On Sundays they bring the baby home from the nursery school, where one-third of Beijing's babies live. They all dress up and go to the park, which has several plots of flowers.

The writer impressed me by how much I learned about today's China in so short a paragraph. I can imagine some other writer faced with giving basically the same amount of information, but unable to put it down simply. Such compression (while retaining some gracefulness of expression) could only be accomplished through such conscientious attention to those details that said something directly (without extra words of explanation) about life at that place at that time. She didn't, for example, contrast that twig- and stone-laced rice with Americans' snow-white, pure rice; no discussion about the comparative nutrient value of the two rices; no long political explanation of "rationed rice"—just the plain, clearly expressed images of what she saw and heard. She took me with her when she ended on the quiet irony that this park for which everyone dressed up has but several plots of flowers.

Sara Davidson, a novelist, has also published articles in many of the magazines that appreciate creative nonfiction writing, magazines such as *Ramparts, Harper's, Esquire, Rolling Stone*, and *Ms.* In *Real Property*, a book that presents many of these articles, she includes the following piece about group life in Venice, California, the closest place to downtown L.A. where you can live on the beach—and the only place in that giant, spread-out city where there's real life in the street. As she says in that book, "You are guaranteed to see people outside their cars." Here's part of her presentation of life in Venice.

> Living in Venice is like living in a camp for semi-demented adults. At every hour, day and night, there are people playing volleyball, running, rolling on skates, riding bikes, skateboards, surf boards, flying kites, drinking milk, eating quiche lorraine. Old people sit under umbrellas playing checkers. Body builders work out in a sandy pen, and crowds line up three deep to perform on the paddle tennis courts. When do these people work? I used to wonder.
>
> The residents of Venice fall into two groups: Those who work, and those who don't. The latter includes senior citizens, drifters, drug addicts, hopeful moviemakers and aging hippies and surfers who have made a cult of idleness and pleasure. The other group includes lawyers, dentists, real estate brokers, accountants. Many are workaholics, attached to their jobs as they are to nothing else. They work nights and weekends, eat fast food while driving to and from their work and live alone, longing, in the silence before falling asleep, for connection.
>
> Everyone comes together on the boardwalk. The natives own their own skates, and the tourists rent them from places like "Cheapskates" and "United Skates of America"....

I liked the way Sara Davidson lured me into the paragraph by saying that Venice is "a camp for semi-demented adults." I couldn't resist reading on to learn what she meant (or half-meant). She didn't "tell" me in some sociological fashion, she "showed" me these adults riding their skateboards, flying their kites, and drinking their milk (what a delightful surprise). As I read that paragraph, I began to wonder how all these adults could be out playing around, seemingly all the time—and then she answered me. A sociologist would never do it, but a creative nonfiction writer can do it—divide the population into just two groups, those who work and those who don't. I found it particularly good writing to then bring these divided groups together again—on the famous boardwalk where we've all seen on television news or documentaries those girls in their sequined skimpy tube tops skating so gracefully in and out of the slower pedestrian traffic. My memory even served up a commercial that showed a lovely young woman on skates delivering (. . . a Pepsi, wasn't it?) to customers along that boardwalk. Another example of how the reader's brain will supply bits and pieces of relevant information from memory to make more understandable the new information it is now receiving. That's why such listings of concrete detail are so useful.

These details serve the dual purpose of giving us pieces of the puzzle to put together for comprehension, and of evoking associated memories that will color the present with the emotions that surrounded them when first experienced (and stored) in the past. Someone else will not dredge up that commercial; they'll dredge up the handsome man who so graced a roller rink in Fort Wayne at a church outing ten years ago. Such is the combined power of concrete details and the brain. We're still talking about achieving realism, this time for describing group behavior patterns.

Filling in the Blanks

Dr. Loren Eiseley writes about anthropology and other sciences so that the well-educated nonspecialist can understand him. Like Dr. Lewis Thomas, the medical researcher, he writes clearly and persuasively about sophisticated topics. These eminent scholars are able to go beyond so-called sophistication and come back to what I consider true sophistication—writing that's clear, interesting, witty, and graceful. They usually write on serious topics which, in other hands, might put the reader to sleep. In the following excerpt from his book *The Night Country*, Loren Eiseley writes about the elderly poor and ill who live in the railroad terminals of many major cities. He compares them to dying old brown wasps he's observed in midwinter. Like them, these old folks prefer to die in the center of things, not somewhere in lonely isolation.

Now and then they sleep, their old gray heads resting with painful awkwardness on the backs of the benches.

Also they are not at rest. For an hour they may sleep in the gasping exhaustion of the ill-nourished and aged who have to walk in the night. Then a policeman comes by on his round and nudges them upright.

"You can't sleep here," he growls.

A strange ritual then begins. An old man is difficult to waken. After a muttered conversation the policeman presses a coin into his hand and passes fiercely along the benches prodding and gesturing toward the door. In his wake, like birds rising and settling behind the passage of a farmer through a cornfield, the men totter up, move a few paces and subside once more upon the benches.

One man, after a slight, apologetic lurch, does not move at all. Tubercularly thin, he sleeps on steadily. The policeman does not look back. To him, too, this has become a ritual. He will not have to notice it again officially for another hour.

Once in a while one of the sleepers will not awake. Like the brown wasps, he will have had his wish to die in the great droning center of the hive rather than in some lonely room....

Perhaps the most important point to take from this particular image of group life is that Eiseley does not lecture us about the plight of these poor, feeble, old folks. He simply paints for us a realistic (though impressionistic) picture of the policeman making his round, and the responses (and nonresponses) of those who huddle on those hard benches. Because he doesn't clutter up his writing with excess words, we can see the gray old heads tilted back against the hard benches, mouths forced open. Note that he didn't supply those open mouths—I did. As a reader, I brought to his simple, clear image something from my memories of seeing folks just like these in Grand Central Station. Had he put in many, many descriptive words, as some of us are prone to do, I wonder whether I'd have supplied that associated memory. When too much description is presented the reader, he or she thinks, subconsciously, that it's all there—no other details are needed.

Everyone's brain, as a creative, problem-solving device, enjoys filling in details—a primitive form of problem solving. These brains of ours are made to solve problems—and they'll do it when given the least encouragement. We can give that encouragement by providing only the minimum (yet carefully selected) information. Have you ever noticed how attractive a photograph can be of a person's face seen through a rain-streaked, misty window? We like it because we get to create—we fill in the missing information about the face and experience joy in doing so.

Jane Howard, writing in *Esquire*'s June 1985 issue writes about a group not often written about in so interesting and straightforward a way, "The Mormons of Salt Lake City." Naturally, it takes more than one paragraph to give us a comprehensive picture, but this one does give us a thumbnail sketch. She told about awaking in her hotel at 3:00 A.M. to a disturbing series of beeping sounds.

The beeping sounds turned out to be traffic signals telling the blind when to cross the streets. Nobody jaywalks. Shoppers, emerging from malls that smell of fudge, wait patiently for lights to change, clutching parcels. What is in them? Maybe Jots and Tittles: The Trivia Game for Latterday Saints (Mormons), from the Deseret Bookstore. (*Deseret* is the Mormon word for "honeybee," which is what Utahans in general and Mormons in particular are supposed to be as busy as.) Maybe something from ZCMI, Zion Cooperative Mercantile Institution, the oldest department store west of the Mississippi, where you get a discount on a new coat if you bring your old one in to donate to the needy. Maybe embroidery supplies; as the Mormon Handicrafts Center behind the hotel suggests, this is a very big town for sewing.

Jane Howard manages to tell us in this short paragraph, mainly by showing us, a fair amount about the lives lived by Mormons—and by others who live among them in Salt Lake City where their influence pervades. Perhaps through their influence, the city has installed beepers for the few blind folks in the city; the people are described indirectly as law-abiding, through that powerful, short sentence—Nobody jaywalks; she implies that the people are wholesome, in that their malls smell of fudge; that they lead a life similar to other Americans, yet distinct—they have their own brand of trivia game; they are practical and concerned—you can get a discount if you'll bring in clothing for the needy; and they lean toward austerity, or at least away from flamboyance—the citizens are big on home sewing. All this information came across, not by formal lecturing, but by the inclusion of telling details of everyday life.

I cannot, by the next juxtaposition, be accused of taking sides in contrasting these two groups (since I have a Mormon son-in-law in Australia and a daughter-in-law from Brazil), but I'm sure that those two personal facts led me to read these two descriptions in the first place. This world is certainly full of the varied realities of group life, but who'd want to live in a less variegated world?

Warren Hoge wrote about Rio de Janeiro's better-off citizens in an article for "The Sophisticated Traveler" (the *New York Times* special section) in October 1983:

> Don't be bothered by the way Brazilians litter their beaches with paper wrappers, soft-drink cans and other disposables. In the early evening, when the veil of mist from the surf and the fog off the mountains meet and soften the edges of vision, platoons of sanitation men in bright orange uniforms rake the beach of the day's debris. Aside from leaving things clean for the next morning, their gentle march across the sands is also a reminder that in Rio the most commonplace things can borrow grace from natural splendor ...
>
> Ricardo Amaral, owner of Rio's hottest nightspot, the Hippopotamus discotheque, rolls his eyes to the heavens at mention of the 4:00 a.m. closing time in New York (he is also proprietor of Club A in midtown Manhattan). Walk out of Hippopotamus at an hour when runners are already in the street, calisthenics classes have commenced on the beach and vendors are setting up their stalls in the farmers' market, and, if you glance behind, you'll see that the frolic inside is still pulsating as if there weren't already a tomorrow.

The first paragraph gives us a quick look at two groups of people living in Rio, the "Cariocas" who seem always to live on the beach, and the army of sanitation men who clean up after them. The image of mist and fog merging to soften the edges of vision was inspired, but I was put onto the beach by his men in orange uniforms that captured the red rays of the setting sun, all softened by the misty air. Yes, I supplied that part about how the red rays of a setting sun move anything orange closer toward red. I don't think I've ever seen orange uniforms in the sunset, but I do see almost every night how the setting sun turns the hairy bark of my red cedars nearly flame red. Truly inspired was Hoge's metaphor of a gentle march across the sands. This book does not promise to make you write as well; it can only hope to inspire you to write to the best level you can. In all the millions of words I've read over a lifetime, I'm sure I've never seen paired up the words *gentle* and *march*. They belonged together here. Perfect. Evocative. *Accurate*.

Beach swimmers in another part of the world live a different life. In fashionable Newport, Rhode Island, the wealthy belong to the Spouting Rock Beach Association and swim at its Bailey's Beach. Until you've managed to get a cabana at Bailey's Beach, you haven't arrived, according to Cleveland Amory, who writes so well about the wealthy and their strange group behavior patterns. In *Newport: There She Sits*, he writes:

> Like other Newport clubs Bailey's is run on a double-membership basis; in other words, one must become first a seasonal subscriber, then a stockholder and full-fledged member. Supporting a cabana at Bailey's often runs as high as $1,500 a year, because they are owned outright and the upkeep and all improvements are in the hands of the owner, not the Beach Association. All cabanas have locks, but not to keep outsiders out; they are to keep the owners out. The superintendent of the beach keeps all keys and every night at seven locks all cabanas; then, all night long every hour, a watchman makes the rounds to see that no owners have tried to get in. Bailey's wants no part of after-dark bathing or cabana courtships, and the fact that the younger generation does not like the beach's blue laws bothers *eclat*-minded Newporters not at all. "Young people have a good time at Bailey's," declares Mrs. George Tyson, a sister of Mrs. (Perle) Mesta and a woman whose cottage overlooks the beach, "but it is a good time in an awfully nice way."

The main point a writer can learn from this paragraph is that Amory does not tell us how to feel about these strange goings-on at Bailey's Beach. He simply lays out the facts accurately and interestingly, leaving the figuring-out to us readers. Beginning writers (and some not-so-beginning) think they have to interpret the meaning behind everything, almost as if they think we have not the intelligence or imagination to attack it ourselves—a good way to lose friends and readers.

One group that needs its balloons punctured more often is the highbrow intellectuals, especially academics. As a professor I know what a long, weak branch I'm crawling out on, but I loved the way Russell Lynes, former managing editor at *Harper's*, stuck needles in our puffed-up egos. The following is from an article he wrote in 1949, "Highbrow, Lowbrow, Middlebrow":

> There is a certain air of omniscience about the highbrow, though the air is in many cases the thin variety encountered on the tops of high mountains from which the view is extensive but the details are lost.
>
> You cannot tell a man that he is a lowbrow any more than you can tell a woman her clothes are in bad taste, but a highbrow doesn't mind being called a highbrow. He has worked hard, read widely, traveled far, and listened attentively in order to satisfy his curiosity and establish his

squatters' rights in this little corner of intellectualism, and he does not care who knows it. And this is true of both kinds of highbrow—the militant, or crusader, type and the passive, or dilettante, type. These types in general live happily together; the militant highbrow carries the torch of culture, the passive highbrow reads by its light. The carrier of the torch makes a profession of being a highbrow and lives by his calling. He is most frequently found in university and college towns, a member of the liberal-arts faculty, teaching languages (ancient or modern), the fine arts, or literature. His spare time is often devoted to editing a magazine which is read mainly by other highbrows, ambitious undergraduates, and the editors of middlebrow publications in search of talent. When he writes for the magazine himself (or for another "little" magazine) it is usually criticism or criticism of criticism. He leaves the writing of fiction and poetry to others more bent on creation than on what has been created, for the highbrow is primarily a critic and not an artist—a taster, not a cook. He is often more interested in where the arts have been, and where they are going, than in the objects themselves. He is devoted to the proposition that the arts must be pigeon-holed, and that their trends should be plotted, or as W. H. Auden puts it—

Our intellectual marines,
Landing in Little Magazines,
Capture a trend.

In my opening comments to this excerpt, I said that Lynes stuck needles in our puffed-up egos. Actually, of course, he didn't do it—I (the reader) did. He pointed to the behavior patterns of this group and I provided the needles from my own prejudices—and that is typical of today's writers of creative nonfiction. As did Cleveland Amory in describing the behaviors of the wealthy at Bailey's Beach, Lynes only put forth some observations, interestingly and accurately, and the reader interprets their meaning. Perhaps a true highbrow would not feel the needles at all—as Lynes said, the highbrow doesn't care who knows what he or she is.

Entertaining Thoughts

Creative nonfiction writers sometimes feel they can get at the realities of group life by looking at what people do for entertainment. William Least Heat Moon, for example, wrote in *Blue Highways* about his drive toward New Orleans and "Cajun Country":

I switched on the radio and turned the dial. Somewhere between a shill for a drive-up savings bank and loan and one for salvation, I found a raucous music, part bluegrass fiddle, part Texas guitar, part Highland concertina. Cajun voices sang an old, flattened French, part English, part undecipherable.

Looking for live Cajun music, I stopped in Opelousas at The Plantation Lounge. Somebody sat on every barstool; but a small man, seeing a stranger, jumped down, shook my hand, and insisted I take his seat. In the fast roll of Cajun English, he said it was the guest stool and by right belonged to me. The barmaid, a woman with coiled eyes, brought a Jax. "Is there Cajun music here tonight?" I asked.

"Jukebox is our music tonight," she snapped.

Moon not only succeeded in telling (showing) us something about the musical entertainment of some rural Cajun people in Louisiana, he also informed us about their unusual speech patterns. A few paragraphs later, he managed to slip in several more bits about their "entertainment" in a listing of references to Evangeline, who had come down from Nova Scotia (Acadia) in 1755.

If you've read Longfellow, you can't miss Cajunland once you get to the heart of it: Evangeline Downs (horses), Evangeline Speedway (autos), Evangeline Thruway (trucks), Evangeline Drive-in, and, someone had just said, the Sweet Evangeline Whorehouse.

In an article David Halberstam wrote for *Esquire* in June 1985, "The Basket-Case State," he described at length the love affair Indiana has with basketball—its chief entertainment. By concentrating on even one form of entertainment, he manages to tell us something about life in Indiana (at least in his view):

... It was a sport for the lonely. A kid did not need five or six other friends; he did not need even one. There was nothing else to do, and because this was Indiana, there was nothing else anyone even wanted to do. Their fathers nailed backboards and rims to the sides of garages or to nearby trees. The nets were waxed to make them last longer, and the kids spent their days shooting baskets in all kinds of weather. This was the land of great pure shooters, and the true mark of an Indiana high school basketball player was hitting the open shot.

A few paragraphs later, Halberstam claims that basketball game-going is a custom of the state:

> Basketball worked in Indiana not just because kids wanted to play it but because adults needed to see it, needed to get into a car at night and drive to another place and hear other voices. So it began, and so it was ingrained in the customs of the state. What helped fan the flame was the instant sense of rivalry, the desire to beat the next village, particularly if it was a little larger. The town of five hundred longed to beat the metropolis of one thousand, and that metropolis ached to beat the city of three thousand, and the city of three thousand dreamed of beating the big city of six thousand. If it happened once every twenty years, said Hammel, that was good enough. The memory lasted, and the photograph of the team members, their hair all slicked down, stayed in the local barbershop a very long time.

Just after reading that fine article in 1985, I took a vacation trip through the Midwest (including Indiana) and found that the memory lasted not only because of the barbershops but because of the very large highway signs just outside town. There, we tourists with our lamentable lack of knowledge about basketball history are informed that this town's high school basketball team won the Regionals in 1980.

Halberstam gave us considerable insight when he told us that the people *needed* to see it, *needed* to get out of the house and hear other voices. I appreciated also the carefully selected verbs by which he described the emotional states of the various sized towns—the smallest *longed*, the next *ached*, and the next to largest merely *dreamed*. Not simply an attempt to vary the verbs, this was writing (and thinking) at its best. I found this progression of emotion accurate. Such subtle accuracy must be strived for. A progression like that does not simply arrive on the page; it's sought. When finally found, it's a thrill only a writer can fully appreciate. Such are the rewards of writing.

Many creative nonfiction writers (including Norman Mailer) seem to enjoy writing about the celebrities of this world. In this final section about how writers frequently describe a group's entertainment as a way to understand the group, Norman Mailer tells us about the dangers of celebrity in an *Esquire* (December 1983) article, "The Prisoner of Celebrity," about Jackie Kennedy Onassis:

For celebrities are idiots more often than you would expect. Few of one's own remarks should still offer pleasure, but I do like, "Fame? Fame is a microphone in your mouth." To celebrities, the wages of success are those flashbulbs in the eye. If one were hit with no more than ten good jabs every day, the brain would soon reflect its damage; the flashbulbs are worse than jabs and sear one's delicacy. They even jar the last remains of your sensibility. So celebrities are surprisingly flat, bland, even disappointing when you talk to them. Their manner has something in common with the dull stuffed-glove feel in the handshake of a professional boxer. His hands are his instrument, so a fighter will guard his hands. Personality is the falling currency of overexposed celebrities, so over the years they know they must offer less and less to strangers. Those flashbulbs cauterize our souls.

Dress as a Badge of Group Life

In addition to looking at a group's methods of entertaining itself, writers frequently look at the way people DRESS. Only an individual, not a group, can dress, of course, but if the individual is a member of some more-or-less identifiable group, he or she will likely dress like others in that group. In *Zen and the Art of Motorcycle Maintenance*, for example, its author, Robert M. Pirsig, and his son Bill are sitting at lunch in Miles City, Montana, when Bill says: "This is a great town, really great. Surprised there were any like this left. I was looking all over this morning. They've got Stockmen's bars, high-top boots, silver-dollar belt buckles, Levis, Stetsons, the whole thing . . . and it's *real*. It isn't just Chamber of Commerce stuff. . . . In the bar down the block this morning they just started talking to me like I'd lived here all my life." The author (or Bill) mentions only several articles of clothing, but we are already forming a mental picture of how the men dress in Miles City, and we think we know something about their character—a dangerous presumption, of course, but we know enough to await further indications of their true character(s).

In *La Place de la Concorde Suisse*, John McPhee's book about the important role(s) played by the army and its reserves in Switzerland, he focuses in on the realistic, accurate details:

Each wears boots, gaiters, a mountain jacket, and a woolly-earflap Finnish hat, and carries a *fusil d'assaut*, which can fire twenty-four bullets in eight seconds and, with added onomatopoeia, is also known as a Sturmgewehr. Massy wears hobnailed boots. Most of the other soldiers are younger, and when they came into the army were issued boots with rubber soles—Swiss crosses protruding from the soles in lieu of hobnails.

A group forever changing its mind about how to dress is teenagers. According to Charlie Haas in *Esquire* (June, 1985), when any new way to achieve a treat is discovered, its technology is rushed to Westwood, California, which he calls the Silicon Valley of silly delight. In the article, "Tinsel Teens," he describes the teenagers and their latest clothing fad(s):

> On a Saturday afternoon the kids start drifting in from all over the city to kick things off with some serious clothes shopping. Boys who can name you every designer in their outfit, from Generra all-cotton jacket down, are heard to swear undying love for the shoes at Leather Bound. The Limited Express, with technopop on the PA, offers Day-Glo sweat-fleece cardigans and other punch-line looks; a few doors down, at the other Limited store, the emphasis is on foreign designs— Firenza, Kenzo. But what is key for the Westwood girl of the moment—even more key than Esprit—is Guess?, a line of sportswear heavy on soft-shaped whites, pastels, and denims. "They'll buy anything Guess?—the *label* sells," says a seventeen-year-old salesgirl at MGA. "They spend a lot of money, but then, *clothes* are a lot of money now." The biggest hit garment with the girls is a hugely oversize white jacket with overlapping seams, a jacket so shapeless and enveloping that its wearers look like sculpture waiting to be unveiled at adulthood.

In addition to Haas's interesting descriptions of the clothes the Westwood teens are into this season, he uses irony in reporting that boys are heard to swear undying love for certain shoes. He also uses a typographical device to help us hear the teenager's exaggerated voice by italicizing the fact that the *label* sells and *clothes* are a lot of money now. Since the writer is now leaving his discussion of clothing fads and going into a discussion of food fads, he winds it up with a piece of humorous irony: they look like sculptures to be unveiled at adulthood. A perfect metaphor in that we get the image of a teenager's typical posing, as a sculptor's model might, but we also see, through his use of "unveiling," an image of a sculpture hidden until the ceremony in a great, shapeless drape of material, reminding us of how he's just described the shapeless and enveloping white jackets the girls of the moment are probably swearing undying love for—and then he winds up the metaphoric image for us by reminding us quietly that there's hope. These young people will someday shed these cocoons and take wing as full-fledged adults. All those thoughts are (or may be) triggered in the minds of intelligent, imaginative readers. The metaphor, well done, is a powerful device for the creative nonfiction writer.

We tend to think that the form of creative nonfiction we're talking about is a fairly new phenomenon, but here is a portion of an article written for the twenty-fifth anniversary issue of *Esquire*, an article about the then-recent (1959) death of the teenage idol of the moment, movie actor James Dean. He was killed when his white Porsche Spyder hit head-on a car driven by Donald Turnupseed, devastating America's teenagers.

In the article, "The Death of James Dean," the writer used several interesting techniques possibly never used before. He alternated actual newspaper headlines, small sections of the newspaper's text, narrative full of realistic details, and long sections of prose poetry.

TEEN-AGE DANCES SEEN THREATENED
BY PARENTS' FAILURE TO COOPERATE

MOST OFFENDERS EMULATE ADULTS

James Dean is three years dead but the sinister
adolescent still holds the headlines.
    James Dean is three years dead;
    but when they file out of the close darkness and
the breathed-out air of the second-run motion picture
theatres where they've been seeing James Dean's
old films
        they still line up;
        the boys in the jackboots and the leather jackets,
the boys in the skintight jeans, the boys in broad
motorbike belts,
        before the mirrors in the restroom
        to look at themselves
        and see
        James Dean;
        the resentful hair,
        the deep eyes floating in lonesomeness,
        the bitter beat look,
        the scorn on the lip

Their pocket combs are out; they tousle up their
hair and pat it down just so;
      make big eyes at their eyes in the mirror
pout their lips in a sneer,
the lost cats in love with themselves,
      just like James Dean.
The girls flock out dizzy with wanting
to run their fingers through his hair, to feel that
thwarted maleness; girl-boy almost, but he needs a
shave ... "Just him and me in the back seat of a car ... "
Their fathers snort,
      but sometimes they remember: "Nobody under-
stood me either. I might have amounted to something
if the folks had understood."
      The older women struggle from their seats wet-
eyed with wanting
to cuddle,
to mother (it's lack of mother love
makes delinquents), to smother with little attentions
the poor orphan youngster,
      the motherless, brotherless, sisterless, lone-wolf
brat strayed from the pack, the poor mixed-up kid.

LACK OF PARENTAL LOVE IS
BLAMED IN SLAYING

   The writer of that modern-sounding and most creative nonfiction article? John Dos Passos. We can see his creative turn-of-mind at work
here, not to mention his poetic side. The details he singles out, and even
the way he breaks up his lines and thoughts, make clear that the writer
was fully aware of how the younger generation (not to mention its mothers and fathers) were reacting to this young phenomenon of the moment.
As far as I can determine at this remove, no one heralded this article at the
time as some kind of breakthrough into a new kind of reporting. Perhaps
they expected the unusual from this unusually gifted author—we accept
creative efforts by men and women already seen as "creative." Had he
been a "regular" journalist, I wonder whether more might have been
made of this remarkable approach and format. Even today, almost thirty
years later, it seems avant garde. *Esquire* thought enough of it to run the
article again in its fortieth anniversary issue, in October 1973.

Further Dimensions of Group Life

We've seen how creative nonfiction writers get at the heart of groups by writing about their typical daily lives, their entertainments, their dress, and their fads. Let's look now at other dimensions frequently written about: their ornaments, decorations, adornments, architecture, and arts.

As you'll see here and elsewhere, these dimensions include all kinds of things, from furniture to pets. Rex Reed has for many years written interestingly of life in and around Hollywood, succeeding in getting to the heart of the individuals and their society more accurately than many who have attempted the same. In the following paragraph, he opens a piece about Ava Gardner: "Ava: Life in the Afternoon," from his book, *Do You Sleep in the Nude?*

> She stands there, without benefit of a filter lens against a room melting under the heat of lemony sofas and lavender walls and cream-and-peppermint-striped movie-star chairs, lost in the middle of that gilt-edge birthday-cake hotel of cupids and cupolas called the Regency. There is no script. No Minelli to adjust the CinemaScope lens. Ice-blue rain beats against the windows and peppers Park Avenue below as Ava Gardner stalks her pink malted-milk cage like an elegant cheetah. She wears a baby-blue cashmere turtleneck sweater pushed up to her Ava elbows and a little plaid mini-skirt and enormous horn-rimmed glasses and she is gloriously, divinely barefoot.

Reed manages, in this one paragraph, to work in details about her ornaments, decorations, adornments, architecture, and, perhaps subliminally, something of her artistic taste. From a technical standpoint, we writers should notice how much he accomplished with his hyphenated noun coinages. What an excellent shorthand description of the Regency's architecture: gilt-edge birthday-cake hotel of cupids and cupolas called the Regency. We enjoy the words not only for the visual image they combine to create, we love the alliteration he's achieved through *cake*, *cupids*, *cupolas*, and *called*. He could easily have chosen other images, other words, but his ear heard the aural potential in these visual words. The author's creative touch also shows up when he refers to the turtleneck sweater pushed up to her Ava elbows. He uses that idea as a recurrent note throughout the article: "'Hell, I've been here ten years and I still can't speak the goddam language,' says Ava, dismissing him with a wave of the long porcelain Ava arms… " "The Ava legs dangle limply from the arm of a lavender chair while the Ava neck, pale and tall as a milkwood vase, rises above the room like a Southern landowner inspecting a cotton field…. " 'You're looking at me again!' she says shyly, pulling short girlish wisps of hair behind the lobes of her Ava ears." "The Ava eyes brighten to a soft clubhouse green." "She laughs her Ava laugh and the head rolls back and the little blue vein bulges on her neck like a delicate pencil mark."

Seen pulled together like that, the device sounds overly used, but distributed through the article, it surprises us with delight as it pops up unexpectedly. We should take this as a good reminder, nevertheless, that a device like this can easily be overdone, and must be reserved for the appropriate article and audience.

William Least Heat Moon, in *Blue Highways*, shows us a completely different segment of society when he describes some of the ornaments and adornments of people living near Danville, Kentucky:

> The highway took me through Danville, where I saw a pillared antebellum mansion with a trailer court on the front lawn. Route 127 ran down a long valley of pastures and fields edged by low, rocky bluffs and split by a stream the color of muskmelon. In the distance rose the foothills of the Appalachians, old mountains that once separated the Atlantic from the shallow inland sea now the middle of America. The licks came out of the hills, the fields got smaller, and there were little sawmills cutting hardwoods into pallets, crates, and fenceposts. The houses shrank, and their colors changed to white to pastels to iridescents to no paint at all. The lawns went from Vertagreen bluegrass to thin fescue to hardpacked dirt glinting with fragments of glass, and the lawn ornaments changed from birdbaths to plastic flamingoes and donkeys to broken-down automobiles with raised hoods like tombstones. On the porches stood one-legged wringer washers and ruined sofas, and, by the front doors, washtubs hung like coats of arms.

It should be clear by now, especially by these past two examples from the extremes of the social spectrum, that a creative nonfiction writer can tell us, simply by selecting details about the things with which people surround themselves, a great deal about the realities of the group's life, even by telling us about how one person in the group lives. Before going on to a chapter that deals primarily with how the realities of individual lives are shown, let's watch Tom Wolfe, the master of describing what he calls "status life," as he shows us how people in certain strata of society have given up the worship of a spiritual god to take up, instead, the worship of art. The following paragraph comes from an essay Wolfe adapted from the 1983 T. S. Eliot Lectures he delivered at England's University of Kent. This is the adaptation as published in *Harper's* (October 1984), "The Worship of Art: Notes on the New God":

> There was a time when well-to-do educated people in America adorned their parlors with crosses, crucifixes, or Stars of David. These were marks not only of faith but of cultivation. Think of the great homes, built before 1940, with chapels. This was a fashionable as well as devout use of space. Today those chapels are used as picture galleries, libraries, copper kitchens, saunas, or high-tech centers. It is perfectly acceptable to use them for the VCR and the Advent. But it would be in bad taste to use them for prayer. Practically no one who cares about appearing cultivated today would display a cross or Star of David in the living room. It would be . . . in bad taste. Today the conventional symbol of devoutness is—but of course!—the Holy Rectangle: the painting. The painting is the religious object we see today in the parlors of the educated classes.

When Tom Wolfe writes about culture, irony drips from the Cross and the Star alike, but he does paint here a partial picture of one segment of society, one that used to merely collect but now worships works of art. Wolfe goes on in this delightful vein to call the Lincoln Centers and Kennedy Centers of the world the cathedrals of the late twentieth century. When the wealthy of old were in trouble with God, they gave money to support the great cathedrals. When the giant corporations develop an odor today, Wolfe went on to say, they support the arts and Public Broadcasting.

In the following chapter, "The Realities of Individual Lives," we'll find that much can be learned about the realities of group life when the writer describes vividly for us the day-to-day life of one person.

FIVE

THE REALITIES OF INDIVIDUAL LIVES

Sometimes the creative nonfiction writer will give us, instead of a look at how a "group" lives, a glimpse of how an individual member lives. The writer's purpose may be either to provide us insights about that particular person, or to give us an indirect look at the entire group by letting us look in some detail at one member, a member the writer thinks may represent the larger group—not scientifically determined representation, but simply as a more or less typical member. This section deals not with personality profiles or even sketches but glimpses, glimpses you might get from a bus window but from which you make certain initial judgments about the people in the area.

Richard Goldstein wrote a character sketch, "Gear," for the *Village Voice* in 1966 that tells us much about a type of person, or a group of them (older teenagers), by sketching for us one of them, Gear.

He sits on his bed and turns the radio on. From under the phonograph he lifts a worn fan magazine—*Pop*, in bright fuchsia lettering—with Zal Yanovsky hunched over one P, Paul McCartney contorted over the other, and Nancy Sinatra touching her toes around the O. He turns to the spread on The Stones and flips the pages until he sees The Picture. Mick Jagger and Marianne Faithfull. Mick scowling, waving his fingers in the air. Marianne watching the camera. Marianne waiting for the photographer to shoot. Marianne, Marianne, eyes fading brown circles, lips slightly parted in flashbulb surprise, miniskirt spread apart, tits like two perfect cones under her sweater. He had to stop looking at Marianne Faithfull a full week ago.

75

He turns the page and glances at the shots of Brian Jones and then his eyes open wide because a picture in the corner shows Brian in Ronnie's pants. The same check. The same rise and flair. Brian leaning against a wall, his hands on the top of his magic hiphuggers. Wick-ked!

A newspaper writer who has made his reputation partly on his insights into the man in the street, Jimmy Breslin, wrote in *New York's Daily News* about a woman police officer, Cibella Borges, who had posed for nude photographs back before she became a cop. At the time of this article, it looked certain that she'd lose her job. In a few short sentences he gives us only a snapshot of her—not enough for us to make any kind of informed judgment about her but enough for us to begin to see some of the realities of her life.

> When she had been asked to pose, back in 1980, Cibella, who had been operated on once for a cyst, had just been informed that she needed another operation and this one probably would end her ability to bear children. "What's the difference. I can't have any kids, so who's going to marry me?" Cibella said. She went to a studio on the West Side, posed for the pictures, put on her clothes, and went home to Orchard Street, where her front door is between two stores, one selling baby clothes and the other men's suits. Clothes hung outside the stores and blew in the wind over Cibella's head as she came home. Her apartment was two floors up.

In this short paragraph, Jimmy Breslin has given us several glimpses of this woman much in New York City's papers at the time—glimpses certainly different, more human, than the usual news reports about her and her problems. He used a number of small, realistic details to focus this glimpse, but I saw her as she hurried into her building greeted by those clothes that blew over her head. I can't explain the workings of my mind; I can only report them. I saw a sunny day with cumulus clouds piling up and gusts of wind snapping those clothes above her head. Now, the writer didn't say any of that, except for the wind and the clothes. I supplied the rest of the image. Perhaps no clouds rose on that day, but my imagination saw them. A writer can't keep readers' minds from doing what they will, but he or she can stimulate them by providing a few concrete details. Naturally, if the writer had thought it significant that it was not a sunny day with gusts but a day of low and ominous clouds with hurricane force winds, he would have told me that. Otherwise, it didn't matter too much how I filled in the image.

Had he given me no details about the weather, I wouldn't have formed that image (or any image at all) of this woman coming home to her apartment two floors up. As it is, he "involved" me and I turned from the sidewalk with her and climbed behind her up those two flights.

V. S. Pritchett frequently writes travel pieces, and, as we might expect, does it with creative flair. In this piece for "The Sophisticated Traveler" (*New York Times* supplement, March 1983), "Pritchett's London," he maintains that Londoners are compulsively eccentric, and describes several individuals as proof of this assertion:

> We have a fair number of that London specialty, the eccentric. Most of us are reserved and dissimilate in the London way, but the eccentric publicly dramatizes his inner life. Why does that man suddenly open his jacket and display a naked chest tattooed with a nest of serpents? Why does that respectable woman with the dog stamp and shout her way into shops denouncing "the technological, scientific, communistic-capitalist society" and scream out that "the blacks, Chinese, Indians, are taking your jobs"? No one takes any notice of her diatribes. We shrug our shoulders; the blacks and Asians politely smile. Who is that tall, ghostly, rather distinguished lady in the long evening dress and satin slippers who once asked me whether I would "adopt" her because she happened to be "temporarily short of funds"? Or that man who steers his way through the crowd, arm outstretched, his finger pointing accusingly at all of us? These people are martyrs to compulsion. They are carrying to extremes something present in most Londoners: a suppressed histrionic gift. London, as Dickens observed in his street prowling, is a theater populated by actors asserting a private extravagance. The desire to be a "well-known character," to enlarge modestly a hidden importance, is endemic.

In *Encounters with Chinese Writers*, Annie Dillard gives us an unusual (and unexpected) glimpse of a Chinese woman writer attending a conference of American writers and the leading members of the Beijing Writers Association.

> Today the usual tea-serving maids do not seem available, so the woman writer pours the tea. There is always one woman. She may have the second-highest rank in the room, or she may have written the novel most admired all over China. It takes her fifteen minutes to pour tea, and she will do this three or four times in the course of the morning.

After she serves, she takes an inconspicuous seat, sometimes on the one little hard chair stuck behind the real chairs.

A short, one-paragraph glimpse of one woman writer doing one simple act, but Annie Dillard has said a great deal about modern China, at least about its attitude toward women writers (and, we might infer, women in general). The technique to note here is that the author did not "tell" us about life in modern China; she "showed" us one woman writer at a conference of Chinese and American writers—and we inferred a message about life for women in today's "egalitarian" China.

SLICE-OF-LIFE WRITING

Cowboy, Jane Kramer's study of Henry Blanton's life, stands as a classic of creative nonfiction. Through this profile of one modern cowboy, Kramer provides us insights into the lives of many cowboys of today's American West. She gives us in her extended profile a good many glimpses of Henry Blanton like the one that follows. Glimpses like this accumulate over many pages to give us the man in all his dimensions:

> Henry valued his authority. He hurried through breakfast so that he could always greet his men with the day's orders looking relaxed and confident. He liked to sit on the wagon, waiting, with his scratch pad in his hand and a pencil behind his ear, and he made it a point to be properly dressed for the morning's work in his black boots, a pair of clean black jeans, and his old black hat and jacket. Henry liked wearing black. The Virginian, he had heard, wore black and so had Gary Cooper in the movie "High Noon," and now Henry wore it with a kind of innocent pride, as if the color carried respect and a hero's stern, elegant qualities. Once, Betsy discovered him in the bathroom mirror dressed in his black gear, his eyes narrowed and his right hand poised over an imaginary holster.

In *The Pine Barrens*, John McPhee describes how he went up to a house in the midst of New Jersey's Pine Barrens to ask for water and met one of Hog Wallow's residents, Frederick Chambers Brown. "I called out to ask if anyone was home, and a voice called back, 'Come in. Come in. Come on the hell in.'"

> I walked through a vestibule that had a dirt floor, stepped up into a kitchen, and went into another room that had several overstuffed chairs in it and a porcelain-topped table, where Fred Brown was seated, eating a pork chop. He was dressed in a white sleeveless shirt, ankle-top shoes, and undershorts. He gave me a cheerful greeting and, without asking why I had come or what I wanted, picked up a pair of khaki trousers that had been tossed onto one of the overstuffed chairs and asked me to sit down. He set the trousers on another chair, and he apologized for being in the middle of his breakfast, explaining that he seldom drank much but the night before he had had a few drinks and this had caused his day to start slowly. "I don't know what's the matter with me, but there's got to be something the matter with me, because drink don't agree with me anymore," he said. He had a raw onion in one hand, and while he talked he shaved slices from the onion and ate them between bites of the chop....

Almost like a cinematographer, McPhee walks with his *cinema verité* camera on his shoulder through the vestibule, the kitchen, and into another room where the camera pans across the overstuffed chairs, one strewn with a pair of trousers, and finally reveals the source of the originally shouted invitation to come on the hell in—Fred Chambers Brown in his undershorts. While Fred redistributes the trousers, he gives a friendly greeting and invites the unexpected visitor to sit down.

A fiction writer could not have written a better line than what Fred Brown says about drink no longer agreeing with him. Would a fiction writer have made up such a scene—a man in his undershorts happily slicing and eating onions in between bites of a pork chop? Yes, some fiction writer might, but this scene appeals to us because we know it's not made up. John McPhee, whom we have learned to trust, simply reports what the man says and each of his actions, as simple as they might be. This is realism because it is real. The fiction writer would have to work hard to create the same feeling of realism; McPhee is observing and reporting the real. His creativity comes in with his selection of the details to be brought before the camera, from all the many he had in his mind and notebook, the sequence with which he brings them on stage, the selection of which captured conversational bits to report, and the word choices he makes.

It's worth noting here how simple and straightforward are McPhee's words, and how simple and clear are his sentences. No fancy footwork, no attempt to show what a clever writer he is and what a power vocabulary he commands. We have here, instead, a careful professional thinking only about the scene at hand and the clarity with which he can transmit that through words alone.

Becoming a "People-Watcher"

To achieve a fully dimensioned character, fictional or real, a writer will watch people closely, much more closely than the average person would. He or she looks especially for anything unusual or distinct about the person or persons involved, but does not ignore what is ordinary and typical. The writer then reports, in as interesting a way as possible, these *poses, posturings, habitual gestures, mannerisms, appearances,* and *glances.* Not that the writer limits observations to these, but these frequently appear in creative nonfiction writing. There's no need to point these out in the following examples, so I'll simply quote the authors.

> In a straight-backed chair near the doorway to the kitchen sat a young man with long black hair, who wore a visored red leather cap that had darkened with age. His shirt was coarse-woven and had eyelets down a V neck that was laced with a thong. His trousers were made of canvas, and he was wearing gum boots. His arms were folded, his legs were stretched out, he had one ankle over the other, and as he sat there he appeared to be sighting carefully past his feet, as if his toes were the outer frame of a gunsight and he could see some sort of target in the floor. When I had entered, I had said hello to him, and he had nodded without looking up. He had a long, straight nose and high cheekbones, in a deeply tanned face that was, somehow, gaunt. I had no idea whether he was shy or hostile.
>
> JOHN McPHEE
> *The Pine Barrens*

> The Geisha's mass of blue-black lacquered hair encloses the painted face like a helmet, surmounts, crowns the slender body's ordered and ritual posturing like a grenadier's bearskin busby, too heavy in appearance for that slender throat to bear, the painted fixed expressionless face

immobile and immune also above the studied posturing; yet behind that painted and lifeless mask is something quick and alive and elfin: or more than elfin: puckish: or more than puckish even: sardonic and quizzical, a gift for comedy and more: for burlesque and caricature: for a sly and vicious revenge on the race of men.

WILLIAM FAULKNER
"Impressions of Japan," *Esquire* (October 1973)

She had shared all the vilification and praise without ever emerging in public as an individual. I was eager to meet her, but all her other interviewers said Mrs. Nixon had put them straight to sleep.

She was sitting in the front of the plane, freckled hands neatly folded, ankles neatly crossed, and smiling a public smile as a sleek young staff man sat me next to her. I didn't want to ask the questions she had answered so blandly and often about her husband ("I just think he'd make a wonderful president") or politics ("You'll have to ask Dick about that"), but to ask about herself.

GLORIA STEINEM
"Patricia Nixon Flying"
Outrageous Acts and Everyday Rebellions

Here's another notable personage, Frank Sinatra, as described by Gay Talese in an article for *Esquire* (April 1966), "Frank Sinatra Has A Cold":

The two blondes, who seemed to be in their middle thirties, were preened and polished, their matured bodies softly molded within tight dark suits.

They sat, legs crossed, perched on the high bar stools. They listened to the music. Then one of them pulled out a Kent and Sinatra quickly placed his gold lighter under it and she held his hand, looked at his fingers: they were nubby and raw, and the pinkies protruded, being so stiff from arthritis that he could barely bend them. He was, as usual, immaculately dressed. He wore an oxford-grey suit with a vest, a suit conservatively cut on the outside but trimmed with flamboyant silk within; his shoes, British, seemed to be shined even on the bottom of the soles. He also wore, as everybody seemed to know, a remarkably convincing black hairpiece, one of sixty that he owns, most of them under the care of an inconspicuous little grey-haired lady who, holding his hair in a tiny satchel, follows him around whenever he performs. She earns $400 a week.

Another dimension a creative nonfiction writer will not neglect is a person's dialect, accent, and colloquial speech patterns. Such detail doesn't really get to the heart of a person, but it does involve us more closely. Jimmy Breslin captures readily the various dialects, accents, and colloquialisms of people on his beat for the *Daily News*. To understand fully the next quote from one of his columns, "Give a Beggar a Horse…," all the reader needs to remember is that he always referred to his wife in his columns as The Former Rosemary Dattolico. In this portion of the column, we're with his mother-in-law, The Former Rose Dattolico's Mother, as she wanders through one of many supermarkets seeking out the best deals.

> She stopped and began scolding a young woman from the neighborhood who came long with boxes of eighty-nine-cent paper napkins atop her shopping cart. The former Rosemary Dattolico's mother tapped the paper napkins.
> "Somebody on an income of twelve thousand dollars can't afford paper napkins that cost eighty-nine cents."
> The young woman said, "You're broke, a little fancy you need."
> "Nonsense," the former Rosemary Dattolico's mother said. She sent the young woman back to the shelves to change the paper napkins and her ultimate advice followed the young woman: "You're cheaper off."

> But, that social life. Where do we all meet? At shops and pubs, of course, but mainly in the street market, the melting-pot in all inner London districts. It is mostly run by the Cockneys, whose aim in life is to shout and play-act at stalls everywhere between Shoreditch and Soho and beyond: "You're in England. Stick to language, carntcher? Speak up! What is it, love?" That final phrase is imposed to heal all wounds. For at the market we are not Mr. or Mrs., Sir or Madam, or even Mum and Dad, but, in the thick wash of sentiment, "love," "ducks," "dear," and "darling" for the women and "guv" for the men. We are people who are used to being rained on and jeered at; the street market is the heart of any London village—and town planners dare not do away with it or impose a cross-channel elegance.
>
> V. S. PRITCHETT
> "Pritchett's London"
> *New York Times*, "Sophisticated Traveler" (March 1983)

And all the while we listen to the cowboy come on over the radio like Red Barber announcing the Yankees as the other hunters rack up their coyotes for the afternoon: "THERE HE COMES, LES, OUT THAT SOUTH FENCE—GO SOUTH, LES! GO SOUTH, GO SOUTH, HE'S CROSSED THE ROAD, HE'S IN THAT SOIL BANK IN THE NEXT SECTION, BETTER GO WEST AND HEAD HIM OFF, LES, JOHNNY WAGONBLAST, WHERE ARE YOU? YOU OUT ON THE WEST ROAD? COME NORTH, JOHNNY, HE'S IN THE NORTHWEST QUARTER, COME NORTH," and Harold nudging me, Harold in love with his radio, "See, I told you he was a real good boy, regular sportscaster," and then the sound, sweet jealous sound now, of the dogs dropped from Johnny's truck, and cowboy's back on the horn, "HE'S GOT HIM, JOHNNY WAGONBLAST'S GOT HIM, THEY GOT THE COYOTE!"

RICHARD RHODES
Death All Day

Creative nonfiction writers pay close and appreciative attention not only to regional and local variations on the mother tongue, they listen and write to capture for us the specialized languages and jargons of the specialists among us. The writer listens carefully to the specialist's language partly to learn enough to be able to use some of it in the narrative portions of the article or book, and partly to select quotes and partial quotes from all those the specialist may have used, in order to simulate a fuller conversation with the specialist. Up to a point, the reader doesn't mind not understanding fully the jargon or specialized language—in fact, as we've said earlier, its very obscurity lends credibility to what's being read by the nonspecialist.

The writer must be careful, however, not to go beyond that point because the reader may soon be totally lost—perhaps never to be found again. Just enough to intrigue and provide credibility. The writer is not obliged to explain all the jargon for the nonspecialist reader, if its purpose is to establish mood, setting, or character. Naturally, if the meaning of the specialized language is essential to understanding what follows, the meaning must be somehow put across, preferably as succinctly as possible, else the piece becomes a textbook or specialist's manual.

John McPhee wrote a fascinating profile of an ecologist as she went about her field work. In this excerpt from *Travels in Georgia* we hear them working a swamp at night:

Silent ourselves, we pushed on into the black. Carol moved a flashlight beam among the roots of trees. She held the flashlight to her nose, because the eye can see much more if the line of sight is closely parallel to the beam. She inspected minutely the knobby waterline of the trees. Something like a sonic boom cracked in our ears. "Jesus, what was that?"

"Beaver."

The next two slaps were even louder than the first. Carol ignored the beaver, and continued to move the light. It stopped. Out there in the obsidian was a single blue eye.

"A blue single eye is a spider," she said. "Two eyes is a frog. Two eyes almost touching is a snake. An alligator's eyes are bloody red."

Two tiny coins now came up in her light.

"Move in there," she said. "I want that one."

With a throw of her hand, she snatched up a frog. It was a leopard frog, and she let him go. He was much within his range. Carol was looking for river frogs, pig frogs, carpenter frogs, whose range peripheries we were stalking. She saw another pair of eyes. The canoe moved in. Her hand swept out unseen and made a perfect tackle, thighs to knees. This was a bronze frog, home on the range . . .

McPhee knows that his writing gains authority not only through his use of a specialist's jargon but through evidence of specialized knowledge. When we read that Carol held her flashlight up to her nose in the middle of that swamp at night, we see we're with a woman who knows her job. This evidence is reinforced when we hear the conversation about eyes in the dark, and later the list of frogs most of us have not met.

Notice that McPhee does not "tell" us that the way to catch a frog is to grab it just above the knees; he "shows" us Carol sweeping her hand out, unseen, and tackling a frog. He can't resist describing that perfect tackle in football terms. Perhaps he should have resisted this next one, but he tells us that the frog she's tackled so nicely can be thrown back because he's not beyond the peripheries of acceptable frog wanderings; he's home on the range. Little sparks of wit like this keep people reading John McPhee. We learn all kinds of specialized knowledge in his books and articles, but it's not like learning it in a classroom—it's leavened with wit. Not heavy-handed humor, but wit.

Specialized knowledge and its concomitant jargon has probably reached an all-time high in the space exploration business. Everyone has been infected by its way of shorthanding and acronymizing everything.

Norman Mailer gained authority in his *Of a Fire on the Moon* by capturing faithfully this specialized knowledge and language. In writing about the first moon walk, he reported part of the effort in this way:

> ...Star checks were taken. Meanwhile, Armstrong was readying the cameras and snapping photographs through the window. Now Aldrin aligned the Abort Guidance Section. Armstrong laid in the data for Program 12, the Powered Ascent Guidance. The Command Module came around again. The simulated countdown was over. They had another Stay. They powered down their systems.
>
> In the transcript the work continues minute after minute, familiar talks of stars and Nouns, acronyms, E-memory dumps, and returns to POO where Pings may idle. They are at rest on the moon, but the dialogue is not unencumbered of pads, updata link switches and noise suppression devices on the Manned Space Flight Network relay.

I'm discussing these elements of language use as though the writers use one, then another, then another. In practice, of course, all these elements and many others talked about in this book work together, even within one paragraph. A section dealing with a specialist's knowledge and specialist's language may also let us hear that specialist's own accent, dialect, or colloquialisms. The specialists I refer to are not necessarily scientific or other high-flying people; they can be specialists of any stripe. For example, William W. Warner's Pulitzer Prize-winner, *Beautiful Swimmers*, takes us into the far reaches of the Chesapeake Bay to learn how the watermen and their crabs live. In the following excerpt, Warner works in specialized knowledge, fisherman jargon, and local dialect.

> "...Some people are plain feared of crabs, though Lord knows they can't hurt you much."
>
> Mike grins from one jug ear to another. "Sometimes they get to you," he says.
>
> Indeed they do. Maine lobstermen can safely remove the much smaller numbers of lobsters found in their pots with bare hands, seizing them from the rear. Chesapeake crabbers cannot do this. Unlike the lobster, the blue crab has excellent rear vision. There are too many crabs in each pot in any case for such individual seizure. You simply plunge in with both hands and separate the tangling masses as best you can, suffering an occasional bite from a big Jimmy (male) that will make even the most hardened crabber wince. Between such bites and the constant handling of pot wire the fabric-lined "Best" rubber gloves last no more

than two weeks during periods of heavy catches. "You get a hole in them," Grant adds. "The crabs will find it."

We pull up a shiny new pot set down a few days ago. It is absolutely jammed. Maybe fifty sooks (females). "New pots seem to attract females this time of year," Grant observes. "Don't know why. Ain't nobody really knows about crabs."

William Warner describes vividly for us a Chesapeake crabber's life. He accomplishes that partly through the concrete details of how a crab behaves and how the crabber works with the captured crab; partly through sensory details like the bite; and partly through letting us hear Mike's voice through bits of captured dialog. The next chapter emphasizes the power of including in your writing: captured conversations (dialog in fiction); short snatches of conversation (as in the Warner quote above); quotes from letters, memoirs, journals, etc.; and words heard over the phone, radio, and television.

SIX

DIALOGS, MONOLOGS, AND OTHER LOGS

Fiction writers have always known that the most effective technique for involving the readers, making them feel as though they are right there *on* the spot, as distinct from being readers *about* the spot, is well-written dialog. Creative nonfiction writers (or writers of creative nonfiction) also realize the power of *captured conversation* to make a scene come alive for the reader. I've decided not to use the word "dialog" in the context of this book because the connotation of scripted dialog for films or plays may be so strong as to make the reader think that I'm talking here of "created" dialog. I'm not. I'm talking here of "captured" conversations, conversations overheard (or taken from a formal interview) while conducting research for an article or book.

The writer does not use all the conversations captured during research. He or she selects carefully those bits of conversation that seem most illustrative of the subject matter under consideration or revelatory of one or more of the persons involved in the conversation. The writer must be careful not to distort matters by this selection. Everyone can seem stupid, brilliant, humorous, humorless, obfuscatory, vague, or otherwise unusual in any single bit of conversation, so the writer must be alert to the possibility of unintentional, as well as intentional, distortion—and assiduously avoid it. YOU MUST NOT LET THE DESIRE TO WRITE INTERESTINGLY AND DRAMATICALLY MAKE YOU SELECT THOSE CONVERSATIONS THAT SERVE DRAMA OVER TRUTH.

People reveal themselves not only through regular conversations but through *monologs*, bits of conversation where one participant goes on at such length that his or her parts in the dialog resemble more a series of monologs.

People reveal themselves and situations through other devices that provide the writer many opportunities to make his or her work more varied, more vivid, more dramatic, more involving, more interesting. They tell us something directly, or indirectly, through *historic letters, court records, memoirs, journals, diaries, reminiscences, official letters* and *telegrams,* and even what they've said on *radio, television* and *telephones.* Finally, we feel we even learn a little something about them by bits or *snatches of conversations* we hear, overhear, or even read in *newspapers.* We believe we understand a people or a region a bit better by the *signs and symbols* we read along the road or in the hotel room—not to mention *graffiti* we read on their walls. All these devices of revelation provide grist for the word mills of creative nonfiction writers. Let's look at some examples of how our better writers have used these devices, beginning with the major one—captured conversation.

CAPTURED CONVERSATION

Joe McGinniss, in his bestselling book, *The Selling of the President,* captured many conversations that seem (especially in hindsight) to reveal Richard M. Nixon. In the following excerpt, Mr. Nixon has come to the Green Room of the White House to make a political (commercial) videotape.

He took his position on the front of the heavy brown desk. He liked to lean against a desk, or sit on the edge of one, while he taped commercials, because he felt this made him seem informal. There were about twenty people, technicians and advisors, gathered in a semi-circle around the cameras. Richard Nixon looked at them and frowned.

"Now when we start," he said, "don't have anybody who is not directly involved in this in my range of vision. So I don't go shifting my eyes."

"Yes, sir. All right, clear the stage. Everybody who's not actually doing something get off the stage, please. Get off the stage."

There was one man in a corner, taking pictures. His flash blinked several times in succession. Richard Nixon looked in his direction. The man had been hired by the Nixon staff to take informal pictures throughout the campaign for historical purposes.

"Are they stills?" Richard Nixon said. "Are they our own stills? Well then, knock them off." He motioned with his arm. "Can them. We've already got so goddamned many stills already." Richard Nixon turned back toward the cameras.

"Now, when you give me the fifteen-second cue, give it to me right under the camera so I don't shift my eyes."

"Right, sir."

The entire chapter about the taping or filming of commercials showed the president trying to look his best, but Joe McGinniss has included this captured conversation to illustrate Nixon's concern about his notoriously shifting eyeballs. Many advisers told him he must control those inadvertent shiftings because close-up camera shots magnify their shiftiness—and people tend to associate shifty eyeballs with "shifty" character. Note that Joe McGinniss didn't write all this that I just wrote about shiftiness; he simply quoted Nixon. Mr. McGinniss did, of course, select this particular conversation to report on, so apparently he did hope that his readers would pick up on that concern of the president.

"Nixon's Neighborhood," one of Paul Theroux's articles collected in *Sunrise with Seamonsters,* tells of Theroux's interviews with men and women in the streets of San Clemente, where Nixon resided when not at the White House. He asked them, among other things, about the book Mr. Nixon was writing.

The book was mentioned by many people I met in San Clemente. In southern California, a book is considered a mysterious thing, even by college students who gather on Nixon's beach to turn on. One of these, Martin Nelson ("I think Nixon's a real neat guy. If you could see his house you'd know it was a prime place."), majors in Ornamental Horticulture at Pasadena. He hopes to get an M.A. and possibly a Ph.D. in Ornamental Horticulture and become America's answer to Capability Brown. He spoke with awe about Nixon's book, so did Mr. Phillips, the security guard, and Brian Sardoz, the scuba diver, and Mrs. Dorothy Symms of San Clemente Secretarial Services, publisher of *Fishcarts to Fiestas, the Story of San Clemente.*

"I met the man who's writing Mr. Nixon's book," said Mrs. Symms.

I said, "Isn't Mr. Nixon writing the book?"

"No. There's a man doing it for him. He writes all the movie stars' books. He's a very famous writer. You say you're from England? Oh, this man wrote Winston Churchill's memoirs, too."

I imagine that Churchill's heirs would be surprised to learn from the author of *Fish carts to Fiestas* that Winston had to rely on a ghost writer for his memoirs.

Gay Talese wrote "The Silent Season of a Hero" about the great baseball player, Joe DiMaggio. This excerpt comes from *Fame and Obscurity*, the book that presents many of Talese's excellent pieces about people who've come and gone. DiMaggio and several old pals are leaving a golf course to go to a banquet when Talese captures the following conversation:

Later, showered and dressed, DiMaggio and the others drove to a banquet about ten miles from the golf course. Somebody had said it was going to be an elegant dinner, but when they arrived they could see it was more like a county fair; farmers were gathered outside a big barn-like building, a candidate for sheriff was distributing leaflets at the front door, and a chorus of homely ladies were inside singing "You Are My Sunshine."

"How did we get sucked into this?" DiMaggio asked, talking out of the side of his mouth, as they approached the building.

"O'Doul," one of the men said. "It's his fault. Damned O'Doul can't turn *anything* down."

"Go to hell," O'Doul said.

Soon DiMaggio and O'Doul and Ernie Nevers were surrounded by the crowd, and the woman who had been leading the chorus came rushing over and said, "Oh, Mr. DiMaggio, it certainly is a pleasure having you."

"It's a pleasure being here, ma'am," he said, forcing a smile.

"It's too bad you didn't arrive a moment sooner, or you'd have heard our singing."

"Oh, I heard it," he said, "and I enjoyed it very much."

"Good, good," she said. "And how are your brothers Dom and Vic?"

"Fine. Dom lives near Boston. Vince is in Pittsburgh."

"Why, hello there, Joe," interrupted a man with wine on his breath, patting DiMaggio on the back, feeling his arm.

"Who's gonna take it this year, Joe?"

Talese does a fine job setting the scene for us, and then simply records what he heard of several conversations, all of which add up to banality, but he does not tell us that all this is banal.

His simple, straightforward description put me right in step with this small group approaching the barn. Until he told me that Joe had said something out of the side of his mouth, I was up in a tree watching the scene of the men approaching, but as soon as he told me how it was said, I was right down there close—involved. Although Talese slipped out of the objective gear and into the subjective when he told me that Joe smiled and claimed he'd enjoyed the ladies' rendition of "You Are My Sunshine," I loved it. When he added that Joe was forcing that smile, of course, he stopped objective reporting and began subjective reporting. A subtle example of the fine line that sometimes divides the two.

Michael Herr's "Khesanh," as collected in Tom Wolfe's *The New Journalism*, gives us some of the most involving writing ever done about the Vietnam war. He's writing in this excerpt about a U.S. Marine nicknamed Day Tripper (because of his hatred for the night hours and his desire to get everything done during the safer daylight hours) who keeps excellent mental records (as though on a built-in chronometer) of the days, hours, minutes, and seconds he has left to serve.

> ... He [Day Tripper] had assumed that correspondents in Vietnam *had* to be there. When he learned that I had asked to come here he almost let the peaches drop on the ground. "Lemmee ... lemmee jus' hang on that a minute," he said. "You mean you doan' *have* to be here? An' you're *here*?" I nodded.
>
> "Well, they gotta be payin' you some tough bread."
>
> "You'd be depressed if I told you."
>
> He shook his head.
>
> "I mean, they ain' got the bread that'd get me here if I didn't have t' be here."
>
> "Horse crap," Mayhew said. "Day Tripper loves it. He's short now, but he's comin' back, ain't you Day Tripper?"
>
> "Shit, my momma'll come over here and pull a tour before I fuckin' come back."
>
> Four more marines dropped into the pit.
>
> "Where's Evans?" Mayhew demanded.
>
> "Any of you guys know Evans?"
>
> One of the mortarmen came over.

"Evans is over in Danang," he said. "He caught a little shit the other night."

"That right?" Mayhew said. "Evans get wounded?"

"He hurt bad?" Day Tripper said.

"Took some stuff in the legs. Nothing busted. He'll be back in ten days."

"That ain't bad enough, then," Day Tripper said.

"No," Mayhew said. "But ten days, sheeit, that's better'n nothin'."

As a writer, try to imagine getting across through straight explanatory reporting all the attitudes and feelings that come across so vividly in that conversation among men at the front. Try writing, for example, a summary explanatory paragraph that gets across what's expressed in the final three lines of that captured conversation. It could be done, but it would lack the vividness, the believability that these three lines possess—because they are real. These are not abstract thoughts; these ring of the real.

Back across the Pacific, we read of the horrors of fighting the battles of Hollywood filmmaking. Gay Talese wrote a chapter called "The Soft Psyche of Joshua Logan" in his book *The Overreachers*. It's a scene that couldn't be more different from the scene in Vietnam, yet the same technique of letting straight captured conversation tell the story works just as well here.

Now he was back in the dark theatre, the lights of the stage beaming on the actors going through a scene in the garden of their Louisiana shack; Claudia McNeil's voice was now softer because she had had a touch of laryngitis a few days before. But at the end of the scene, she raised her voice to its full power, and Logan, in a pleasant tone, said, "Don't strain your voice, Claudia."

She did not respond, only whispered to another actor on stage.

"Don't raise your voice, Claudia," Logan repeated.

She again ignored him.

"Claudia!" Logan yelled, "don't you give me that actor's revenge, Claudia."

"Yes, Mr. Logan," she said with a soft sarcastic edge.

"I've had enough of this today, Claudia."

"Yes, Mr. Logan."

"And stop Yes-Mr. Logan-ing me."

"Yes, Mr. Logan."

"You're a shocking, rude woman!"

"Yes, Mr. Logan."

"You're being a beast."

"Yes, Mr. Logan."

"Yes, Miss Beast."

"Yes, Mr. Logan."

"*Yes, Miss Beast!*"

Suddenly, Claudia McNeil stopped. It dawned on her that he was calling her a beast; now her face was grey and her eyes were cold, and her voice almost solemn as she said, "You...called...me...out... of...my...name!"

"Oh, God!" Logan smacked his forehead with his hand.

It would be difficult to invent for a fictional story such a petulant conversation. We enjoy it particularly here because we know that it was not "created" by this creative writer of nonfiction but was simply captured at the moment it occurred.

One of the best ways to show the inefficiency, the stupidity, or the absurdity of an institution is to quote accurately its staff as it deals with its public. James Michener does this extremely effectively in the following excerpt from *Iberia*, his study of Portugal and Spain. Merely describing in narrative form the situation shown here could not begin to achieve the reality we feel as we listen in on this captured conversation. We have all faced such Catch-22 situations in our lives. Michener jogs our memories and we bring them to bear on our reading of this passage.

In Badajoz I also learned something about the government of Spain. At the post office I purchased ten air-letter forms and paid six pesetas (ten cents) each for them. I went back to the cathedral plaza and spent most of one morning writing ten letters, a job I find difficult, for words do not come easily to me. The next day I took the ten letters to the post office to mail but a clerk refused them, saying, "The price of air-letters went up this morning from six pesetas to ten."

"All right. Give me ten four-peseta stamps and I'll stick them on the letters."

"We can't do that, sir, because it states very clearly on the form that if anything whatever is enclosed in the form or added to it, it will be sent by regular post."

"Then let me give you the difference, and you stamp them as having ten pesetas."

"There is no provision for that, sir."

"Then what can I do? Mail them as they are and let them go regular mail?"

"No, because they're no longer legal. They've been declassified."

"It took me a long time to write these letters. How can I mail them?"

"Take each one. Place it inside an airmail envelope. Readdress the envelope and place twelve pesetas' worth of stamps in the corner and mail it as a regular air-mail letter."

This I did, and the letters were delivered in various countries, but I was so astounded by the procedure that I called upon a high government official to ask how such things could happen. His answer was revealing. "The clerk did right. The forms you bought were valid yesterday. Today they're not. Each form states clearly that nothing may be added, so there was no way to mail the old forms."

Note that Michener simply reported the conversation. He did not tell us in between the pieces of dialog just how the clerk said the words, nor how Michener could feel his blood pressure rising. He left all that to the reader's memory of similar, frustrating experiences to fill in the physical and other feelings probably going on at the time. The only direct clues we get about his feelings on the matter are that he did then go to a higher-up government official—and he uses the simple word *astounded*—which gives us a clue to the tenor of that second conversation.

C. D. B. Bryan's book *Friendly Fire*, about the Vietnam war and the effects of a son's death upon the family, quotes many people, sometimes to great dramatic effect. Chapter 6 of that book ends with a captured conversation that leaves an impression on the reader more lasting than any summary statement about the awful nature of war and the loss of sons. Peg and Gene Mullen have recently lost their son, Michael, in Vietnam and are shown here visiting a woman who has lost a son in Vietnam on the same day that Michael was killed. They hope to comfort her by sharing their thoughts with her, as they have with other distraught mothers and fathers who have suffered the loss of sons in Vietnam.

The Mullens followed the man along the dirt section roads, zigged and zagged until finally they reached a dilapidated and paint-peeled farmhouse and a broken-down barn. When Peg and Gene came up to the door, the woman invited them in right away. The Mullens explained why they had come, that Michael had died on the same day as their son, and Peg noticed that here, too, no one had visited or brought food. The mother thanked and thanked them for coming, explained that she was on welfare, and it had been very hard on them lately, but she hoped things would be better. "You know, Mrs. Mullen"—the woman sighed—"this was the third of my sons to go to Vietnam."

"Your *third*?" Peg asked.

"I have seven sons," she explained, "and I prayed the first two out of the war, but when they drafted my third son, I was so discouraged.... He was my best son, mentally, physically, in every way, and when they drafted him, too, well I kind of lost faith in God. I guess I couldn't pray hard enough to pray him back home. "But," she said, smiling bravely, "the draft board is so kind. When I went to visit with them, they told me they would only draft five of my sons for Vietnam."

MONOLOGS

"Monolog" may not be the technically accurate word to cover what I have in mind here, but I refer to a speech given by one person. It may be a formal speech, or an excerpt from it, or it may simply be a lengthy speech by one person within a lengthier conversation between two or more people. It could also be a lecture, or a part of one, given by a professor, a minister, or a drill sergeant. They come in many variations and disguises, but I've given below three that illustrate how the writer can say a great deal about a person simply by recording accurately what he or she says, especially when speaking at length.

In the "Delhi" chapter of her book *Destinations*, Jan Morris captures the flavor of India through a monolog given by a government spokesman.

"Certainly," said the government spokesman, perusing my list of questions, "by all means, these are all very simple matters. We can attend to them for you at once. As I told you, it is our duty! It is what we are paid for! I myself have to attend an important meeting this afternoon—you will excuse me I hope?—but I will leave all these little matters with our good Mrs. Gupta and all will be taken care of. I will telephone you with answers myself without fail—or if not I myself, then Mrs. Gupta will be sure to telephone you either today or tomorrow morning. Did you sign our register? A duplicate signature if you would not mind, and the requisite application form for a pass—it will make everything easier for you, you see. Have no fear, Mrs. Gupta will take care of everything. But mark my words, you will find the spiritual aspects of our city most rewarding. Remember the River Ganges! As a student of history you will find that I am right! Ha ha! Another cup of tea? You have time?"

We come away from this monolog with some understanding of the government official, especially his feeling of self-importance, but we also come away with a feeling about how it must be to deal with the government of India. I came away wanting to meet our good Mrs. Gupta. Surely she and many other Mrs. Guptas provide the government whatever efficiency and effectiveness it has. Had the author chosen to interrupt this monolog with little summary bits about what the official looked like, what his office smelled like, or to give a glimpse of Mrs. Gupta in the outer office, much more would have been lost than gained.

The following excerpt from "The General Goes Zapping Charlie Cong" by Nicholas Tomalin, as collected in Tom Wolfe's *The New Journalism*, could be put in the section on specialists' language, but it makes better the point about how effective the direct quotation of a monolog can be.

> The General has a big, real American face, reminiscent of every movie general you have seen. He comes from Texas, and he's 48. His present rank is Brigadier General, Assistant Division Commander, United States Army (which is what the big red figure on his shoulder flash means).
>
> "Our mission today," says the General, "is to push those goddam VC's right off Routes 13 and 16. Now you see Routes 13 and 16 running north from Saigon toward the town of Phuac Vinh, where we keep our artillery. When we got here first we prettied up those roads, and cleared Charlie Cong right out so we could run supplies up.
>
> "I guess we've been hither and thither with all our operations since, an' the ol' VC he's reckoned he could creep back. He's been puttin' out propaganda he's goin' to interdict our right of passage along those routes. So this day we aim to zapp him, and zapp him, and zapp him again till we've zapped him right back where he came from. Yes, sir. Let's go."

Creative nonfiction writer Joe McGinniss, in his book about the Alaska of today, *Going to Extremes*, does not use many conversations or monologs, but he does quote one short monolog captured aboard one of Alaska's state ferries. A small group of Alaskans are sitting around the ferry's bar as they prepare to leave Seattle for the north.

> Eddie the Basque moved quickly to a corner table, where he had spotted two heavy young women with teased hair. I sat at the bar and

ordered an Olympia beer. Duane Archer was telling the high state official about his new truck, a Ford, and about the way he had bought it. He had two cigarettes going at once.

"So I said to that son of a bitch, 'Listen, you son of a bitch, I want that heavy-duty bumper on there and I want them studded snow tires on there and I want that extra layer of undercoating on there and I want that auxiliary heater hooked up and I want this taken care of by four o'clock tomorrow when I come back here to pick this baby up and I don't want any more shit about it.'"

The high state official was nodding. Duane Archer took a swallow of his drink. V.O. and water was what he drank.

OTHER LOGS

Since the Greek root word "logos" means such varied things (*word, saying, speech, discourse, thought . . .*), I feel safe referring to the following as other kinds of "logs": *journals, diaries, memoirs, court records, personal letters, official letters* and *telegrams, memoranda* and *messages, headlines* and *news reports*. The writer, whether "creative" or not, finds these written records of people communicating with each other useful in nonfiction articles and books. A fiction writer may invent such communications to lend verisimilitude, i.e., to make his or her story sound real. In nonfiction, of course, they are real, but the writer uses them to help put across the fact that what he or she is writing is the truth, not fiction.

Aside from their factual content, these messages between people add variety for the reader. The creative nonfiction writer deliberately searches out and selects those journal entries, headlines, etc. that reinforce some point he or she is making in the more straightforward summary parts. Because the writer frequently sets these special forms of communication in their original format, even sometimes including photographic reproductions of handwritten diary entries, for example, they serve also to "add light" to the page. The reader, unconsciously perhaps, appreciates these visual breathers in the midst of an otherwise dense page of type. The creative writer uses them for multiple purposes, although usually for one primary purpose—the others being seen as fringe benefits.

In a historical study, such as Evan S. Connell's *Son of the Morning Star*, about General Custer and his last stand, the author uses many historic letters, memoirs, soldiers' reminiscences, and Court of Inquiry records. In the following excerpt, we learn something about Generals Custer, Sheridan, and Sherman. The first short quote is from historian Stephen Ambrose; the major quote is from a communication sent by General Sherman to General Sheridan.

Historian Stephen Ambrose characterized him [Custer] as an obstinate little man, given to intense rages, mad with battle lust during an engagement, quick to censure and slow to forgive, bursting with energy, forever demanding the most of his men ... women found him exciting, and unlike Sheridan, he seldom cherished a grudge; otherwise, they must have been much alike. Custer might erupt at any instant, he loved to fight and was quick to blame. He could be sarcastic and impossibly demanding. They understood each other, these two. Sheridan perceived in the audacious young cavalryman a sympathetic spirit, one who was not reluctant to discipline troops and who thought the best way to handle dangerous redskins was to crush them. Little Phil [Sheridan] was supported by his boss, William Tecumseh Sherman—himself no shrinking violet. He wrote to Sheridan on October 15 that it was up to the Indians themselves to decide whether or not they would be exterminated....

"As brave men and as the soldiers of a government which has exhausted its peace efforts, we, in the performance of a most unpleasant duty, accept the war begun by our enemies, and hereby resolve to make its end final. If it results in the utter annihilation of these Indians, it is but the result of what they have been warned again and again, and for which they seem fully prepared. I will say nothing and do nothing to restrain our troops from doing what they deem proper on the spot, and will allow no more vague general charges of cruelty and inhumanity to tie their hands, but will use all the powers confided in me to the end that these Indians, the enemies of our race and our civilization, shall not again be able to begin and carry on their barbarous warfare on any kind of a pretext that they may choose to allege ... you may now go ahead in your own way and I will back you with my whole authority, and stand between you and any efforts that may be attempted in your rear to restrain your purpose or check your troops."

Historians also make heavy use of historic letters in their research, and frequently quote all or parts of letters that help them make a point. Readers immediately get more involved when they hear people speaking out of the past than they do when reading the historian's words alone. In the following paragraphs from the chapter "The Quarrel with America" in his monumental series *A History of the English Speaking Peoples*, Winston Churchill quotes from an "anonymous" letter by "Junius," and then from a newspaper, *The North Briton*:

> The first decade of his [George III] reign passed in continual and confused manoeuvering between the different Parliamentary groups, some of them accepting the new situation, some making passive resistance to the new motion of the Crown. George was angry and puzzled at the wrangling of the political leaders. Pitt sat moodily in Parliament, "unconnected and unconsulted." Many people shared Dr. Johnson's opinion of the Scots, and Bute, who was much disliked, fell from power early in 1763. His successor, George Grenville, was a mulish lawyer, backed by the enormous electoral power of the Duke of Bedford, of whom "Junius" wrote in his anonymous letters, "I daresay he has bought and sold more than half of the representative integrity of the nation." Grenville refused to play the part of "The Minister behind the curtain"; but for two years he clung to office, and must bear a heavy share of responsibility for the alienation of the American colonies.
>
> There were other conflicts. On April 23, 1763, a newspaper called *The North Briton* attacked Ministers as "tools of despotism and corruption . . . They have sent the spirit of discord through the land, and I will prophesy it will never be extinguished but by the extinction of their power."

We do not usually see Britain's former prime minister, Winston Churchill, described as a creative nonfiction writer. I've included him here to show how a writer of history works in quotes from letters and newspapers of the historic period but also to show that he is, indeed, creative in his writing of history, creative in the sense we use that word in this book—he doesn't "create" history, he's creative in his use of language to tell history.

Sometimes one of the best sources of historic information comes from court records, where the words of men and women were recorded verbatim and preserved. For *Son of the Morning Star*, Evan S. Connell went back to the records of a Court of Inquiry convened by President Rutherford Hayes to investigate the matter of U.S. Army Major Reno's behavior in the battle now known as "Custer's Last Stand" or "The Battle of Little Big Horn." Reno testified at length, partly about the battle itself, partly about General Custer, as we listen in on the following excerpt from his testimony:

> Reno was asked about his relationship with Custer. He replied that he felt no animosity, he and the General got on well enough. But the implication of this was unmistakable, so he added that even if his own brothers had been riding with Custer he could not have done any more than he did.
>
> His response did not satisfy Lt. Lee. "The question is, did you go into that fight with feelings of confidence or distrust?"
>
> Reno again responded that he and the General got along all right: "My feelings toward Gen. Custer were friendly."
>
> "I insist that the question shall be answered," said Lee.
>
> "Well, sir, I had known General Custer a long time," Reno said, "And I had no confidence in his ability as a soldier."

Author Connell, with all those records in front of him, could have simply said something to the effect (taken from the end of that piece of testimony) that Major Reno had no confidence in General Custer's ability as a soldier, but he elected to quote the testimony ahead of that point. I'm speculating, of course, but I imagine that as a creative nonfiction writer (and as a first-rate fiction writer, too) he saw the dramatic possibilities inherent in the way Lt. Lee kept at Major Reno until he said something damaging. Connell let the suspense build, using only the Court of Inquiry's words. He did not invent a sequence of questioning the way a fiction writer would be allowed to. Nonfiction writers also know the value of suspense in involving and holding the reader.

Joseph Wambaugh reported to good effect the verbatim transcript of a criminal's statement to detectives in his nonfiction novel *The Onion Field*. In a "Note to the Reader" foreword, Wambaugh wrote that "The courtroom dialogue was not re-created." He took it verbatim from official court transcript. Wambaugh could have told his readers what he thought was the state of Jimmy Smith's mind as he talked to detectives, but he made the point much more effectively by letting us hear the wanderings of this tortured mind.

> The statement was difficult to follow, at times incoherent, and Pierce Brooks looked at Jimmy Smith and imagined the absolute fear that was on him that night when he huddled there handcuffed, a blanket over his naked shoulders, his feet bloody and painful, while he was

interrogated, not for his usual five-dollar shoplift, but for the *murder* of a cop. He could easily imagine Jimmy babbling incoherently, and he could understand how a man like Jimmy Smith could have survived his wretched life by *never* giving anything *but* an indirect, evasive reply to anything anyone ever asked of him.

Brooks could *understand*, but that was all. He despised the lying coward too much for a quantum leap into pity. Jimmy had blurted things to the Bakersfield detectives: "When I hit the county jail, I'm gonna make them give...give me...I know that I...you know,...that I, you know...that I'm not mental, that I couldn't do it, you know, do *that*. I *hope* I didn't do it. I might do it, you know, in a pinch, or maybe if I was shoved into it, or something, but I mean, as far as just outright, you know, just kill a man, you know. Was there anything else you wanna know?"

Presidents, congressmen, generals, and other notable people tend to write memoirs about their experiences, and writer/historians turn to these written records as research sources. When sections from memoirs are pulled out and quoted in articles and books, they give readers more than facts—they give them human beings. For this reason, creative non-fiction writers frequently quote from memoirs, as in the following excerpt from the Pulitzer Prize-winning historical study of the final year of America's civil war, *A Stillness at Appomattox*, where Bruce Catton quotes from Ulysses S. Grant's *Personal Memoirs:*.

> The pursuit of [Confederate General] Early had been ineffective because too many men were in position to give orders to soldiers like Wright and Emory. All lines of authority were crossed, and the War Department was buzzing and fretting and issuing innumerable orders, taking time along the way to modify, alter, or countermand the orders other people were issuing. Looking back long after the war [General] Grant wrote his verdict: "It seemed to be the policy of General Halleck and Secretary Stanton to keep any force sent there in pursuit of the invading army moving right or left so as to keep between the enemy and our capital; and generally speaking they pursued this policy until all knowledge of the whereabouts of the enemy was lost."

Author Catton wisely mixes quotes from senior military officers like Grant with letters and reminiscences from the lower-ranking officers and enlisted men. In this passage about an ill-fated charge, he draws from Charles H. Banes's *History of the Philadelphia Brigade* (1876).

Down to the right were the troops which had made the unsuccessful attack earlier in the day, and it was resolved to send them back in again. The men had just succeeded in re-forming their lines after the repulse when a staff officer came galloping up, riding from brigade to brigade with orders for a new attack. One of the men who had to make this charge wrote afterward that "there was an approach to the ridiculous" in the way in which these orders were given. He specified:

"No officer of higher rank than a brigade commander had examined the approaches to the enemy's works on our front, and the whole expression of the person who brought the message seemed to say, 'The general commanding is doubtful of your success.' The moment the order was given the messenger put spurs to his horse and rode off, lest by some misunderstanding the assault should begin before he was safe and out of range of the enemy's responsive fire."

The soldier who wrote so bitterly about the way the charge was directed confessed that some of the best men in the army "not only retired without any real attempt to carry the enemy's works, but actually retreated in confusion to a point far in the rear of the original line and remained there until nearly night." Staff officers sent to recall them found the men quietly grouped around their regimental flags, making coffee.

Writers also find that official letters and telegrams are sometimes, as in the following example, of such dramatic content that the writer includes one—even reproducing its actual format. C. D. B. Bryan in *Friendly Fire* did just that with the type of letter no one wants to receive because it's another reminder of what has just happened to one's son or daughter. For that reason, I'll include no other examples of official letters.

DEPARTMENT OF THE ARMY
OFFICE OF THE ADJUTANT GENERAL
WASHINGTON, D.C. 20315

20 Apr 1970

I have the honor to inform you that your son has been awarded posthumously the Bronze Star Medal and the Good Conduct Medal.

Prior to death, Michael had been awarded the National Defense Service Medal, Vietnam Service Medal, Vietnam Campaign Medal, Combat Infantryman Badge, and the Marksman Badge with rifle, automatic rifle, and machine gun bars.

Arrangements are being made to have these awards presented to you in the near future by a representative of the Commanding General, Fifth United States Army.

The representative selected will communicate with you in the next few weeks to arrange for presentation. Any inquiry or correspondence concerning presentation should be addressed to the Commanding General, Fifth United States Army, Fort Sheridan, Illinois, 60037.

My continued sympathy is with you.

Sincerely,
S/Kenneth G. Wickham
Major General, USA
The Adjutant General

People also expose bits of themselves when they talk on the telephone, the radio, or television, so creative nonfiction writers keep their ears alert. Sometimes the writer can hear both sides of a telephone conversation; at others he or she may have to re-create one end from what's heard on the other end; or what one person recalls for him about the other end of the conversation. Reporting only one side of a conversation can also lend drama and verisimilitude to a report on an incident. Gay Talese, in his extended article about bridge building (collected in his book *Fame and Obscurity*) captured this telephone conversation between Chris Reisman and someone named Willy:

The day after Reisman had been hired by the American Bridge Company and sent to Murphy's shack on the Staten Island shore, Murphy's welcoming words were, "Well, I see we got another ass to sit around here." But soon even Murphy was impressed with twenty-three-year-old Reisman's efficiency as a secretary and his cool manner over the telephone in dealing with people Murphy was trying to avoid.

"Good *morning*, American Bridge..."

"Yeah, say is Murphy in?"

"May I ask who's calling?"

"Wha?"

"May I ask who's calling?"

"Yeah, dis is an old friend, Willy... just tell 'im Willy..."

"May I have your last name?"

"Wha?"

"Your *last* name?"

"Just tell Murphy, well, maybe you can help me. Ya see, I worked on the Pan Am job with Murphy, and ... "

"Just a minute, please," Chris cut in, then switched to Murphy on the intercom and said, "I have a Willy on the phone that worked for you ... "

"*I don't want to talk to that bastard,*" Murphy snapped back.

Then, back on the phone, Reisman said, "I'm sorry, sir, but Mr. Murphy is not in."

"Wha?"

"I said I do not expect Mr. Murphy to be in today."

"Well, okay, I'll try tomorrow."

"Fine," said Chris Reisman, clicking him off, picking up another call with, "Good *morn*ing, American Bridge ... "

Not much need be said about that phone conversation except that we learn a fair amount about Murphy and Chris Reisman, and about the general calibre of operation going on. To get so much background information to the reader through straight exposition would have lacked much and would not have put us right there in that construction workers' shack. People seem to enjoy overhearing phone conversations—and we tend to believe what we learn about something in that manner.

In Jan Morris's lengthy study of the inner and outer workings of New York's Port Authority and its ports, *The Great Port: A Passage through New York*, she captures this end of a phone conversation in a union hiring hall somewhere down near New York's piers.

I felt rather like a hoodlum boss myself, as we swept around the docks in the recesses of an immense Cadillac, which if not actually bullet-proof (it was only rented) smelt authentically, I thought, of bourbon and cigars. The hiring hall we visited certainly seemed innocent enough. The hiring bosses looked genteel, and the longshoremen, told there was work at Hoboken or Brooklyn, stepped into their waiting cars rather as though they were off to the office (though, in fact, since they are paid for the time they take in travelling to the piers, they often stop off for unnaturally long coffee breaks). It reminded me of Sotheby's, and was conducted, like that other earthy institution, with a certain ritual urgency. In the office a man was on the telephone, collating the needs of the port for labor that morning.

"Okay, Jersey City wants twelve drivers, eight banana men ... Sure, I got a driver at Bayonne, where d'ya want him? ... No, like I say, they don't want work in the hold ... Yeah, yeah, send him to Berth 7, ITO ... Whassat you say? Sure, category A, yeah ... "

In remote parts of places like Africa, northern Canada, and Alaska, transportation is expensive and difficult and telephone service nonexistent, so many people must depend on radio messages. Joe McGinniss wrote about this in his *Going to Extremes* and captured for his readers some typical messages going out over the open airwaves. Sometimes people without a radio themselves have to depend on someone else's hearing and recording the message—and getting it to them somehow, sometime, somewhere.

Bush Pipeline on the radio: a way to make contact when you are out in the backcountry without a telephone, or when you were trying to reach someone who was.

"For Mom at Shell Lake. I had my physical yesterday and it was all right, except it cost fifty-one dollars. Gordon."

"To Julie at Chase. Ellen will be at Talkeetna Saturday. Would you come down?"

"To Mom and Sparky at Peter's Creek. Come into town as soon as possible. Might have a job lined up for Sparky."

"For David Burns at Gakona, or on the Gulkana River. Call your attorney at 274-7522 at once. From Geri, your attorney's secretary."

"For Boulder Creek Lodge. The transmission won't be finished until tomorrow. I'll be out with fresh supplies if the weather holds and I'm able to make it through the pass."

Sometimes a writer will find that fragments of talk or snatches of conversation may actually be telling, dramatic, vivid, involving—despite their shortness of burst. Joan Didion, in her short study of El Salvador, *Salvador*, collected what professional photographers in the field sometimes call "grab shots." These are photographs made on the run, from the hip—shots which if properly set up would most likely be missed because of the pace of action. With a tape recorder, or a good ear, the writer can grab snatches of conversation, as Joan Didion did here.

There had been, they agreed, fewer dead around since the election, fewer bodies, they thought, than in the capital, but as they began reminding one another of this body or that there still seemed to have been quite a few. They spoke of these bodies in the matter-of-fact way that they might have spoken, in another kind of parish, of confirmation candidates, or cases of croup. There had been the few up the road, the two at Yoloaiquin. Of course there had been the forty-eight near Bar-

rios, but Barrios was in April. "A *guardia* was killed last Wednesday,"
one of them recalled.

"Thursday."

"Was it Thursday then, Jerry?"

"A sniper."

"That's what I thought. A sniper."

Paul Theroux's *Sunrise with Seamonsters*, in a chapter about New
York City's subways, captures for us some of the straaange goings-on
and straaange snatches of conversation we hear on New York's streets
and subways.

> Then a Muslim flapped his prayer mat—while we were at Flushing
> Avenue, talking about rules—and spread it out on the platform and
> knelt on it, just like that, and was soon on all fours, beseeching Allah
> and praising the Prophet Mohammed. This is not remarkable. You see
> people praying, or reading the Bible, or selling religion on the subway
> all the time. "Hallelujah, brothers and sisters," the man with the leaflets
> says on the BMT-RR line at Prospect Avenue in Brooklyn. "I love
> Jesus! I used to be a wino!" And Muslims beg and push their green plas-
> tic cups at passengers, and try to sell them copies of something called
> *Arabic Religious Classics*. It is December and Brooklyn, and the men
> are dressed for the Great Nafud Desert, or Jiddah or Medina—skull
> cap, gallabieh, sandals.
>
> "And don't sit next to the door," the second police officer said. We
> were still talking Rules. "A lot of these snatchers like to play the doors."
>
> The first officer said, "It's a good idea to keep near the conductor.
> He's got a telephone. So does the man in the token booth. At night,
> stick around the token booth until the train comes."

Jan Morris reports in her book *Destinations* that New York City's
daily life is "spattered with aspects and episodes of unhinged sensibility"
and lists a few items that she snatched up during a two-week stay. Here
are some selected items from her list:

> *Item:* At the headquarters of the New York police, which is a func-
> tionary called the Chief of Organized Crime. I heard an administrator
> say to a colleague on the telephone there: *You're going sick today? Ad-
> ministrative sick or regular sick?*
>
> *Item:* A young man talks about his experiences in a levitation group:
> *Nobody's hovering yet but we're lifting up and down again. We're hop-*

ping. I've seen a guy hop fifteen feet from the lotus position, and no one could do that on the level of trying.

Item: An eminent, kind and cultivated actress, beautifully dressed, is taking a cab to an address on Second Avenue. Cabdriver: *Whereabouts is that on Second Avenue, lady?* Actress, without a flicker in her equanimity: *Don't ask me, bud. You're the fucking cabdriver.*

A special category of conversational snatches is the one-sided conversation between the pet owner and pet. Jan Morris, in the same listing of items, snatched this one as it went by on a leash:

Item: I feel a sort of furry clutch at my right leg, and peering down, find that it is being bitten by a chow. *Oh Goochy you naughty thing,* says its owner, who is following behind with a brush and shovel for clearing up its excrement, *you don't know that person.*

I suppose I could write an entire chapter on graffiti found in and around our cities and toilets as illustration of the point that we, as a people, do say something about our society through what some of us write on walls, sidewalks, and subway cars. I'll be content here to add simply the one bit of graffiti given by Jan Morris.

Item: Graffito in Washington Square.
YIPPIES, JESUS FREAKS AND MOONIES
ARE GOVERNMENT OPERATED

People also reveal something by the instructions they write for the public in public places, like hotel rooms, restaurants, and highways. I recall one sign in an English hotel room where my wife and I were staying. On the back of the door was a series of instructions for various things like checkout time and room rates. The instructions on what to do in the event of fire consisted of about six items. Before they instructed us about crawling close to the floor to find unused oxygen, or about not using the lift during a fire, they gave what the English must consider a priority instruction: (1) *Put on your wrapper.*

Not long after returning home, I came upon an article in the *New York Times* by Donald Carroll, author of the book, *The Best Excuse.* I've excerpted several examples of public instruction from his article, "Truly Inspired Gibberish":

Consider, for example, this advice from the brochure of a car rental firm in Tokyo: *When a passenger of foot heave in sight, tootle the horn. Trumpet him melodiously at first, but if he obstacles your passage then tootle him with vigor.*

Back in your hotel room, if the hotel is Japanese, you might well be confronted with a polite warning combined with an impossible request: *Is forbidden to steal the hotel towels please. If you are not person to do such thing is please not to read notis.*

That final instruction says more about the Japanese people's desire never to offend guests than any amount of long, expository writing or lecturing could accomplish. At first, such items seem simply humorous, but then we see something deeper. Sometimes, of course, the mangling of English or other languages leads to something no deeper than a chuckle, such as the sign Carroll reported in the same article: "There is, for instance, a dentist in Hong Kong who advertises: TEETH EXTRACTED BY THE LATEST METHODISTS."

I guess there are one or two things to be learned from all the foregoing. (1) Non-Methodist tourists—better have that six-month check-up before leaving home. (2) If you should be recommending this book to a friend, trumpet its praises at first melodiously; that failing, tootle with vigor.

SEVEN

ANGLES OF APPROACH AND POINTS OF VIEW

The business of point of view seems to confuse most of us when we begin getting serious about our writing. Much of the explanation in textbooks does more to confuse than clarify. Part of any confusion comes from the several different meanings of the phrase "point of view." Everyone, in casual conversation, will say something like: "Well, that's HER point of view; mine's quite different!" or "Everyone has his own viewpoint on that" or, close to that phrase, "What's your view on this, John?" All these variations express the notion that where you stand affects your view—a metaphor that gives us an image of someone, say a military scout, standing atop a rocky point and saying: "From my viewing point (or standpoint) (or vantage point) (from this perspective) I believe we've already lost the battle or we're about to, General." The general, from his point of view down in the forest, had thought everything was going well. Now, seeing things through the eyes of his scout, he has to reconsider. These meanings of point of view are similar to the meanings used by the writer, but the student of writing must set those aside and concentrate on the several meanings the phrase has within the literary world. It's hard enough to keep the following two literary distinctions clear without also carrying along the informal meanings used in casual conversation.

ANGLES OF APPROACH

The phrase "angle of approach" has been invented to help distinguish this concept from point of view, which it resembles in an informal way. A story's angle of approach does not concern itself with who *tells* the story (the concern of point of view) but with *how* the writer approaches it. That approach can be either *objective* or *subjective*.

Objective

In addition to all the other elements he or she has to worry about, the writer must first decide which basic approach to use, objective or subjective. The decision is crucial because the angle of approach determines to a great degree what kinds of facts are relevant and should be included (and, importantly, what should be considered irrelevant and, thus, excluded).

If you were writing as a military strategist, for example, you would adopt an objective angle of approach, and include as relevant how many bombs dropped on the city. You might well include as relevant how many civilians died as a result of the bombing. You would not, however, include descriptions of the children dying in the streets as the bombs fell. In a larger sense, of course, such facts are important and relevant, but when the angle of approach is objective, the facts of how horribly the children died are not relevant. Given the same situation, if you were writing as a psychologist, how the children and their parents suffered would be relevant (and hence included), but the facts about how many bombs of what kind fell that night would be viewed as irrelevant.

Subjective

Given the same bombing scene, a man who had been an ambulance worker might later write an article about the experience—and he might use a subjective angle of approach. If so, his descriptions would not only be vivid, they'd likely be emotional. He would write about his own emotions when he slid the injured children into the back of the ambulance, and he might describe the emotional responses of the parents as the ambulance rushes with sirens to the hospital. An objective angle of approach would not take up such matters. These thoughts and feelings are for the subjective writer. The chances are that an ambulance worker would not write in the same article about the Eighth Air Force's bombing strategy against the cities of western Germany. That would be a more objective than subjective approach.

Most of the time a scientist or other specialist writing an article (especially an expository one) about his or her specialty will decide to write in an impersonal (objective) *voice*. The voice is impersonal in that the specialist writing such a piece will probably not introduce his or her personal, private feelings on the subject, and won't tell the reader how to feel about the subject. Sometimes we can read between the lines and sense personal feelings, but the approach is still relatively impersonal. At least the writer doesn't deliberately make him- or herself the focus of the article, or periodically insert personal reactions or attitudes. If the writer does switch back and forth between impersonal and personal, the reader will end up confused. A writer of creative nonfiction will be apt to write with a personal voice, which is all right, provided it is consistent.

Consistency of approach is important for the reader and for the writer. Given the example of the bombing raid, consider the confusion caused by the military who changes his or her angle of approach in the middle of a narrative and begins describing the horrors of war (i.e., who shifts to a subjective approach). Think of the confusion caused by the psychologist-writer who interrupts a cogent discussion of the mental damage suffered by the dead children's parents to go on at some length about how many tons of bombs fell, from what kind of aircraft, and at what intervals. Relevant for one specialist, irrelevant for the other, yet their angle of approach is the same—objective. It is crucial to make an early decision as to angle of approach, so you won't include materials irrelevant to your audience—and make your writing confusing. Your credibility will slip and you'll likely lose your following.

Beginning writers tend to move inconsistently from angle to angle, usually because they just start writing and putting down thoughts as they occur. A beginning writer with strong pro-life feelings, for example, might feel compelled to insert a value judgment into an official report on the issue of taking away life-support systems from a dying patient. Value judgments and opinions have no place in a piece with an objective angle of approach. They belong in works using a subjective angle of approach.

POINTS OF VIEW

After the writer has made the key decision about angle of approach, he or she must make an equally important decision—from whose point of view shall the article or book be told? We will now discuss what I think should be the only meaning for point of view—through whose eyes the reader views the action. The writer has several possible points of view from which to select, and, as a general rule, he or she must use only one point of view throughout. The selection is crucial. Because a short story or a nonfiction article usually attempts to achieve a single effect, a single point of view becomes essential. To tell a story through more than one set of eyes tends to confuse the reader—a cardinal sin for a writer (especially for a writer of nonfiction). Writers strive for unity; multiple points of view destroy unity. Sometimes a story or article can be divided into two parts, each told from a different point of view, and still be successful, but a piece that switches back and forth between viewpoints all the way through promotes confusion.

First, the writer has to answer the fundamental questions (and the answers are not always immediately obvious): Whose story is this, and who could best tell it? Then, he or she has to decide which grammatical person should be used in the writing.

The story might, for example, be George Orwell's story, but after some thought, the writer may decide that George's story might be more interestingly, or more effectively, told by someone other than George. If George tells it, the writer uses the grammatical first person, but if someone else narrates Orwell's story, the writer must use the grammatical third person. If first person is chosen, the narrator says "I" throughout; if third person, the writer does not refer directly to him- or herself, and refers to people written about as "he," "she," or "they."

First Person Point of View

In the case of George Orwell's book *Down and Out in Paris and London*, he was the writer and the main character; and he told his story in first person.

I travelled to England third class via Dunkirk and Tilbury, which is the cheapest and not the worst way of crossing the Channel. You had to pay extra for a cabin, so I slept in the saloon, together with most of the third-class passengers. I find this entry in my diary for that day:

"Sleeping in the saloon, twenty-seven men, sixteen women. Of the women, not a single one has washed her face this morning. The men mostly went to the bathroom; the women merely produced vanity cases and covered the dirt with powder. Q. A secondary sexual difference?"

Another early question the writer must ask (and answer) is: What is the relationship between who tells the story and the story itself? In the above case, the narrator is the main character, so almost everything relates to him in one way or another. If someone else observes and narrates the action that relates to the main character, the writer may also use the first person. If, for example, George Orwell had had a friend, Bill, traveling with him, and Bill was now writing a book about their experiences living down and out, he would narrate the story. It might still be George Orwell's story, but told by an observer, a fellow participant. Such a passage might sound like this:

WE travelled to England third class via Dunkirk and Tilbury, which is the cheapest and not the worst way of crossing the Channel. You had to pay for a cabin, so *WE* slept in the saloon, together with most of the third-class passengers. I find this entry in *MY* diary for that day:

"Twenty-seven men and sixteen women slept with *US* in the saloon. In the morning *GEORGE* and I used the bathroom, as did the other men, but not a single woman did; they simply produced vanity cases and covered the dirt with powder. *GEORGE* asked whether I thought this might be a newly discovered secondary sexual difference."

My italicized words show that this hypothetical Bill, too, would use the first person, but by referring directly to "George," he makes it clear to us that George is not the narrator, not the "I" in the story. Such a short passage could not make it clear that it is still George's story his companion is narrating, but it would soon be apparent by the emphasis he would give to George rather than to himself.

One great danger in writing first person narrative is the tendency for the "I" person to take over the limelight, rather than keeping the focus on the main character. Nonfiction and fiction writers run this risk every time they elect to write in the first person. Naturally, when the piece is auto-biographical, the central character is automatically kept in the limelight by the first person technique—just where he or she should be. The problem comes only when the narrator is an observer reporting on the main character through first person point of view.

William Zinsser likes to write in a personal voice and often in the first person, yet he keeps the limelight on the character or thing he's writing about. His presence is felt, but not intrusively so. In his profile about two great jazz musicians, Willie Ruff and Dwike Mitchell (*Willie and Dwike—An American Profile*), Zinsser goes with them on concert tours, but he's not forever telling us about himself, what he did, how he reacted. We just sense that he's with them through the occasional reference to himself in first person:

> Mitchell and Ruff go to the auditorium early to look it over. It's handsome, like the rest of the building, but with the intimacy of a small concert hall. Backstage, it has a door big enough for the biggest combine to drive through—this theatre can present a full cast of Deere's green and yellow tractors, works of art in themselves.
>
> The piano is an almost seven-foot grand, and Mitchell tries it out before he even takes off his coat. It hasn't been tuned. "The piano's got eight A's, all different," he tells *ME*. Ruff is hailed from the highest tier by a young man who says he will be operating the lights. Ruff shouts up to him that whatever he wants to do will be fine. The hall begins to fill up with men and women who have driven out from the Quad Cities. I recognize quite a few who were at the Sunday afternoon concert. Lois Jecklin works the house, asking the new arrivals whether they are on the mailing list of Visiting Artists. They gladly fill out a card for her; in America the arts have one sacred text—the mailing list.

I examined *Willie and Dwike* for several pages surrounding that passage and found that the "ME" and the "I" (that I've italicized above) were the only first person references to Bill Zinsser's presence. Those two totally unintrusive references were enough to keep the personal voice and the first person point of view throughout. I would be hard put, however, to say that the book was written in the first person, despite the occasional "I", "me," and "we." Zinsser has written there, and elsewhere, in the personal voice without writing totally in the first person. Again, not much about writing is clearly one thing and not another. Rather, writing is sort of this way, and not really that way. Like my hypothetical companion to

George Orwell, Bill Zinsser accompanied Willie and Dwike and wrote the Willie and Dwike story as an observer, not as a deeply involved observer, but simply as observer. Many writers don't have as much control as Zinsser, and write their pieces either intrusively in first person, or in the third person where it's easier to remain unintrusive. I think the Zinsser approach works best, if you can maintain control over that limelight.

The choice of first person or third person centers on distance. Do you want close-up, intimate, immediate, involved writing? First person does a better job of that. Do you want to stand back for an overview, deal with more characters, more descriptions of people and settings? Third person is a better choice.

Third Person Point of View

When the "New Journalists" of the early sixties were experimenting with the kind of creative nonfiction writing we're talking about here, they were criticized for putting the journalist too much in the forefront. In a sort of overreaction to all the years when journalists had to stay totally, absolutely invisible, some writers did push themselves so much stage-front that the limelight fell on them rather than on the events or the characters about which they were writing. Tom Wolfe led the way at the time, but in his more recent work, including *The Right Stuff*, he stays largely in the background, although we know he's present. We like having Tom Wolfe present. He says in his *New Journalism* that some of the best writing of this "new" kind has been done in third person. He mentions writers like Capote, Talese, and John Gregory Dunne as examples of people who write in a personal voice but use third person.

Third person point of view has less immediacy than first person, and always has an impersonal voice. The narrator seems to stand above it all, but there are limits to how much he or she is "allowed" to observe as a nonparticipant in the action. Literary convention allows the third person narrator some latitude. In fiction, the omniscient narrator may enter any or all characters' minds. He or she may observe any action anywhere. In creative nonfiction, however, the writer has less latitude, less omniscience. He or she is limited by the facts available to a character, or reasonably deducible by that character. Historical biographies, for example, use this kind of third person narrator, a narrator whose camera has a wide-angle lens. Other writers of nonfiction carry a literary camera with interchangeable lenses, one of which is a close-up lens. The best way to make clear this distinction between third person (close-up) and third person (panoramic or wide-angle) may be through two passages from the same book (*The Right Stuff*), each dealing with Alan Shepard's first orbital flight. The first takes place within the tiny capsule where we not only see Shepard close up, we go inside his mind (the ultimate close-up). The second passage shows us what happens soon after when Shepard arrives in New York City. Tom Wolfe takes off the close-up lens and inserts the wide-angle lens to enable the narrator to watch Alan go by on parade, and then he widens his lens to include Alan's hometown and New England—all in the same third person.

Shepard had forgotten to take the filter off the capsule's periscope, so he was seeing everything on Earth in black and white—yet he knew that the folks back home wanted to hear about it in color:

> "What a beautiful view!" he said. He could hear Slayton say: "I bet it is." In fact, there was a cloud cover over most of the East Coast and much of the ocean. He was able to see the Cape. He could see the west coast of Florida . . . Lake Okeechobee . . . He was up so high he seemed to be moving away from Florida ever so slowly . . . And the inverters moaned up and the gyros moaned down and the fans whirred and the cameras hummed. . . . He tried to find Cuba. Was that Cuba or wasn't that Cuba? Over there, through the clouds. . . . Everything was black and white and there were clouds all over. . . . There's Bimini Island and the shoals around Bimini. He could see that. *But everything looked so small!* It had all been bigger and clearer in the ALFA trainer, when they flashed the still photos on the screen. . . . The real thing didn't measure up. It was not *realistic*. He couldn't see anything but a medium-gray ocean and the light-gray beaches and the dark-gray vegetation. . . .

We know Tom Wolfe has snapped on the close-up lens as soon as we hear the inverters, gyros, fans, cameras. Then he really goes in tight on Alan Shepard when we hear the astronaut thinking about Cuba and whether he's seeing it or not. Then the irony of his thought that the flight simulation had been more realistic than the real thing. The scene is even more personal and up close than if Wolfe had used first person and had Alan Shepard *telling* us what he'd thought back then in the capsule. Instead, Wolfe *shows* us Shepard's thought processes. Naturally, Wolfe had not been inside Shepard's mind. He interviewed Shepard about his thoughts, and then re-created them for us in this interior monolog. The beauties and difficulties of using this technique in creative nonfiction will be taken up later in this book because it deserves some focused attention.

Now, let's watch as Wolfe shows us the Broadway ticker-tape parade with his wide-angle lens:

> . . . The next day New York City gave Al a ticker-tape parade up Broadway. There was Al on the back ledge of the limousine, with all that paper snow and confetti coming down, just the way you used to see it in the Movietone News in the theaters. Al's hometown, Derry, New Hampshire, which was not much more than a village, gave Al a parade, and it drew the biggest crowd the state had ever seen. Army, Navy, Marine, Air Force, and National Guard troops from all over New England marched down Main Street, and aerobatic teams of jet fighters flew overhead....

These two passages show the versatility of third person point of view. The first stayed in close with sounds that Alan Shepard could have heard (and no sounds that he could not reasonably have heard), and then entered right inside the man's mind as he watched the world through his periscope. We eavesdrop on a brain at work—the ultimate in personal writing, yet in third person, which we tend to think of as the impersonal point of view.

Multiple Points of View

I made the point earlier that a writer should not switch points of view in a piece, because it tends to confuse the reader. The crime is to switch frequently back and forth, but some creative nonfiction writers have switched points of view successfully, i.e., without confusing the reader. C. D. B. Bryan in *Friendly Fire* wrote in the third person as he told about how the young soldier, Michael Mullen, was killed accidentally by our own guns. As soon as the writer went to visit Michael's parents, however, he switched to the first person. Because this was the first time he had come into the story himself, the switch to first person seemed totally natural. No reader could have been confused by that switch—and he didn't switch back to third person.

A similar type of single switch occurs in Joe Eszterhas's much-praised story, "Charlie Simpson's Apocalypse," (collected by Tom Wolfe in *The New Journalism*, Harper & Row, 1973) when he tells the story in third person until the end. At that point, he does come into the story to explain to his readers how he happened to come upon the story and how he worked on it. Again, this kind of simple, single shift of point of view is allowable because there's no danger that the reader will wonder what's going on.

Jane Kramer begins her book *The Last Cowboy* in first person, telling us how she came to write about cowboy life and, particularly, why she selected Henry Blanton to write about. After she explains a bit about her method of working with Henry and his wife, she ducks out of the limelight and lets it fall almost totally on Henry for the remaining 95 percent of the book. No problem here.

Michael Herr's excellent book *Dispatches*, reporting on life for the U.S. Marines fighting in Vietnam during the Tet Offensive, uses multiple points of view as Herr switches from talking about specific marines in the third person to giving his own, noncombatant's feelings in the first person. Wisely, he kept the limelight on the fighting marines most of the time, only returning occasionally to himself. By doing it proportionally like that, he accomplished two objectives. First, we believed what he wrote partly because of the captured conversations with the marines, which kept our eyes and ears on the young fighting men. Second, by occasional references to himself he reminded us, unobtrusively, that this was not a secondhand report written in a Saigon bar; this man was sitting there in the slit trench, head down, talking with these men. So, it's a matter of proportion. Keep in mind whose story you're telling, and keep the grammatical person appropriate for telling that particular story. Then, if needed (and only if needed), switch point of view.

Then there's the very deliberate, very conscious, very artistic use of multiple points of view. Tom Wolfe makes an art of switching points of view in the middle of a story, in the middle of a paragraph, in the middle of a sentence. At times the reader is confused, I imagine, but Wolfe is always going for the overall effect, a tone, a feeling for the scene, rather than trying to keep the reader right on track every moment. In his book *The New Journalism* he writes about an article he wrote: "I began a story on Baby Jane Holzer, entitled 'The Girl of the Year,' as follows:"

Bangs manes bouffant beehives Beatle caps butter faces brush-on lashes decal eyes puffy sweaters French thrust bras flailing leather blue jeans stretch pants stretch jeans honeydew bottoms eclair shanks elf boots ballerinas Knight slippers, hundreds of them, these flaming little buds, bobbing and screaming, rocketing around inside the Academy of Music Theater underneath that vast old moldering cherub dome up there—aren't they super-marvelous!

"Aren't they super-marvelous!" says Baby Jane, and then: "Hi, Isabel! Isabel! You want to sit backstage—with the Stones!"

The show hasn't even started yet, the Rolling Stones aren't even on the stage, the place is full of a great shabby moldering dimness, and these flaming little buds.

Girls are reeling this way and that way in the aisle and through their huge black decal eyes, sagging with Tiger Tongue Lick Me brush-on eyelashes and black appliques, sagging like display-window Christmas trees, they keep staring at—her—Baby Jane—on the aisle.

After Tom Wolfe's clever opening paragraph that presents the reality of the teenagers' lifestyle through a disembodied narrator in a third person point of view, he switches to Baby Jane's third person point of view. The switch occurs with the phrase, "aren't they super-marvelous!" When the text gets down to "they keep staring at—her—Baby Jane—on the aisle," Wolfe has switched the point of view again. This time, we're seeing the scene through the eyes of the young buds as they look at Baby Jane. He uses three points of view in this piece—his own, the young girls', and Baby Jane's. It's all rather subtly done, and we end up with an understanding of how it must have felt to be there in the Academy of Music surrounded by all those noises and bobbing buds.

Tom Wolfe went on to say: "Eventually a reviewer called me a 'chameleon' who constantly took on the coloration of whomever he was writing about. He meant it negatively. I took it as a great compliment. A chameleon... but exactly!"

Pseudo-Point of View

I have coined the name for this almost-point of view because I'm unaware of an "official" name for it, although I suspect it's what Tom Wolfe labeled the *downstage* voice, not a bad label for people familiar with the stage. What I'm about to describe also has a chameleon look about it. Tom Wolfe is one of the few writers who make artistic use of this technique, as he does in this excerpt from a piece that helped earn him a reputation for innovation back in 1965. "The Last American Hero Is Junior Johnson. Yes!" chronicles the lifestyle of Junior Johnson, the famous stock car racer and former moonshine runner. Wolfe uses the first and the third person as called for, but then he periodically switches to what at first sounds like a different point of view, like someone else at the race. Reading on, we find that the narrator is still Tom Wolfe, but now he's talking just like a good ol' boy. So, it's not truly a different point of view, it's a pseudo-point of view, a sort-of-but-not-quite-new-point-of-view. We're sort of hearing (not viewing) from a new angle, a new perspective (maybe I should call it point of hearing). Wolfe accomplishes this sometimes with a single word that we realize immediately is not the sophisticated, East Coast Tom Wolfe-with-the-white-shoes voice, yet we can hear that he's still there in the sentences, guiding things along. Sometimes, of course, he lets us hear long passages in the local lingo.

> ... God! The Alcohol Tax agents used to burn over Junior Jackson. Practically every good old boy in town in Wilkesboro, the county seat, got to know the agents by sight in a very short time. They would rag them practically to their faces on the subject of Junior Johnson, so that it got to be an obsession. Finally, one night they had Junior trapped on the road up toward the bridge around Millersville, there's no way out of there, they had barricades up and they could hear this souped-up car roaring around the bend, and here it comes—but suddenly they can hear a siren and see a red light flashing in the grill, so they think it's another agent, and boy, they run out like ants and pull those barrels and boards and sawhorses out of the way, and then— Ggghzzzzzhhhggggzzzzz eeeeong!—gawdam! there he goes again, it was him, Junior Johnson!, with a gawdam agent's si-reen and a red light in his grill!

Perhaps we can't tell immediately that Wolfe has switched into a pseudo-point of view, but we can certainly tell when we get down to "Finally, one night they had Junior trapped. . . . " From there on, the almost continuous run-on sentence of about one hundred words sounds like someone telling a tale. We hear the pseudo-narrator imitating the sound of Junior ripping through the would-be roadblock. Then Wolfe hits us with a couple of gawdams and the sound of a si-reen. We know it's not Wolfe, yet it's no one else identifiable. We know that Wolfe lurks nearby, nevertheless.

Joe Eszterhas opened his article "Charlie Simpson's Apocalypse" with an excellent example of a pseudo-point of view. It starts out sounding like a normal third person narrative in a personal voice, but it gradually becomes something else.

> Right after the sun comes up, first thing folks do around Harrisonville, Missouri, is to go up to the barn and see if the mare is still there. Horse-thieves drive around the gravel roads and brushy hills in tractor-trailers looking to rustle lazyboned nags. Then they grind them up into bags of meat jelly for the dogfood people. It's getting so that a man can't live in peace anywhere, not even on his own plot of land.
>
> Harrisonville is 40 miles southeast of Kansas City along Interstate 71, just down the blacktop from the red-brick farmhouse where Harry S. Truman, haberdasher and President, was born. The little town is filled with weeping willows, alfalfa, Longhorn steer, and Black Whiteface cows. Life should be staid and bucolic, a slumbering leftover of what everyone who buys the $3.00 Wednesday-night Catfish Dinner at Scott's Bar B-Q calls Them Good Old Days. But it isn't like that anymore.
>
> There's always some botheration to afflict a man these days and if it isn't the horse-thieves or the velvetleaf that plagued the soybeans last year, then it's them vagrant tornadoes.

I've arbitrarily broken his text into paragraphs that illustrate how he's used a combination of normal, third person point of view and pseudo-point of view. In the final sentence of the first paragraph we can hear clearly the voice of someone local, even though the first few sentences are not too clearly third or pseudo.

The second paragraph is straight, third person point of view. We hear the voice of the outside writer-narrator. It's written in a personal voice, but it's not the voice of the local person we think we heard at the end of the first paragraph.

The third paragraph (in my arbitrary break-up of his text) sounds like a local person's point of view, yet he or she's not identified. It's the writer deliberately making the narrator sound more in touch with the place and the people—a pseudo-point of view.

It takes a writer with a sensitive, well-tuned ear to simulate a local person's voice. Not very many writers attempt it, but it seems to me an excellent technique available for the creative nonfiction writer—if he or she can handle it cleverly and in good taste.

VOICE

In objective (impersonal) writing, the writer/narrator writes about thoughts shared by many people, ideas available in the literature, the newspapers, and in the general public opinion. The impersonal narrator never gets "personal" by voicing his or her emotions or deeply held thoughts about the topic at hand. Journalists have been told to write in this impersonal voice so as to maintain an "objective" tone—the reader should not know how the journalist feels about the subject, only what others say about it.

Writing done in a subjective (personal) voice, which the New Journalists said was the better way to write about journalistic subjects, does allow the writer to inject openly his or her feelings on the subject to let the reader know whose mind the ideas are filtering through. The New Journalists (or parajournalists) thought this was the honest way to report the world to the public. They got into trouble sometimes by injecting themselves so much into the story that they became the center of it. They wrote so "personally" that all eyes focused on them and their (sometimes) histrionics. Tom Wolfe, often called the father of parajournalism, was so happy to get out from under the fetters of traditionally impersonal journalistic writing, that he wrote wildly (wonderfully, but wildly in the eyes of traditional journalists). He tried his wings, and he flew in great style to great heights. Neither of these "voices" is the voice I'm taking up here.

Lewis H. Lapham (editor of *Harper's* magazine, and a creative nonfiction writer of consummate skill) wrote several years ago in his column, "Notebook," a piece called "On Reading." His opening paragraph says as well as can be said just what "voice" means:

> On first opening a book I listen for the sound of the human voice. By this device I am absolved from reading much of what is published in a given year. Most writers make use of institutional codes (academic, literary, political, bureaucratic, technical), in which they send messages already deteriorating into the half-life of yesterday's news. Their transmissions remain largely unintelligible, and unless I must decipher them for professional reasons, I am content to let them pass by. I listen, instead, for a voice in which I can hear the music of the human improvisation as performed through 5,000 years on the stage of recorded time.

... As a student, and later as an editor and occasional writer of reviews, I used to feel obliged to finish every book I began to read. This I
no longer do. If within the first few pages I cannot hear the author's
voice ... I abandon him at the first convenient opportunity.

Those words were so refreshing to my tired eyes, I cut out the column
and saved it, not knowing how or when I would use it. Now I realize that
these words express perfectly what I wanted to say in more halting
words.

Before I cloud the matter, all creative nonfiction writers do not write in
the personal voice, but the ones this book celebrates do write in a voice of
their own that we can hear. We may or may not immediately recognize
the voice as Hemingway's, for example, but we do recognize that a
human being is at work. One group of creative nonfiction writers believes that writers should subordinate themselves, telling the story in its
own terms, not theirs. They intend to portray reality just as it is, not interpret it for the reader. Not altogether possible, of course, but they try.

Writers in the other group do insert themselves and approach reporting the world as an art. They make it clear that things are being filtered
(and very likely distorted) through their unique intelligence, and they try
to write it in language that approaches literature. Writing of this latter
kind, of course, calls attention to itself, and the reader enjoys it partly for
the information and partly for the intellectual joy of hearing it filtered
through a respected intelligence. The former group believes, like the min-
imalists in fiction, that the writing should be transparent, not calling attention to itself by its fanciness, its beauty. These two groups belong
under the same creative nonfiction tent because they do write with the
voice of a human being, not an institutional non-voice, what Wolfe calls
the "beige" voice. Neither group writes in beige. Their writing is vivid
writing, writing that brings the subject alive. It vivifies a subject. Traditional journalism and nonfiction writing in general avoid vivification.
When we read a piece that lives, that has a human sound to it, we know
we're reading creative nonfiction—writing with voice.

I'll end this discussion of voice with words and ideas from Mark
Kramer, as reported in Norman Sims' book *The Literary Journalists*. The
introduction of personal voice, according to Mark Kramer, allows the
writer to play one world off against another, to toy with irony. "The
writer can posture, say things not meant, imply things not said. When I
find the right voice for a piece, it admits play, and that's a relief, an antidote
to being pushed around by your own words," Kramer said. "Voice that

admits of 'Self' can be a great gift to readers. It allows warmth, concern, compassion, flattery, shared imperfections—all the real stuff that, when it's missing, makes writing brittle and larger than life."

EIGHT

CHARACTER DEVELOPMENT

Traditional nonfiction, particularly journalistic nonfiction, never concerned itself with "developing characters." Fiction writers worked at characterization; nonfiction writers concentrated on events. Creative nonfiction writers say that because so many "events" occur as the result of human interactions, the event cannot be fully understood without also understanding something of the people (characters) surrounding it. The word "character," unfortunately for this book, has been so long associated with fictional characters that I hesitated to use it in this nonfiction context, but I couldn't find a suitable substitute. Please bear in mind that the "characters" talked about here are real people, and most of the time I'll be referring to their character—what makes them tick.

When I write about "character development," I'm talking about how the writer goes about revealing a person's character—how the writer "develops" that revelation, not how that real person develops character over a lifetime.

The "creative" nonfiction writer does not "create" characters; he or she reveals them to us in ways as honest and accurate as possible. The better writers use a variety of techniques to accomplish this. Like most modern fiction writers, they, too, believe that character should be revealed much as it is in real life—bit by bit.

When we first meet a character (person) in real life, no one reads to us his or her résumé, curriculum vitae, or life story. We learn a few tidbits about that person's background at our first meeting; we form some initial impressions about the person's "character" by what we talk about, what that person said in response to what we said, how it was said, what words were used, etc.; before the next meeting, we hear what other people (friends and others) say about the person; and in subsequent meetings we form more impressions and revise earlier ones. In the case of spouses, for example, we may go on learning more and more for fifty years as his or her character is revealed, bit by bit.

Article or book authors don't usually have fifty years to collect data, so they must collect what they can, and then, very selectively, choose those bits that seem best to reveal character the most accurately. They then reveal the bits in a sequence that seems reasonably connected with the unfolding narrative. Most modern writers (fiction and nonfiction alike) will not lay out all characterization in one place, but will simulate life in its nonlinear, unpredictable revelations, and spread through the article or book pieces of characterization.

Writers of creative nonfiction have available to them a variety of devices and techniques for revealing character: *Dialogs, Monologs, and Other Logs; Angle of Approach/Point of View/Voice; Realities of Group Life; Realities of Individual Lives.* These devices look familiar because I've discussed them in earlier chapters. The potential for each of these devices or techniques to serve several functions makes them extremely valuable to know about and use. In a single captured conversation, for example, we might hear references to several concrete details that resonate in our memories and stir up emotions while, at the same time, the diction and the specialist language used may give us one or more dimensions of the character—all in one piece of captured conversation. The careful writer selects from all the conversations captured those that serve as many functions as possible simultaneously. A fiction writer creates dialog that will serve several of his or her narrative purposes. The creative nonfiction writer cannot create dialog; he or she can only select those captured conversations or comments that do some of the narrative work. Why select one conversation or comment that serves only one purpose, when you could just as easily select a multi-purpose one?

DIALOGS, MONOLOGS, AND OTHER LOGS

Dialogs (Captured Conversations)

Teachers of fiction writing usually tell new students that they can "characterize" best by showing a character in different situations and letting us note how he or she behaves—and what he or she says. Fiction or nonfiction writers have a basic choice to make when faced with establishing character: They can do it "directly" through a written summary of traits (telling) or "indirectly" through dialog and action (showing). The modern way is to show, not tell, the reader about the character. One fundamental reason for this is that we readers begin to suspect a writer who keeps tugging at our elbow and telling us, in effect, how to think about this character. That's bad enough in fiction writing; it's very questionable in nonfiction. Fiction writers have as part of their responsibility to tell us how we should think about a character so as to draw some moral point; nonfiction writers are not in business to instruct us in moral behavior. Nonfiction writers limit themselves to showing us how things really look to them in the world, leaving the reader to interpret what it all means. Reporting as accurately as possible what people say is one of the best ways to establish a person's character; we all tend to reveal ourselves through our speech—even when, for some reason, we want desperately not to.

The writer must stay close to the action to take down by tape recorder, notes, or memory what everyone is saying. At first, this may sound no different than any traditional reporter who is forever "going after quotes." The difference is great. The traditional, hard-news reporter on deadline seeks answers to questions he or she poses in order to get quotable quotes. He or she doesn't also record all the other things people say. The reporter looks not for quotes that characterize but for quotes that explain. The creative nonfiction writer, too, listens for quotes that may explain, but he or she also listens to everything else, knowing through past experience that some unsolicited comments by "unimportant" people may explain even more than those received from the "notables." Reporters tend to quote the notables—the lawyers, the officers, the preachers, the drug pushers. The creative nonfiction writer knows that these people can give only parts of the story—in some cases, they deliberately give only certain parts of the story. Sometimes the enlisted men provide more useful quotes and better insights than the officers. They see the event through a different point of view. They may see it from a foxhole, while the general sees it from an aerial photograph.

We learn about characters not only through *what* they say; we learn from *how* they say it. The ancient Greeks said: Speak so I may see you. Exactly. Until a character (real or fictional) speaks, he or she is but an abstraction for us. From the moment the character begins speaking, we believe we're beginning to know the person. We also know through experience that we can be deceived by what a person says and how he or she says it, but we also know that there's little hope of fully understanding someone until we listen to what he or she says.

Although the following attributes of human speech do not give us a full understanding of a person's character, they do help us see the speaker. The creative nonfiction writer, more than a traditional reporter, tries hard to capture the speaker's *accent, dialect, colloquialisms, jargons, specialist language, rhythms, color, tone, emphases, diction, mood.* The writer must be careful, however, not to stereotype by emphasizing too much the idiosyncrasies of a person's speech. The careful writer uses just enough of these attributes to give the flavor of the person. Not that the writer makes up "dialog"; he or she is simply selecting from all the quotes taken down those that give an accurate, undistorted view of the person speaking. To take an exaggerated case—even though the quoted person had used foul language in practically every sentence, the careful writer will not report every one of them, but will use some to get across the flavor of the conversation. It would be a distortion to clean up every sentence to make them acceptable to every possible reader. Some writers, of course, get carried away and report every foul word used—in the interest of accuracy and what they claim as "objectivity." Most readers are intelligent enough to get the point without being hit over the head with every four-letter word some person can think up.

Rex Reed reported in *Do You Sleep in the Nude?* a conversation with Ava Gardner. She didn't speak in four-letter words, but she did speak colorfully—and Reed captured the color:

> Don't look at me. I was up until four A.M. at that goddam premiere of *The Bible.* Premieres! I will personally kill that John Huston if he ever drags me into another mess like that. There must have been ten thousand people clawing at me. I get claustrophobia in crowds and I

couldn't breathe. Christ, they started shoving a TV camera at me and yelling, "Talk, Ava!"

John McPhee in *The Pine Barrens* reported the following captured conversation with Bill and Fred. Here, the writer captured the essence of conversation with these men, both as to level of discussion and as to mode of expression.

> Eventually, I made the request I had intended to make when I walked in the door. "Could I have some water?" I said to Fred. "I have a jerry can and I'd like to fill it at the pump."
> "Hell, yes," he said. "That isn't my water. That's God's water. That right, Bill?"
> "I guess so," Bill said, without looking up. "It's good water, I can tell you that."
> "That's God's Water," Fred said again. "Take all you want."

The main purpose of using captured conversation is to discover and report by *indirect* means what a person is thinking. The only means more *direct* would be to tune in on the person's brain and mind—to write an internal monolog.

Internal Monolog

Fiction writers have long been "allowed" to use internal (interior) monolog as a technique to reveal a character's mental state, but nonfiction writers have been told in the past to stay out. After all, the traditionalists said, nonfiction deals with facts, truth, and objectivity, so how could it use something so subjective, so speculative, as reporting what a person "thought"? Besides, they said, it's impossible. You can't know what another person thinks.

Tom Wolfe, one of the early writers to claim this territory as legitimate ground for the nonfiction writer to explore, said that you could indeed know what a person thought. All you had to do, he said, was to ask them what they were thinking, and ask them in depth, not in the superficial way the deadline reporter had to.

The interior of the mind was a new beat for the average journalist. Reporters didn't know their way around in that quagmire; it was a frightening country; and it was best left to fiction writers who felt at home there.

Tom Wolfe, Gay Talese, and a handful of others decided in the sixties, as part of New Journalism, that the inner life was accessible—but only to serious, highly professional writers with high ethical standards.

Of all the techniques borrowed from fiction writers by nonfiction writers, this one of entering the mind of another (their internal monolog) met the most objection. Wolfe's early, persistent, and wonderfully innovative use of the technique almost led to the early demise of the parajournalism movement. It was simply too great a leap for most people, even those sympathetic to this new approach to journalistic writing. In clever hands like those of Wolfe and Talese, the internal monolog can be the most effective technique for revealing a person's character. We hear his or her innermost thoughts, something we're not normally privy to.

Tom Wolfe claims that he doesn't "create" what he puts down as the person's thoughts. He says that the thoughts are expressed to him during a long (sometimes weeks or months) series of conversations, through letters or diaries. During that extended period of time the writer also learns how the person expresses himself or herself under various conditions of relaxation and stress. This enables the writer to make the internal monolog sound "right." The reader has to feel that this is probably just the way that person's internal, pre-vocal thoughts sound. It's all speculative, of course, since no one knows what thoughts "sound" like before they're said aloud.

Most of the devices used by fiction writers to make internal monologs credible serve nonfiction writers as well. Nonfiction writers, in one sense, have an easier time of it. They don't have to invent the thoughts (they mustn't invent them). All they have to invent are the words, rhythms, diction, emphases, repetitive patterns, the unusual punctuation, or lack of it, and other devices traditionally used more by the fiction writer. The well-written internal monolog sounds like unedited, uncensored, unspoken human thought—at least, what we think it might sound like if we could tap the brain.

Joseph Wambaugh, after considerable interviewing and research, wrote from inside Jimmy Smith's mind as he ran away from *The Onion Field* where the murder occurred:

> En route he thought that maybe Powell will get *himself* killed. Sure, why not? The cop'll make his call and in fifteen minutes there'll be squad cars crawlin' over every inch of that miserable farmland. Powell is nuts. He might try to shoot his way out. Sure.

Or maybe Powell will try to give himself up and the cops might shoot him anyway. Sure. Yeah. The fuckin' cops'll be ready to kill anybody over this. Yeah. And maybe they'll just go ahead and dust him anyway. And then I made it for sure. The other cop won't know nothin' about me. How could he? He knows I'm called Jimmy, that's all. And I kept my hat on and my mouth shut most of the time so he won't even know what race I am. "I got a chance, baby, a hell of a chance!"

An interesting variation on the use of internal monolog is the writing about what goes on (or might go on) within the brain of a non-human being. In the first example, Loren Eiseley, the anthropologist who wrote so creatively about scientific matters, wrote in his book *The Unexpected Universe* about his relationship with his big shepherd dog Wolfe. Eiseley had laid on the floor a ten thousand-year-old bison bone that normally sat on his desk. The dog grabbed the bone and mouthed it with sharp fangs. When the master asked Wolfe to put it down, he was met by such low and steady rumbling he couldn't believe it was the same dog. Eiseley decides that we'll understand better what was happening if he writes for the dog an internal monolog:

As I advanced, his teeth showed and his mouth wrinkled to strike. The rumbling rose to a direct snarl. His flat head swayed low and wickedly as a reptile's above the floor. I was the most loved object in his universe, but the past was fully alive in him now. Its shadows were whispering in his mind. I knew he was not bluffing. If I made another step he would strike.

Yet his eyes were strained and desperate. "Do not," something pleaded in the back of them, some affectionate thing that had followed at my heel all the days of his mortal life, "do not force me. I am what I am and cannot be otherwise because of the shadows. Do not reach out. You are a man, and my very god. I love you, but do not put out your hand. It is midnight. We are in another time, in the snow."

"The other time," the steady rumbling continued while I paused, "the other time in the snow, the big, the final, the terrible snow, when the shape of this thing I hold spelled life. I will not give it up. I cannot. The shadows will not permit me. Do not put out your hand."

Another world-renowned scientist, Dr. Lewis Thomas, wrote in *Lives of a Cell* about how animals (including man) emit odors that communicate. Pheromones, the molecules that create these odors that communicate very specific messages, work under very low concentrations—eight or ten molecules in a chain are enough to do the job. He wrote about the thoughts a male moth might have as he got a whiff of bombykol, a pheromone released by the female moth when it would like to be visited by a male. Dr. Thomas is not sure whether the male knows why he's being summoned; all the male moth knows for sure is that he's going!

> The messages are urgent, but they may arrive, for all we know, in a fragrance of ambiguity. "At home, 4 P.M. today," says the female moth, and releases a brief explosion of bombykol, a single molecule of which will tremble the hairs of any male within miles and send him driving upwind in a confusion of ardor. But it is doubtful if he has an awareness of being caught in an aerosol of chemical attractant. On the contrary, he probably finds suddenly that it has become an excellent day, the weather remarkably bracing, the time appropriate for a bit of exercise of the old wings, a brisk turn upwind. En route, traveling the gradient of bombykol, he notes the presence of other males, heading in the same direction, all in a good mood, inclined to race for the sheer sport of it. Then, when he reaches his destination, it may seem to him the most extraordinary of coincidences, the greatest piece of luck: "Bless my soul, what have we here!"

This may not have been the perfect example of internal monolog, but I included it because it's a perfect example of how writing about science can be done in a creative way—the writing of these two men entertains as it informs. Some scientists would never write an internal monolog for a dog or a moth because, after all, how would anyone know how (or even whether) a moth thinks. That's what makes this kind of nonfiction writing creative.

Discussed more fully under "Realities of Individual Lives" and "Dialogs, Monologs, and Other Logs," dialects, foreign accents, regional accents, and many other variations of human speech patterns seem sometimes to show us something about the character—if not about his or her "character," then about the person. The writer should always be wary of the potential that these elements have to stereotype a character—even to ridicule the person. Too much emphasis, for example, on someone's poor grammar may make the person seem unintelligent when he or she is merely ignorant. If the person is unquestionably intelligent but unschooled, the writer must get this distinction across, probably not by direct statement but by showing us through a scene that raw, uncultivated intelligence at work.

Occasionally, a person's character can be partly developed for readers by letting them hear the character deliver either a formal speech or a shorter but still longish, uninterrupted mini-speech (monolog) in the midst of what tried to be a conversation. Character comes out through the content of the speech, its level of diction, its method of delivery, and audience reactions.

Historic or everyday letters (even love letters from the attic) when quoted in part or in toto can add some dimension. In an article about someone's arrest, quoting from *official court records* can shed light on things. Important people may write *memoirs* that make revealing comments. When *personal journals* or *diaries* become available to the writer, they may be quoted to give further insights, perhaps into the developing character.

Although snatches of conversation could logically be subsumed under "captured conversations," *snatches of conversation* can reveal something of a character, and should be mentioned here. Short phrases, outbursts, cursings, etc. captured on the fly make interesting and perhaps revelatory reading. These should be used only if the writer believes them habitual or typical for the character. Examples of snatches of conversation are given in the chapter "Dialogs, Monologs, and Other Logs."

ANGLE OF APPROACH /
POINT OF VIEW / VOICE

The potential for a writer to develop for readers a person's character is affected, among other things, by the writer's decision on the angle of approach. If, for example, the writer plans to approach an article about the meltdown of the Soviet Union's atomic power plant at Chernobyl in terms of what it means for the future of the world's atomic power industry, he or she will have no logical way to develop the character of Chernobyl's chief construction engineer, chief engineers in other plants, or any other individuals.

If, instead, the writer decided to approach the article by writing about poor construction of the Chernobyl plant, he or she would be "allowed" by literary convention to bring into the story the chief engineer's childhood in Siberia; his problems with certain math courses that seemed, then, unimportant; his attitude toward the Communist Party; and his drinking problems during the hectic days of Chernobyl's construction. All of this background information would gradually develop for the reader an understanding of this man now under a cloud for the rest of his life as "the person responsible."

The potential to develop a character is affected, too, by the point of view selected. Unless the writer happens to be intimately connected with Chernobyl's chief engineer or with the construction activities and personnel, or did considerable background research, the first person point of view is not the most likely choice.

If the writer did happen to be assistant chief engineer at Chernobyl, of course, he or she could write an article from the first person point of view, and could readily develop for us the character of the chief engineer. The writer would say things like: "I could tell 'way back in high school that he'd become an important person someday—not so much because of his academic abilities but his 'political prowess.' Political in the sense that kids always wanted to do what he said would be fun to do, or the right thing to do. I could see that my friend was a born leader, and that I was a born follower."

If the writer was not so involved with the person and the situation, the usual choice of point of view would be third person. Then the writer would decide whether to write it with an "objective" or "subjective" voice. If "objective," the assistant chief engineer would use only reports and other information available to anyone technologically capable or well informed. If "subjective," the writer would be allowed by literary convention to write about his or her own thoughts on the matter, personal knowledge about the chief engineer's early background, private conversations he or she had had with the chief, and other information not generally available.

A subjective *angle of approach* written in the *third person* seems, therefore, the best way to write this piece that wants to stress not only the construction activity but the character of the man (or people) involved with it. Other ways are possible, but this combination seems to offer the writer the most flexibility to write technologically and psychologically.

REALITIES OF GROUP LIFE

I've used this title to remind the reader that a fuller treatment can be found earlier in this book, but it's worth highlighting some points here in the specific context of character development.

Since the writer's intention is always to get the reader "involved" with the character, he or she will deliberately put in concrete details that will evoke emotions which will help the brain bring up for the reader other characters in its memory bank who resemble in some way the character being developed. In earlier chapters we have seen how simple details simply listed can conjure up emotions, emotions that surrounded the details when they were first experienced and stored in memory.

Among the categories of concrete details used by creative nonfiction writers are the somewhat indirect details that come from a consideration of the group(s) the character is a member of. No single detail does it, of course, but the writer's faith is that enough may accumulate in the reader's mind to give an accurate impression of the character. Showing us a scene at the noon meeting of the local Kiwanis, that the character is an officer and has been active for years in all the good works of the club, tells us something about the person's character. I suppose a man could participate in all the charitable activities of a Kiwanis Club and still be a less than desirable citizen, but the chances are slimmer. When we find that the character also works hard for his Congregational Church, acting as Superintendent of Religious Education, we see another dimension of the man. If we read about his dancing only with his wife at the country club's annual dance, and about his drinking only Diet Coke, we see other dimensions. If, instead, the writer shows him working hard for Kiwanis, and working hard for his church, but in the scene at the country club we see him sloppy drunk and making passes at every unmarried woman there, and his wife sits out the dances sipping her Diet Coke, we form another impression of the character.

We can't make a final judgment from these pieces of evidence, and the writer probably doesn't present his or her own judgment either, but we do have a gradually fuller image of the character. The best technique to reveal these bits of "character" (if that's what they are) is to write scene by scene. The scenes "show us"; they don't tell us. Naturally, the writer could summarize (instead of dramatize) and "tell" us that this character is *the type of guy who attends Kiwanis meetings, teaches Sunday School, and gets smashed at country club dances,* but by putting it that way, we have the feeling that the writer has already judged the man, and is "leading the jury." In the other case, we feel more like a jury that's heard the evidence and comes to a decision based on deliberation and careful thought.

Writers will sometimes give the realities of the character's group life by describing the group's entertainments, its clothing fads, fads in vacation destinations, architectural fashions in offices and homes, its "in" sports, its "in" books, and its "in" celebrities. If the character is shown fitting perfectly into these group behaviors, that shows us one thing about the individual; if the character stays away from the activities of the group he or she might be expected to be within, that shows us something different.

REALITIES OF INDIVIDUAL LIVES

The modern method in fiction and nonfiction is not to describe a character in detail at the beginning of a piece, or in any one place within the piece. Rather, physical details of a character are doled out by the writer one or two elements at a time—and, if possible, where logic dictates they should appear. Most writers of today will save the mention of hair color, for example, until a sensible place:

> *... his long, yellow mane streamed out behind his golf cap in the wind that picked up as they approached the ninth hole....*

> *... the sun glinted from her so-perfect teeth as she took off her glasses and began to speak to the crowd....*

> *... tripping on the rug. He complained to no one in particular that these damned size fourteens have given me problems since I was fourteen myself....*

The writer will watch for any elements that seem to describe the character more accurately for the reader. If the character "characteristically" poses with an elbow resting on the mantle, and holds a martini in a certain way, the writer may mention it—only, however, if it seems truly habitual.

There's not much sense in wasting precious words on poses that are coincidental and might imply too much by their mention.

Other kinds of gestures can also be used to help create an image for us—but only if they seem habitual. Some people have minor mannerisms that may delight (or bug) people around them: *He lets his cigar ashes drop wherever gravity dictates.* In one case, this might mean that the person is deliberately insensitive; in another case, the same mannerism may be simply the behavior of a theoretical physicist whose mind is not on his ashes—or even on gravity. Only by the gradual accumulation of other characteristic behaviors can the reader legitimately begin to form an understanding of the person's character.

NINE

STRUCTURES

Structure is what gives overall coherence to a piece. Many devices and techniques exist for achieving coherence between sentences and paragraphs, but the governing element is the grand, overall structure. Coherence cements together the individual bricks that make up the structure.

The architecture analogy is not a bad one. Given the purpose of a building, the number of people who will use it, what those people will do in it, the area allotted it, the architect makes an overall decision on design. Will it scrape the clouds or hug the ground? Many factors enter into the decision. Some, like the above, are imposed externally, some the architect imposes from within—the aesthetics of the building and the kind of structure he or she wants to play with this time. Once all these decisions that determine the structure and foundation have been made, the architect brings in other people to make it work, make it hang together. The engineers, carpenters, electricians, and plumbers give it coherence—they cement it together to give it strength and functionality. It works.

Then the architect goes another step and invites in the interior decorators who give each floor and the total building an aesthetic unity. The writer does much the same. Within the grand structure of an article or book, the writer works within each section to make each cohere within itself, cohere with the other parts, and give some measure of aesthetic beauty and unity to the whole. A more delicate metaphor says that good writing requires a thread of coherent logic along which are strung beads of thought. Done well, the necklace coheres (i.e., doesn't cascade all over the dance floor) and gives beauty to its wearer and the evening.

A writer of nonfiction will often spend a great amount of time considering structure before ever beginning the composition itself. Some writ-

139

ers claim that they just start writing, and that a structure gradually imposes itself. The trouble with this method is that it may result in a lot of wheel spinning, revision, and rewriting once the structure magically emerges from the mist. From what I've read and experienced, most professional writers of creative nonfiction will have a structure well in mind before writing at length. They've found that all the thinking about structure in advance is not wasted; it has value beyond structure considerations. By continually turning over the compost of the mind, all the materials therein become more firmly entrenched in memory—and by being in the brain, rather than merely on paper, thinking is promoted in the subconscious. There's no predicting what will grow in this repeatedly plowed and harrowed ground with all its varied nutrients. In such fertile soil sprout the seeds of serendipity.

Faced with the search for structure, sit back and sift, shuffle, and stack. Do any patterns, or things that look like possible patterns, take shape?—even a vague shape that promises structural potential? Keep at it as long as possible within the situation you find yourself. And don't stop sitting and sifting just because one structure occurs to you. Whoever said that the first one to arise is the best? Consider as many as come to the surface, and think about the possible implications and ramifications of putting each into effect. Don't consider only the problems each presents; think about the positive possibilities. Anyone can think of negatives; think creatively about the possibilities. It's normal for any idea to have both negatives and positives; it's a matter of imagining and weighing, discarding and keeping. It could go on forever, but at some point, usually dictated by deadline or economic pressures, you have to fish or cut bait. I believe that the waiting and weighing pay off.

I believe that you should know the ending before you begin the writing itself. Knowing this and knowing how to get into the piece make the middle rather easy to write. After all, the middle must somehow take off logically from the opening, and it must lead with some inevitability toward the ending you've decided on. Not that you'll necessarily know the actual words of the ending (although you may), but the general thought behind the ending will have been in mind all along, unconsciously, if not consciously, guiding your choice of words and ideas from the beginning. If the ending is there, it'll act as a magnetic pole drawing everything toward it, at first gently, and then as the ending nears, irresistibly.

When you know reasonably well how the piece of work will end, you can relax in the knowledge that everything is nailed down (well, tacked down). You can now concentrate your worrying on one section at a time. Returning to the architecture metaphor—the steel is up and foundation poured, so you can now put all your thought into creating one floor at a time, secure in the belief that things won't fall apart before you can get to them.

My suggestion that you establish the structure before beginning may sound terribly mechanical and too linearly organized for the creative mind, but I don't believe that's so. It seems to me that having the security of structure (even one not fully figured out) enables the writer to relax and play with any number of creative possibilities to perk up each floor (paragraph). To solve any problem (in writing or anything else) you have to let the mind periodically go wild and woolly. This is difficult to do when you're uncertain and worried about what will come next, and what after that, and how it will all end. You are forced to keep asking yourself: If I go with this crazy but interesting idea that seems right now to be evolving, where could I go from there? This continuous, haunting uncertainty dampens your ability to let loose the fetters of conventional thinking. If, however, you are safe within one small segment (floor or paragraph) of the overall structure, and the free-thinking, wildly imaginative moments turn up nothing, all is not lost. Either you can try some more of that kind of thinking, or you simply turn to conventional solutions (the kind some writers turn to right at first for fear of falling fetters). (See—sometimes the playful, alliterative mind dredges up something you'd just as soon it didn't!)

Let's look first at a few structures a writer can consider in the search for structure; then we'll look at a group of strategies he or she might use to support the structure.

CHRONOLOGIC STRUCTURE

The logic of time (chrono-logic) is perhaps the oldest structure for a story, going all the way back to the storyteller at the fire in front of the cave. I woke when the sun woke. I left the cave and walked over the mountain and down to the big river. Then I saw a deer come down to drink. I crept up close on quiet feet . . . and so on until the embers glow and the story ends, probably with the storyteller's arrival back at the cave. This follows that, and then this is followed by . . . and later . . . The listener (reader) can follow the tale readily because of its logical, easily followed "and then" structure. Even before time measurement came along, people knew about life's passage of time—a sequence of just one damned thing after another.

Modern, sophisticated human beings concerns themselves with various segments of time. Bruce Catton's *A Stillness at Appomattox*, for example, treats one chunk of time—the last moments of the Civil War. He opens the book with a scene at Washington's Birthday Ball in an army encampment near the Rapidan River south of Washington, D.C. We meet some of the young officers having what for some of them will be the last joy of their lives on Earth. The author then takes us in ensuing chapters down various war roads until the final scene in the town of Appomattox Court House, Virginia. We watch as the Union commanders ride in to accept the sword of surrender from General Robert E. Lee.

A chronologic structure like that brings contentment to the mind. It brings closure, which psychologists say the human mind naturally seeks. (Gestalt psychologists would say that our minds demand closure—will even create it where it doesn't exist.) Our comfort comes not only from closure (the resolution of a problem) but from the linear development. Our understanding increases as we move from cause to effect, from A to B to C. We understand C because we've already grappled with and comprehended B, and before that, A. By the time we reach Z, we can apprehend the entire progression from A to Z. We see it then, not as A to Z, but as *alphabet*. We've understood the constituent parts as we went along, so now we see the whole for what it is. The trouble is that this attractively simple, linear sequence is sometimes simplistic, not simply simple.

In the nonsimplistic world of human affairs, events are not necessarily caused by the immediately preceding event. Sometimes, for example, actions are caused by someone's perception, someone's speculation, about what the future might be—thus the future determines the present as people adjust to prepare for that speculated future. When this is the case, a straight logic of time may be an absolutely inappropriate structure to use years later when trying to explain why what happened happened.

A shorter passage of time may call for a straight chronologic structure. The story of a plane crash, a ship collision, or a bank robbery, for example, may use the device that shows us at the beginning of a paragraph the precise time—11:43 A.M. As we make our way toward the climax, the time increments may lessen, so that by the end we're seeing the time change every few seconds, while at the beginning it may have been by month, day, or hour. In nonfiction, we readers often know the ending already, yet we're fascinated by the inexorable march of time. Filmmakers love to show us the clock face or the digital counting mechanism on a time bomb ticking, ticking, ticking. The camera keeps cutting back and forth between the mounting action and the ticking time bomb. Suspense mounts. We're affected emotionally by the merciless sweep of time.

Fiction writers have used time devices to create suspense ever since they first began writing suspense stories. Only fairly recently have nonfiction writers lifted these devices from the fiction writer's toolbox. Suspense, deliberately planned, was not considered appropriate for nonfiction work until fairly recently. Sometimes nonfiction writers would emphasize the passage of time, but he'd be using it simply as a coherence device, something to tie things together—using time as the narrative string. Today's creative nonfiction writers use the device both for the coherence it gives and for the suspense it can develop.

Gloria Steinem used a similar time device in an early article that exposed the lifestyle of one segment of America—"I Was a Playboy Bunny" (collected in her book, *Outrageous Acts and Everyday Rebellions*, New American Library, 1983). Ms. Steinem deliberately (and clandestinely) signed on as a Bunny to conduct research for the article, an article that helped make her reputation as a writer in the feminist cause. She worked as a Bunny mole for about a month (long enough, she said, to increase her foot size several times after all the walking and carrying heavy trays), so she structured her article chronologically, heading up each minor section with time data: AFTERNOON TUESDAY 5TH; WEDNESDAY 6TH; etc. Some suspense develops as time goes by and we wonder when they'll discover her role as mole.

Ms. Steinem structured another article, "Campaigning," around a number of essays she'd previously written about the general topic of political campaigning. She used dates as headlines: JULY 1965 (about George McGovern on the trail) and so on, through various other campaigners such as Eugene McCarthy, Robert Kennedy, and Richard Nixon, until the final date, JULY 1972, when the Democratic National Committee convened in Miami. The dates stressed her point about how the women's movement grew into platform planks over that seven-year period of hard work by many men and women. She ended with the significant statement: *But women are never again going to be mindless coffee-makers or mindless policy-makers in politics. There can be no such thing as a perfect leader. We have to learn to lead ourselves.*

The same sort of device may be used to cover longer periods of time. The well-known naturalist and philosopher Joseph Wood Krutch named a collection of his essays *The Twelve Seasons: A Perpetual Calendar for the Country*, each chapter named for a month. This works well for coherence and structure in a book where there is no intention of urgency or suspense.

Some of our finest works of nonfiction have followed the seasonal march because it provides a convenient, easily followed structure. Not only farmers see life as a series of seasons. Old people speak of how many summers old they are. Many have seen the spring season as metaphor for beginnings, new beginnings, renewal. January arbitrarily claims to mark the beginning of new years; our bodies and our ancient brains tell us that spring, not winter, marks a new year. This gut reaction to our lives and nature's seasons makes warmly satisfying a book organized in some fashion around the seasonal flow.

Two familiar books that seem to go on and on being enjoyed by all kinds of people, Henry Beston's *The Outermost House* and Henry David Thoreau's *Walden*, each chronicles the life of its author deliberately isolating himself from ordinary city and village life to confront nature head-on in a simple cabin. A structure that follows the flow of the seasons seems a natural for such subjects. *The Outermost House* takes us with the author through a year on Cape Cod, as Beston experiences firsthand the wonders and mysteries of migrating birds, moving dunes, and thundering waves. In his foreword to that book's eleventh printing, he recounts the thoughts called forth by rereading his own words of twenty or so years before:

> As I read over these chapters, the book seems to me fairly what I ventured to call it, "a year of life on the Great Beach of Cape Cod." Bird migrations, the rising of the winter stars out of the breakers and the east, night and storm, the solitude of a January day, the glisten of dune grass in midsummer, all this is to be found between the covers even as today it is still to be seen. Now that there is a perspective of time, however, something else is emerging from the pages which equally arrests my attention. It is the meditative perception of the relation of "Nature" (and I include the whole cosmic picture in this term) to the human spirit. Once again, I set down the core of what I continue to believe. Nature is a part of our humanity, and without some awareness and experience of that divine mystery man ceases to be man.

In books like that and *Walden*, the authors not only structure the book tightly (or loosely) around the seasons as a natural order for talking about nature, they also draw from the seasons much that becomes content for the book. Such authors typically take off from their contemplation of a specific reed bending (or not bending) in the wind to make a more universal point about the advisability of yielding to superior force if you wish to survive to win another day. Thoreau would straighten up from watching, with a child's curiosity, an ant's activities, and let his mind spin out universal thoughts.

Diaries, journals, log books, daybooks, and similar writings may eventually be published, even though not written with the public reader in mind. Sometimes they'll be published exactly in the chronology written: day by day, year by year, or, in the case of a ship's log, watch by watch. We enjoy seeing how things evolve, especially when we know how everything has since worked out, but the keeper of the diary had no idea what life would bring right around the corner. When the diarist speculates about what the future will bring, and we see how close (or far off) the mark he or she was, we enjoy it. The diary gets some of its strength by its innocent march into the unknown future, step by step, day by day.

The keeper of the diary, journal, or some other form of log may use it someday simply as one source of information to help him or her write an autobiography or memoir. In other cases, a biographer or historian may use the log as just one research source, and may jump around through time in his or her own book, quoting now from the diary, now from a journal, now from a local newspaper account, frequently not following the logic of time, at least not a straight-ahead logic. The biographer may use a diary entry from one day to reinforce some speculation of his or her own about how the diarist "may have been thinking" at some earlier point. An entry at age fifty might be thought by the biographer to provide insight into the motivation or behavior of the diarist at age twenty-five. Chronology may be reworked, reshaped, reorganized for artistic purposes—within reason.

REWORKED CHRONOLOGICAL STRUCTURE

For any number of logical, aesthetic, or other reasons, the creative nonfiction writer may decide that a linear, straight-ahead chronological structure seems wrong for a particular piece of writing. He or she may turn to the fiction writer again for a structure that may work better for a given purpose. The writer may drastically reorder chronology by opening up an article or book with a scene that in real life belongs somewhere else in the story, even at the very end. As we mentioned in the chapter on openings, the "jumping into the middle of things" (or even the end of things) is often called by its Latin equivalent, *in medias res*.

Tom Wolfe opened *The Right Stuff*, for example, right in the middle of an emotionally moving episode in the life of Jane Conrad, as she awaits possible news that her husband's plane has just crashed. The episode is not truly "in the middle of things," but the later chapters do go back to earlier years. Wolfe didn't open by telling us that he was about to tell us the story of the astronauts' lives; didn't tell us about the structure of NASA or the navy fighter pilot training program; not even that Pete Conrad would survive to become an astronaut. Wolfe took us first into the emotions of this twenty-one-year-old wife of a twenty-year-old fighter pilot as they began married life, a life that would bring many moments of terror to Jane Conrad.

The result—we're immediately engaged, immediately involved. We're not concerned that we don't know all the background. We can't get interested in the astronaut training program until we get involved at a human level with the people participating in it—and Tom Wolfe does this for us. He does it throughout this exemplary book of creative nonfiction, always getting us into the mind of someone and then coming out to look around at what's happening.

CONVERGENT NARRATIVES STRUCTURE

The convergent narratives structure is another form of reworked chronology available to the creative writer. This structure is usually called "parallel structure," but it seems to me that this geometry metaphor is inaccurate—parallel lines do not converge, according to the geometry axiom. Parallel narratives would best describe stories like those on "Hill Street Blues" or "St. Elsewhere," in which several stories run side by side with cinematic cross-cutting between them. In most episodes, these stories stay truly parallel and never cross each other—never converge. A story can gain in interest when we find out at the last possible minute that two narratives that seemed totally unrelated are, in fact, very dramatically related—and are, unsuspected by us, rapidly converging. In both forms, parallel and convergent, suspense is effectively promoted and entertainment heightened.

THE FLASHBACK

Another fiction device, the flashback, finds itself now in the toolbox of the fully prepared creative nonfiction writer. Not exactly the opposite of *in medias res*, the flashback is another example of how you are allowed to rework chronology, re-create *time*. This device is subject to abuse. It should be used for artistic reasons, not for lack of foresight, the writer finding frequent narrative need to go back in time to cover something he or she forgot to set up earlier.

Starting out a piece *in medias res*, and then going back to pick up the story for a subsequently straight chronological development, is not a true flashback; it's more often called a "frame." *In medias res* is more a *flashforward*. A true flashback interrupts a narrative or a scene, but we're soon returned to where we were.

The flashback device, while available to the nonfiction writer, seems not too often used. I had to search to find these examples of its proper use and several methods for using it. In Bruce Catton's *A Stillness at Appomattox* we find, in the midst of a discussion of how Confederate General Early had sent General Gordon in behind the federal troops to open an attack, a flashback to the day before. The flashback is signalled by the opening words of the second paragraph in the excerpt below.

> So the army moved. Very early on the shivery, misty dawn of October 19, with fog hanging in the low places and the darkness lying thick in the graveyard hour between moonset and dawn, the Confederates rose up out of the gorge and came yelling and shooting on the drowsy flank of Sheridan's army.
>
> The day before, certain election commissioners from Connecticut had come into the Yankee lines to take the presidential vote of Connecticut soldiers, and they remained in camp overnight as special headquarters guests. They liked what they saw of army life, and to their

hosts at supper they expressed regret that they could not see a fight before they went home. The officers who were entertaining them said they would like to accommodate them, but there just wasn't a chance: "It seemed very certain that Early would keep at a respectful distance."

At the end of the subsequent paragraph, author Catton takes us gradually and smoothly out of the flashback with the image of the commissioners leaving, more rapidly than they'd arrived.

> Then, suddenly, artillery began to pound, the infantry firing became sustained and intense, and a wild uproar came through the dark mist—and the election commissioners quickly found their clothes and ballot boxes and horses and took off for the North just as fast as they could go.

Loren Eiseley, the anthropologist who wrote a number of creative nonfiction books about science (e.g., *The Immense Journey*, *The Unexpected Universe*, and *The Invisible Pyramid*) also wrote his autobiography creatively (*All the Strange Hours: The Excavation of a Life*). That fascinating book follows a generally chronological structure, but the author occasionally inserts a flashback to earlier times in his life. In the chapter "The Laughing Puppet," he writes about his problems dealing with college. When other students stumbled into a course they immediately hated, they'd go directly to their adviser and legally drop the course. Loren Eiseley would simply walk away from it, leaving a black mark on his record. Bureaucracy intimidated him. Having set us up with this attitude of his, he writes a flashback to take us back to his high school days. He signals it through the simple phrase, "Once, in high school…" Since readers know that Eiseley is talking about his own college days, they know that this is the beginning of a flashback:

> Once, in high school, I had written, more or less blindly, an essay for an English teacher. "I want to be a nature writer," I had set down solemnly. It was at a time when I had read a great many of Charles G. D. Roberts' nature stories and those of Ernest Thompson Seton. I had also absorbed the evolutionary ideas of the early century through Jack London's *Before Adam*, and Stanley Waterloo's *Story of Ab*. None of this had come from high school. It had come from books I brought home from the local Carnegie Library to which I used to pedal my coaster wagon. "I want to be a nature writer." How strangely that half-prophetic statement echoes in my brain today. It was like all my wishes.

There was no one to get me started on the road. I read books below my age, I read books well beyond my age and puzzled over them. In the end I forgot the half-formed wish expressed in my theme.

I had to seek food, shelter, and clothing. I remember a philosophy professor for whom I had once read and graded papers....

He reminds us that the high school flashback is over by bringing up the philosophy professor in the first sentence of the third paragraph. A good (i.e., thoughtful) writer always makes certain that flashbacks are clearly entered and exited.

Structuring an article or book around chronologies, or their reworked versions, remains popular with creative nonfiction writers because life does proceed chronologically (it can't help it), although writers at times find it more interesting for the reader if they move the story around through time. Other structures may seem chronological, in that they move forward in time, but sometimes the emphasis or intent is not so much upon the march of time as upon how the person functions over time.

STRUCTURE BY FUNCTION

When a writer describes in great detail how something is made or done, he or she is said to write a "how to" book. When a writer writes a book that shows the reader how to make something perform its intended function, it's called a "technical manual." I'm not referring in this section to those types of writing about function. "How to" books and "technical manuals" (and I've written both) are generally not written "creatively"; their purpose is not to entertain but to instruct. Once in a great while, one may be entertaining as well as instructive (I think right away of Peter McWilliams's *The Personal Computer* [Doubleday, 1984], book on how to use computers and how computers function), but as a genre, they're usually more informative than entertaining (and, hence, are not treated in this book on creative nonfiction writing).

Books (and documentary film narratives) have taken us on innumerable tours through the button factory and the meat packing plant to inform us how parts of our variegated world function. These, too, tend toward information, not entertainment. Rarely would they be described as "creative." Sometimes the cinematography will be handled creatively, while the narrative voice-over drones on with its frequently prosaic, even pedantic, prose (more often than not "telling" us what the visuals are already "showing" us much more effectively and attractively).

Two popular variations on "structure by function" are: "How Things, People, or Systems Function" and "How Things, People, or Systems Come to Be." These are not academically pure categories, but they do give us one way to discuss structure by function.

Structure by Function: How Things Function

John McPhee has written many articles and books about how individuals function in the world, frequently people working at seldom-heralded occupations. His pieces end up as "profiles" of these individuals, but very often the piece is constructed not so much around the chronology of their lives as around their occupations (functions). He did vary from this focus on the individual to a wide-angle focus on a large system—the Swiss Army.

In *La Place de la Concorde Suisse*, he didn't follow precisely a structure by function, but many of the chapters concentrated on army units with specialized functions. As we might expect, McPhee also finds ways to pull away from talking about this unusual army, an army organized only to forestall invasion by an enemy, to give us fascinating descriptions of terrain, geologic history, and individual officers and men. He gives us a popular Swiss expression, which could have been the book's subtitle, "Switzerland does not *have* an army; Switzerland *is* an army," and gives us detailed glimpses of *Section de Renseignements* whose function it is to provide all other army sections with important intelligence information: Which farmhouse could shelter how many soldiers? What are the coordinates of that large barn over there where enemy soldiers might stay? How much ammunition and explosives of what type are stored in that camouflaged cave carved out of solid granite? Another chapter gives us an understanding of the important function horses have in such steep terrain; and which farmers' horses are certified as suitable should the invasion come today.

In another chapter we learn about the possibilities and problems of armored tank warfare in this mountainous land, while another takes us into the artillery units. We find out, too, how the annual maneuvers involve two "armies," the Blue and the Red. Since the Red Army is always the enemy force, communists in the Federal Assembly complain each year, but their 1 percent vote sways no one.

McPhee, in a less well known article (the title story in the collection *Giving Good Weight*), gives us a fine "profile" of New York City's "Greenmarket." He opens the piece *in medias res* with a scene in that open-air market—people squeezing the melons, pulping the nectarines, rapping the sweet corn, and speaking in New York dialects. After we know how such a market functions with its shoppers, he takes us outside the city to other people and places that work to keep the Greenmarket functioning effectively: the huge packing house at Van Houten's farm in Orangeville, Pennsylvania, where cabbage, cucumbers, broccoli, eggplants, and other produce are grown and packed; then on to an area along the New York-New Jersey line where towns stand like small islands in the midst of a black-dirt sea—especially to Pine Island, New York, the largest and most productive muckland of them all. From this fertile black muck come many of the vegetables bound for the Greenmarket: celeries, moist beets, iceberg lettuce, carrots—and above all, onions. McPhee says, "What the beluga is to caviar, the muckland is to the onion."

From this ugly black soil come the Red Globes, White Globes, Yellow Globes, Buccaneers, Bronze Age, Benny's Reds, and the Tokyo Long White Bunching onions. This soil functions as onion heaven, a soil so organic it'll burn. By the time the article finishes, we know not only what a greenmarket feels, sounds, and smells like, we understand how it functions as a system with lines radiating out from New York City to the still agricultural lands surprisingly nearby.

In his recent collection with the unexpected title *Table of Contents*, McPhee's major piece is a study of a new breed of doctor in rural communities engaging in what's called "family practice." In this long article, "Heirs of General Practice," he lets us watch how these hardworking, often young, doctors function. We learn that these "generalists" have to know so many different specialties that they are now Board Certified as "specialists" to legitimize the fact that they're not. These "comprehensive specialists" practice family medicine in the belief that if the doctor treats your grandmother, your father, and your niece, he or she will be better able to treat you. These doctors are responsible for the total health care of the individual and the family—and, where feasible, the extended family of two, three, or four generations. Although the piece not structured totally on a function basis, McPhee does walk us around with these doctors, listening in and watching them perform many of their multiple functions.

Mark Kramer provides us with a look at a more traditional medical specialist, the surgeon. In this first book by Kramer, *Invasive Procedures,* he takes us into diagnosis sessions with the patient and the surgeon. That's fairly unusual, but then he takes us on a most unusual journey right into the operating arena. We watch the surgeon, doctors, and nurses perform their individual and teamwork functions. I recommend reading in tandem McPhee's "Heirs of General Practice" and this book by Mark Kramer.

Burton Bernstein, in a major article in the *New Yorker,* "A Reporter Aloft: Small Airports" (August 26, 1985), flies his readers to a number of what he calls "tenuous airports" in the Northeast. Although he ties the article together organically by flying us to each airstrip, his real purpose is to show us all the various functions involved in the "small airport system." We learn, in a most interesting style, all kinds of functions performed by the pilot, the air controller, airport manager, and others pivotal or peripheral to the system. We also learn about gliders, ultra-lights, flying boats, and how these function differently.

Structure by Function: How Things Come to Be

The second variation on structure by function, "How Things, People, or Systems Come to Be" differs from "How Things, People, or Systems Function" primarily in its purpose. Articles and books of the second type are structured largely around functions but with a primary concern, too—the early development of a thing, person, or system: how a new house comes to be; how a new kind of computer comes to be; how a minihydro power generation system develops; how Olympic champions develop; and how one goes about selling to the public a presidential candidate.

Tracy Kidder has written two excellent books that deal with two completely different subjects—houses and computers, but he structured each largely by function. In his book *House,* he chronicles the entire house-creating process from the clients' first dream about a new house; working with the architect toward a design to approximate the dream; and both groups working with the craftsmen involved to carry out the collaborative vision. Kidder treats other subjects, such as the lumber industry and architectural trends, but he structures the book around three major functioning groups: clients, architects, and builders. This triangle of sometimes opposing, sometimes cooperating forces has the strength inherent in the physical triangle. These major functions, of course, are performed by people, and Kidder does a fine job of making us understand what makes these individuals tick, i.e. function. This book could be a textbook on how to write nonfiction creatively. At first blush, one would think it unlikely that a writer could treat this topic "creatively," but listen to some of the words from *House*:

> The air has some winter in it. On this morning in mid-April, 1983, a New England spring snow is predicted. The sky looks prepared. It has a whitening look. Several weeks must pass before dandelions appear, but the urge to build has turned April into May.... Locke [the carpenter] is wearing jeans and work boots and an old brown jacket, a workingman's uniform. His clothes are clean and he is clean-shaven. He has straight brown hair, neatly trimmed and combed, and a long, narrow jaw. There is a delicacy in his features. You can imagine his mother in him. He has a thoughtful air. He studies his transit a moment, laying two fingers to his lips. Then, as he bends again to the eyepiece, he wipes his hair off his forehead and for a moment he looks boyish and defiant. The ceremony can begin as soon as the bulldozer arrives.

Tracy Kidder received a Pulitzer Prize for *The Soul of a New Machine*, his earlier book about how Data General Corporation's new computer, the Eagle (MV-8000), came to be. That book was not so purely structured by function, but much of it was. Chapters take up such computers, computer people, and computer functions as: "The Wonderful Micromachines," "The Case of the Missing Nand Gate," "Midnight Programmer," and "La Machine." Within each chapter Kidder also gives the reader profiles of the key people providing the various functions involved in the design of a brand new type of computer. The book achieves tension and suspense because the teams are working on a new computer concept while the corporation's administrators believe the teams are simply trying to improve the existing product to compete against rival Digital Corporation's super-minicomputer VAX. By showing us the individuals and teams functioning, Kidder has shown us how a computer came to be.

To demonstrate the all-inclusiveness of structuring by function, consider the bestselling *The Selling of the President—1968* by Joe

McGinniss. The book detailed, as no book had before, just how a presidential candidate is "sold" by the mass media to the American voting public. McGinniss structures the book around various media specialists and their functions in the "selling" or "marketing" of the candidate—in this case, Richard M. Nixon.

The author, by scenes as often as possible, shows his readers specialists at work, "functioning." He opens *in medias res* with a scene in the Hotel Pierre, where television directors, camera people, lighting experts (we mustn't see perspiration glistening on Nixon's upper lip, gentlemen), stage managers (we must have cue cards in the center, gentlemen, so we won't see the candidate's eyes shifting), and others function in order to produce a one-minute political commercial.

Elsewhere in the book we learn how an advertising executive from Madison Avenue functions at higher levels as he tries to sell a man. We listen in, too, as one of the world's most famous still photographers, Eugene S. Jones, is brought aboard to prepare short commercials. His commercials used the then-new techniques of "moving on" the still shots to give the impression of motion pictures, but with the advantages inherent in still photography. We're even introduced to an "ethnic specialist" performing his function of critiquing the ten panel shows produced by the campaign group, on which men and women from various ethnic backgrounds speak out in behalf of the Republican candidate. McGinniss supplements his vivid descriptions of functions with a lengthy appendix that presents simply, with no comments or opinions by him, memoranda and reports associated with the campaign.

The cumulative effect of these eighty-two pages of appendixed real documents from the Nixon campaign is so devastating that any authorial comments would have been superfluous. McGinniss was wise enough to see that, and to stay out of the appendix.

ORGANIC STRUCTURE

Most of the structures so far discussed follow human logic, but an organic structure is a more natural one, one that's somehow inherent in the subject, one that grows out of it. It could be called "natural structure" but for the unhappy extension of that thought—that all the other structures are unnatural.

In my book *Getting the Words Right*, I wrote about the various "logics" a writer can use to promote unity and coherence. My example there was of a glaciologist wanting to describe the surface features of a valley glacier. He or she could, of course, use a "chrono-logic" to describe these features on the basis of "when" they form. The features could, instead, be described more organically by following the flow established by the natural downhill direction of the ice's flow. The glaciologist could, of course, begin at sea level, where the ice falls into the water as icebergs, and then talk about the glacial forms all the way back up to the glacier's mountain origins. That would be "logical" but not "organic." The organic way would take into account the direction the glacier flows and comes down from the high-altitude *snow fields* above. The glaciologist might begin with the wind-blown *sastrugi* forms; work downhill with the glacier's flow, describing *ice falls* and the chaotic *crevasses* where the glacier fractures as it bends around corners; then describe the *moraine*-forming materials created where tributary glaciers coalesce; and end where the sea cuts a notch in the ice front, giving birth to great icebergs as the giant blocks *calve* into the sea.

To tie this in with structure by function, a glaciologist might in some case need to describe how a glacier came to be and how it works. In that event he or she might write first about the origin and morphology of the snowflakes that fall high in the mountains; then about how they are gradually converted to ice; then about how the pressure of thousands of feet of ice and snow on top combine with gravity to give the ice its initial shove downhill; and then how that motion causes friction that causes melting which provides lubrication that promotes more rapid movement downhill which causes more melting, more lubrication, more movement, and so inexorably to the sea.

To clinch the difference between this structure by function and organic (natural) structure, note that although the glaciologist above was describing "natural" processes, the structure of the writing was not "natural"; it discussed naturally occurring glaciers in conceptual terms—human terms, logical terms, scientific analysis terms—structures and terms nature knows not of. Either structure is valid; it's the writer's choice.

John McPhee seems to enjoy finding in his research materials the possibility of an organic structure, but he warns us not to use it too compulsively. If it works, it works, but we should not become slaves to it, the way some poets enslave their minds to the geometrically shaped poetry format (concrete poetry). He wants to work within a form that's logical, yet unobtrusive. Even when we do elect to use an organic structure, we should allow ourselves some flexibility within it when something unexpected pops up.

After Richard West published "Richard West's Texas," he wrote about a completely different but powerful "state"—New York City's restaurant "21"—and published it in *New York* magazine as "The Power of '21.'" He structured this study of a world-class restaurant organically, using the same system as the restaurant's maître d' in seating guests. Depending on your "status," you are seated on a particular floor, in a particular section, and at a numbered table. The table also bears a name: *Maxwell's Table of Happy Memories, New Yorker Table, Richard Milhous Nixon President's Table.*

Although the hosts like to say, over and over again, "The man makes the table, not the table the man," not everyone believes that wholeheartedly. Writer West moves his "21" story from floor to floor and table to table spinning fascinating anecdotes about people who at various times during the restaurant's past fifty years have occupied each table. Because this restaurant is hierarchy-conscious and seats patrons accordingly, it was natural for West to structure the story by locations that reflect the elitist, hierarchical system. Had he written about a fast-food eatery, hierarchy would have played no role and the structure would have been different. If nothing else, fast-food places treat us all—prince and pauper—alike.

THE TRIP STRUCTURE

One type of organic structure that has always appealed to people is "the trip." The story of any kind of trip, usually told from the beginning to the end, has the advantage of following the logic of human thought (it proceeds from 1 to 10 or A to Z) combined with the organic logic of following the physical structure of the topic (the trip). This dual logic may explain the continuing popularity of "the trip"—beginning, perhaps, way back with the *Odyssey*. More likely, it began even before the invention of writing—the returning hunter telling the clan around the fire about a trip, its dangers, its failures, and in greater detail, its successes.

Some trip reports concern themselves with the trip itself, a sort of scientific report: where the rivers' rapids run; where hostile tribes lurk; where a factory's falls require a portage; where industrial pollution prohibits drinking from a cup over the side of the canoe; what natural resources line the river; what tourist attractions are near I-95; how many icefalls occur on the Beardmore Glacier before the South Polar Plateau is reached; or where the Blue Nile begins to trickle out of Uganda.

Other stories of trips document not so much the physical side of the trip as what happened along the way. John Steinbeck's *Travels With Charley* tells us some of the physical details of the highways followed, motels visited, etc., but not enough for it to fall into travelog. He tells us more about the people he and his poodle, Charley, meet along the way, his thoughts about them, and about the mood of the nation. As he said near the beginning of that book:

> My plan was clear, concise, reasonable, I think. For many years I have traveled in many parts of the world. In America I live in New York, or dip into Chicago or San Francisco. But New York is no more America than Paris is France or London is England. I, an American writer, was working from memory, and the memory is at best a faulty, warpy reservoir. I had not heard the speech of America, smelled the grass and trees and sewage, seen its hills and water, its color and the quality of light. I knew the changes only from books and newspapers. But more than this, I had not felt the country for twenty-five years. In short, I was writing of something I did not know about, and it seems to me that in a so-called writer this is criminal. My memories were distorted by twenty-five intervening years.... So it was that I determined to look again, to try to rediscover this monster land. Otherwise, in writing, I could not tell the small diagnostic truths which are the foundations of the larger truth.

Steinbeck structured the book around the trip, but he didn't care whether we could repeat the same trip ourselves without getting lost on the road. He just wanted the state of the union revealed to us in the same sequence he experienced it. The phrase "creative nonfiction" may not have been around at the time, and I don't know whether he'd approve of it, but that's the kind of writing he was doing in that book.

John Steinbeck seemed to appreciate the organic structure of a "trip." His greatest fiction, *The Grapes of Wrath*, "reported" on farmers driven off their farms near Sallisaw, Oklahoma, forced by the dust to make the arduous trip to Weedpatch, California, the land of plenty. Their trip gave him an organic structure along which to string his observations about these people, the economy, and the government during those terrible years. Although he wrote a work of fiction about that "trip," Steinbeck had done what a writer of creative nonfiction would have done—he traveled with these "Okies" as they moved westward. He immersed himself in the realities before writing. *Travels with Charley* gave him a nonfictional way to update himself and us—not a true sequel to *Grapes of Wrath*, but another look, another chance to feel the country. Recognizing this, his editors gave the book its descriptive subtitle, *In Search of America*.

Steinbeck's *Travels with Charley: In Search of America, The Log from the Sea of Cortez,* and *A Russian Journal* all use the trip as an organic structure, but their nonfiction purpose is to tell us something more than details of the trip itself. Sometimes, as in those listed, the author tells us about things that have not much to say about the author. Others, however, have as their primary purpose to describe an odyssey of personal growth, an odyssey toward a new understanding of Self, of Life. *Zen and the Art of Motorcycle Maintenance*, for example, takes us along with the author, Robert M. Pirsig, and his son, Chris, as they bike and hike around America. The book's subtitle says better what I'm trying to say about the book's real purpose—"An Inquiry Into Values." The writer of creative nonfiction articles and books Edward Hoagland said in praise of that book that it was "A magic book, full of the elixir of originality, about the majesty of the continent and the frights of the mind." Books structured around a trip but concerned primarily with matters that transcend the geographic are sometimes called "quests," this is an ancient way to structure an odyssey of understanding, an exploration of inner lands.

William Least Heat Moon's bestselling book, *Blue Highways*, chronicles his trip in a van around the perimeter of America, much like Steinbeck and Charley's peregrination. *Blue Highways'* subtitle is an accurate one—*A Journey Into America*. Not a journey *around* America, not a journey *through* America—a journey *into* America. Although he undoubtedly learned things about himself, he certainly learned a great deal about this land, this monster land, and its people. He talks on the first page about the night the idea for the trip occurred to him—and why the concept of a circular route appealed to him:

The result: on March 19, the last night of winter, I again lay awake in the tangled bed, this time doubting the madness of just walking out on things, doubting the whole plan that would begin at daybreak—to set out on a long (equivalent to half the circumference of the earth), circular trip over the back roads of the United States. Following a circle would give a purpose—to come around again—where taking a straight line would not. And I was going to do it by living out of the back end of a truck. But how to begin a beginning?

Blue Highways earned great praise from many quarters. A review by Robert Penn Warren said, in part: "A masterpiece . . . Least Heat Moon has a genius for finding people who have not even found themselves, exploring their lives, capturing their language, and recreating little (or big) lost worlds, or moments. In short, he makes America seem new, in a very special way, and its people new. . . . " Annie Dillard said of the book: " . . . his uncanny gift for catching good people at good moments makes *Blue Highways* a joy to read."

To bring the circle full circle, William Least Heat Moon (William Trogdon) makes clear on the book's final page what he had learned from his quest:

> The circle almost complete, the truck ran the road like the old horse that knows the way. If the circle had come full turn, I hadn't. I can't say, over the miles, that I learned what I had wanted to know because I hadn't known what I wanted to know. But I *did* learn what I didn't know I wanted to know.

ECCENTRIC STRUCTURES

Your writing must be unusually good to succeed with one of the slightly off-center, eccentric structures that follow. Your style, the vividness of your writing, must be of such high quality that your reader will happily (or tolerantly) put up with some vagueness of direction. Your writing must be so enjoyable that the enthralled reader goes along for the ride, figuring you'll end up at a destination at least as interesting as each of the intervening ports-of-call. Not that all writing must be fun, fun, fun; you could be writing about some very serious matters, yet your comments, your imagery, your accurate language, your insights, are so interestingly presented that the reader will know you're going to end up at a very interesting, even important destination—so the reader has faith enough to overlook the lack of some more logical, more linear, more expected, more "normal" structure.

Spiral Structure

One of the most favorably reviewed books in recent times was *Arctic Dreams* by Barry Lopez. This book provides us with much information about arctic regions, and the author presents it with authority and attractive images. Lopez celebrates the arctic, its flora, fauna, and peoples, but under it all lie three thematic questions: How does the arctic landscape (and perhaps any landscape) influence the human imagination; when we desire to put a landscape to human use, does that desire affect how we evaluate the environment; and what does it mean to "grow rich"—are we here on Earth to lay up treasures, to hunger, instead, after what is truly worthy, or to live at moral peace with our natural world?

Those questions give us significant themes to ponder in a book, and some authors might have structured such a book in a formal way (to match the important themes), but not Barry Lopez. Perhaps it's reasonable or expectable that a book with a title involving dreams should use a structure that mimics the way the brain processes thought—by associational chaining from thought to thought.

One theory of brain processing says that all our thoughts are stored in some unknown type of files according to what memories are associated with which other memories—from a lifetime. The theory also says that we can think only by associating new information coming into our brains by taking from our brain files memories of any kind of previous experiences that just might help us understand this new experience.

Our language and our thinking seem dependent upon the way our evolutionary ancestors created, from their associated memories, metaphors. Through metaphors we can move more easily from this thought of the moment to relevant, associated memories. Metaphors of all kinds are shorthand equations to help us quickly locate in the brain the associated memories needed to understand the moment.

Casual conversation between intelligent, articulate people will proceed from associated thought to a connected thought. This process frequently manifests itself in a conversation when one participant says, "Speaking of *that*, did you hear about . . . ?" A good writer like Barry Lopez would not write that as a transition, but he does, in effect, do just that. He moves from one topic to the next by association—one thing makes him think of the next thing.

In Chapter 1 of *Arctic Dreams*, for example, his associational chaining runs something like this, although his transitions are much more skillfully handled: Standing under the moon of an arctic winter afternoon, Lopez reflects on the fact that the bright moon allows no depth to the sky, but that the stars shine brightly. This thought about stars, associated in his mind (and ours) with the moon, leads him to a description of stars in the arctic sky; this leads him after a while to another natural association, the North Star (Polaris), which leads him, logically enough, to another associated thought—the North Pole itself; once into that, it's natural enough to go into a scientific review for us of the meaning behind the five different north poles; and writing about the migration of one of those poles, the North Magnetic Pole, leads him into a discussion of some early scientific expeditions that tracked that migration from the year 1600 to modern times.

Before long, he's talking about the sun and its seasonal migrations across the meridians. Through that discussion we learn about the "meaning" of the Arctic Circle, the winter and summer solstices, and even something about the Dutch explorer Willem Barents and his icebound (and finally wrecked) ship in 1597.

As he takes us on a hypothetical trip from the North Pole south along the 100th meridian, he soon associates the variations of sun positions and its length of stay anywhere with how the various ecosystems have adapted to the seasons—everything from the stunted growth of the subarctic's trees to the retarded development of the region's soils. These are all associated in nature (and in his mind) with rainfall, which gives him a logical opportunity to bring up the fact that the arctic receives no more precipitation per year than the Mojave Desert—and so the associational chaining goes. Each leap across an associational synapse is logical enough that the reader accepts each of these mini-structures and stays with the writer despite an apparent lack of overall structure—but only, I think, because Lopez writes every word, every sentence, every image so well.

Because associational thinking is so central to all thought, I've decided not to label this variety of eccentric structure "associational" but "spiral." I call it spiral because the writer, like a hunting hawk, spirals around and around the topic, viewing it from different altitudes and distances, different angles, different perspectives. Once certain that the truth or the goal has been spotted and identified, the writer/hawk swoops in and makes the point. During the long, looping, spiralling descent, it may not have been apparent where the hawk might finally strike (or what his prey would be), but the aerial views were attractive all along the way—and we went along its for the ride. We had ridden on the hawk's back before, so we knew that we'd find the truth down there somewhere and with greater clarity as we swooped down in such dignified swirls. As a hawk has an identifiable shriek while searching, a writer like Lopez has a voice we can hear. This kind of eccentric structure allows the writer's voice to be heard.

Again, my warning—if you have reason to believe that you have not yet achieved an identifiable voice, you'd best stick for the time being with one of the less eccentric, more formal structures discussed earlier in this chapter.

Orchestrated Structure

We can certainly hear Annie Dillard's voice when she writes in her wonderful, sometimes off-center way. Although she uses associational, highly metaphoric writing that swoops slowly in on the subject, I'll not put it in the spiral category. In her chapter "Seeing," as in many of the other chapters in *Pilgrim at Tinker's Creek,* she has been said by James Moffett to "orchestrate" the piece. In a very instructive book, *Points of Departure—An Anthology of Nonfiction,* James Moffett, its editor, writes:

> Instead of telling several incidents that show the same thing, Dillard accumulates various firsthand experiences that show different things about the same basic phenomenon. The title indicates the theme, which Dillard develops gradually from different starting points—old memories, recent observations, passages in books.

Her essay advances in a circular way like a musical composition in which motifs once sounded are picked up and developed further later, each motif giving new meaning to the others as the whole fills out. She tightly alternates particular and general, instance and idea, playing freely up and down the abstractive scale. This draws the reader into the very inductive process of generalizing. . . No doubt the practice of calling student essays "themes" recognizes that the traditional essay has from its inception with Montaigne—through Hazlitt and Lamb, Emerson and

Thoreau—tended toward this musical structure rather than toward either chronology or logical organization.

Mosaic Structure

Writers use this eccentric structure in several ways. When an article has many quotes from a number of people, often with varied, even conflicting views, it may not be clear at first just where the writer is heading, what his or her overall view will be. Each tile of this mosaic may not make total sense, but after more and more tiles are laid and grouted by the writer's narrative skills, we see the pattern emerge, perhaps a pattern we would never have expected by projecting from the first few tiles.

This structure is seen very often in articles about a catastrophic event. The writer interviews the survivors; talks with the victims' relatives; interviews the police, the Coast Guard pilot, etc. When all the tiles are put together by the writer, there's a cumulative effect that affects our emotions and improves our comprehension of the event.

Another situation also suggests the possible use of a mosaic structure—multiple scenes. In *The Executioner's Song*, Norman Mailer structures it first into two equal halves; then, within each half, uses a mosaic structure. His tiles are scenes. In filmic terms, he cuts rapidly among scenes, each scene short, sometimes only several lines long. Where a filmmaker might dissolve, or even fade to black, between scenes, Mailer accomplishes the same effect typographically by simply using extra white space after each short scene. This structural technique to create for us the character of convicted murderer Gary Gilmore is dramatically, cumulatively effective.

Memoir Structure

Not to be confused with "diaries," which I've placed under chronologic structure, memoirs do not necessarily follow a strict, linear chronology, the way a diary typically does. They generally proceed from youth to old age, but a lot of jumping around through time may happen in a memoir. Tradition allows a memoirist to follow his or her own eccentric route down through the halls of time. Russell Baker's well-received memoir, *Growing Up*, for example, reads almost like a novel except that all the characters are real, and made real for us by Russell Baker's narrative ability. He takes us from his youth (and a little bit before) up until his mother, the main character in this story, dies in 1981. Baker's voice is heard throughout the book, as exemplified by the following paragraphs that open Chapter 3:

> My mother's efforts to turn poor specimens of manhood into glittering prizes began long before she became my mother. As the older daughter in a family of nine children, she had tried it on her younger brothers without much success. When she married she had tried it on my father with no success at all.
>
> Her attitudes toward men were a strange blend of twentieth-century feminism and Victorian romance. The feminism filled her with anger against men and a rage against the unfair advantages that came with the right to wear trousers. "Just because you wear pants doesn't mean you're God's gift to creation, sonny boy," she shouted at me one day when I said something about the helplessness of women. Of a man vain about his charm with women: "Just because he wears pants he thinks he can get through life with half a brain."

Some memoirs will read almost like a diary expanded by later thoughts. Others are more like a historic narrative, one that draws on several sources.

Those Days, by Richard Critchfield, carries the interestingly descriptive subtitle *An American Album*. This chronicle of three generations (his own, his parents', and their parents') resembles an old family album in that it includes photographs, diary entries, old newspaper clippings, and letters. It differs from the ordinary family album in that it also includes narrative by the memoirist, interviews by him, and even internal monologs created by the memoirist to bring alive long-dead relatives. This latter album element removes *Those Days* from the category of history or biography, and places it comfortably within this book as an excellent example of responsibly written, creative nonfiction.

The chapter "Anne" even ends with a few lines from a familiar song of the day:

> *... they'll never want to see rake or plow*
> *And who the deuce can parley-vous a cow?*
> *How ya' gonna keep 'em down on the farm*
> *After they've seen Paree?*

TEN

STRATEGIES

Books on rhetoric sometimes call the following strategies "methods of development," "rhetorical modes," or some other phrase, but the popular word these days is "rhetorical strategies," or "strategies." Let's consider now a number of strategies from which you can select the one (or several in combination) you'll use for a particular article or book. Certainly a book will use more than one of these strategies within its overall structure, but an article might need only one strategy to develop the story within its selected structure.

The fact that the following are rhetorical strategies may at first confuse those who have heard the word "rhetoric" only in reference to inflated political language—or outright lying. Rhetoric is not that: Rhetoric is the art of using language effectively. Period. The following series of strategies for using language effectively has proved useful to writers of fiction and nonfiction since the early Greeks, strategies so fundamental to human thought that they may not be safely ignored. Narration may be the most basic form of written human discourse.

NARRATION

Narration is storytelling.

We all get hooked on narration as children—and we remain kids in this regard. We like a good story, and we like a good storyteller. Some people may think they've outgrown narration when they quit reading fiction, but they continue to enjoy nonfiction that "tells a story" and tells it well. They especially appreciate the nonfiction story told vividly, one that uses

165

some of fiction's techniques, i.e., creative nonfiction, the great new American literature.

Narration answers the basic question: What happened? It answers it not by telling *about* a story: It *tells* a story. It gives us the story one moment to the next—life in motion. Narration is not a still life; it's a moving picture. Pure narration presents ACTION, not description. *Description*, another basic mode of discourse, helps give immediacy to a story, but its purpose is to get at the *quality* of an action or event. Description's not after movement; narration is.

Narration concerns itself mainly with *what* happens along a timeline. Although it may sometimes talk about *how* things happened, if its emphasis falls on the how, it impinges on the strategy called *analysis*. It may sometimes allude to the why of the situation, but if the emphasis falls primarily on the why, it impinges on the strategy here called *cause and effect*.

Narration may follow a timeline, but it does not simply report on a chain of events; it must lead to a result the reader can see. Something must change by the end. Frequently, the main character changes, perhaps only by a bit, but he or she will never again be the same. In other narratives, the world changes in some tiny or huge way by the end.

All this can happen effectively only under a plan the writer designs. The general plan, organization, or structure for almost any piece of fiction or creative nonfiction work is simple (although carrying it out may be neither so simple nor so easy). You have to devise a plan that will provide your story:

1. an OPENING (or lead) that pulls potential readers into your story as soon as possible;

2. a MIDDLE that sustains, supports, develops the story effectively and attractively;

3. an ENDING that has an identifiable climax, one that's intellectually satisfying. Readers know they've read a story, and they know it's over.

That's all you have to accomplish.

You'll make many decisions during the course of writing a piece, but a few decisions are so fundamental that they must be made even before beginning: How shall I handle time? From whose point of view shall I narrate it? How should I work in the expository material I've collected? (Read up on time in the structure section, there called "chronology" and "reworked chronology." Point of view and angle of approach make up Chapter 7. You can find information about expository material in practically every chapter.)

Note that we refer here to narration as a "strategy" that typically follows a timeline, and yet we spoke earlier of chronology as "structure." Let's clear up any confusion brought on by that similarity. If, for example, you've selected a chronologic structure for a piece, your structure would not need the support of a "strategy" also based on time—it would just happen because of the overall structure by chronology. If, however, you had elected to use some other structure, say, function, by which you would describe all the functions performed by some person or some thing, you might then decide that it would be most useful for the reader if you related it according to what minute, hour, or day the function begins and ends, i.e., time.

Since it might take many pages to discuss fully any one strategy for development, I suggest that you consult any of the many textbooks on rhetoric or fiction-writing guides to learn more about using the following strategies.

DESCRIPTION

You'll find description extremely useful in almost any kind of writing and within almost any kind of structure. Except in school, you'll rarely write a long piece that could be categorized as "pure description." You'll find description woven into pieces largely expository, or even in argumentation, the description passages perhaps used as a lead or opening that sets in context the event discussed.

Description provides context for content. An article about the dangers to a community from a nuclear power plant, for example, might open with a description of the lovely countryside about to be invaded by a huge atomic power plant. A profile article about a person will often have descriptive sections, not only about his or her appearance but about the building where the person works, his or her private office, or the bungalow where he or she grew up.

Except for most technical writing, writers use description as a strategy for developing ideas within the structure; they write not for the sake of description itself but to put the reader right in front of what's described.

To the extent the writer writes well and the reader reads well, the reader will share the experience the writer had when originally observing. To the extent the reader feels the description's secondhandedness, the writer has failed. The reader wants to "participate" in the experience described. He or she wants to "feel" it, not just be told about it. That's the writer's goal—the reader's involvement.

Description strategies are of two basic types: *technical* (or scientific) and *suggestive* (or artistic). This pair has also been described as: *objective* (technical or scientific) and *subjective* (artistic or suggestive). This book concerns itself with the type known as subjective (or artistic, or suggestive), because a writer writing objectively about science or technology for a professional publication, or writing a manual describing equipment and how to use it, will try above all else to be clear and precise. Creative nonfiction writers (about whom this book primarily concerns itself) may, of course, sometimes write about science and technology for those of us not involved with such technical matters, but they will write about science and technology more emotionally, more suggestively, more metaphorically, more poetically than prosaically. This section concentrates on description that's more suggestive, more subjective, more artistic.

The "artistic" writer wants (as do other "artists") us to experience the object of a description as directly as possible (recognizing the limitations imposed by using words only). He or she usually accomplishes this immediacy of experience by presenting the reader specific details, avoiding too many generalizations.

Description concerns itself mainly with: shape, line, contour, color, sound, touch, light, smell, texture, movement. These more or less tangible sensations stir in the reader's brain memories that help him or her re-experience.

I'm discussing here in only a few words what, in fact, much of this book is about—the value of presenting all kinds of concrete details and sensory details about life. Creative nonfiction gains much of its power to persuade, entertain, and inform through the writer's ability to conjure up in the reader's brain memories of similar experiences that enable him or her vicariously to experience what the writer describes.

The writer often tries through the description of physical and sensory details also to evoke in the reader a feeling, atmosphere, or mood—a sense of a place, person, object, or event. An experienced writer knows that the best way to do this is to decide, early in the observing-thinking-writing process, the *dominant impression* he or she received at the time and now wants to leave with the reader.

Finding this dominant impression takes standing back from the experience, avoiding too much thought about the details, and reflecting on what tone, mood, and meaning dominate. Once this key understanding comes, the writer can begin "writing to that."

The writer will now organize the details collected, so that the lesser details will stay subordinated to that dominant impression. (The beginning writer often tries to show off and detracts from the impression that is supposed to play the leading role.) Now there is a rationale for deciding which details to include—and which to exclude. Unless certain details help "build a case" for the dominant impression, the writer will probably not use them. After all, it's impossible to say everything about everything (although the beginning writer tries to), so the writer has to have a method for deciding which to include, which to exclude.

One guiding principle for writing description is that you are not, through description, trying to make the reader know the facts about something, so much as trying to make him feel some emotion (or have some attitude) toward it.

You'd think there existed a guiding principle claiming that the success of description writing comes from knowing many, many adjectives and adverbs—and using them as lavishly and as often as possible. If anything, the modern guiding principle says the opposite—use as few as you can.

I'd recommend that in your first draft you go ahead and let all the adjectives and adverbs tumble from your pen, and then revise them at leisure, substituting whenever possible more accurate nouns and verbs. Beginners' descriptions tend not only to have every noun modified by an adjective, they tend also to have every modifier modified, resulting in little strings of adjectival words and phrases preceding every noun. Professional writers advise that your writing will gain in strength through accuracy, not by adding modifiers but by rethinking the noun. In revision, always ask yourself whether you couldn't find a more accurate noun, one that has the idea of the adjective right there inside itself.

Don Murray, author of excellent books on writing, says that we should feel a tiny sense of failure when we use an adjective or an adverb. Naturally, sometimes you absolutely must modify a noun or a verb, but hold the fort against adjective and adverb abuse. Ernest Hemingway minimized the use of adjectives (or any excessive use of words in general). William Zinsser in *On Writing Well* pokes away at our adjectival (and other) clutter. Raymond Carver uses a minimum of adjectives and adverbs, depending instead on accurate (and simple) nouns and verbs to give vividness and strength to his short stories.

If people like that, along with Eudora Welty, Somerset Maugham, John Ciardi (who once said, "Never send an adjective on a noun's errand"), and John Steinbeck, all advised against adjective abuse, shouldn't we all take note?

William Strunk wrote in *The Elements of Style* (and I'm sure co-author E. B. White agreed) that adjectives are "the leeches that infest the pond of prose, sucking the blood of words." What could be more descriptively accurate and persuasive than that statement?—and not an adjective or adverb swimming anywhere in that pond.

Another principle is that you must *organize* the presentation of details. A mere accumulation of details, a cataloging, a listing, an enumeration of concrete and sensory data will not build up to a dominant impression; you have to be artistic about it. You can't use an aerosol can full of adjectives and adverbs to spray among the nouns and verbs, hoping for a unified, dominant feeling or impression.

All these wonderfully descriptive details have to work together coherently, and only you can impose the logic that glues them together to create a unified impression. You may want to organize them to mimic closely the way the details originally struck your senses, but you needn't feel obliged (by a misapplied honesty or accuracy) to stick to that original sequence. You may come up with a better system for exposing the reader to the details, hoping to build interestingly and effectively toward that dominant impression—that impression you hope, should all else be missed or forgotten, will stay with the reader.

You might decide to "build your case" by moving the reader's inner eye (and other senses) from far to near; from left to right; up to down or down to up; from outside to inside; first to last or vice versa; soft to loud, etc. These logics of perception are all valid choices; they are simply more effective in one case than in another. Only you can decide: you the writer; you the artist.

One final principle. Don't confuse "completeness" of description with "effectiveness" of description. Sometimes we're so complete and thorough that we bore, so complete and thorough that we disguise our main point—the dominant impression. Know when to stop.

The success of your description strategy comes not so much from how many details you use as from which details you select to use. Then comes the business of how creatively you present those details selected. This sensitive selectivity combines with creativity to develop your style. By your style shall they know you.

COMPARISON AND CONTRAST

The consideration of how two things compare and contrast with each other (i.e., how they are similar and different) has roots deep in the brain/mind complex. This kind of thinking goes way back to the early days of the brain's development, when the ability to compare quickly something new on the horizon, and perhaps take cover or prepare for defensive action, helped determine which animal (and later, man) would survive to fight another day. Considering how an indistinct form on the far horizon resembled a potential enemy was performed first by noting its similarities with the familiar. Figuring out how this new animal differed in its form, movements, and smell was probably reasoning of a higher order that came later in the brain's evolution. When a man of today wants to tell another person about something new, he's apt first to tell the other person how the new thing is similar to something else he or she already knows well. Then, to reinforce that understanding, he tells that person also what the new thing is not. Surprisingly, knowing what something is NOT (contrast), is one of the better ways of figuring out what it IS.

This capability to compare, this drive to compare the unfamiliar with the familiar, evolved into the human brain's unique capability to create metaphor. Knowing how something "new" (a problem) is similar to what we're already familiar with makes man a problem-solving animal. Naturally, something so fundamental to our survival stays with us today as a basic way we think. We want to understand the similarities and differences in everything we come across. Without these basic underpinnings to thought, we feel we don't have a real grip on the matter at hand. For this reason, we find writers employing a strategy of comparison and contrast in all kinds of writing and in all kinds of structures. Sometimes, comparison and contrast will be the principal strategy, but it's very often used to complement, to shore up, another strategy that might remain weak without it.

Any one of three different purposes might lead a writer to use the comparison and contrast strategy to develop his or her idea:

1. The writer might want to present to his or her reader data or information about one "item" by relating it to something the reader is already very familiar with;

2. he or she might want, in another situation, to tell the reader about both items by relating them to some broad idea or principle with which the reader is familiar enough to understand more readily something about the two items; or

3. the writer might want to compare and contrast both items to build a case for a new idea, or to prove the validity of an existing idea.

As with most other elements of writing, you must organize by some logic your presentation of the several comparisons and contrasts. It must not be a haphazard arrangement of comparisons and contrasts, each of different levels of significance (from trivial to crucial). Rhetoricians have come up with four basic methods for organizing your strategy:

1. You can first discuss one and then the other item fully, with continual references to the similarities and differences. This works best when the extent of comparisons and contrasts is small.

2. When, however, the comparisons and contrasts go on at considerable length, too long for any brain to retain all the similarities and differences, you should take up just a part of the first item. Then, take up one part of the second item and discuss their similarities and contrasts before moving on to a second part of each.

3. You can, instead, present one item totally. Then, when discussing the second item, keep cross-referring each similarity and difference back to the initial discussion of the other item.

4. If your purpose is to build a case for an idea or a universal principle of some kind, you can take the reader through all the comparisons and contrasts, leading him or her inexorably to the grand idea—or you can work backward from your premise or idea, showing how the similarities and contrasts support or don't support the idea.

Some things to keep in mind when preparing a strategy of comparison and contrast:

1. Compare and contrast only two items at the same time. Who could keep straight for long a three-way analysis of how A, B, and C are similar in some ways and different in others? It's likely that A is different in some

way from the same part of B, while being similar to the same part of C. On the other hand, C could be entirely unlike both A and B on a whole number of parts but be very similar on a few others. Imagine comparing and contrasting even more such items, each with many parts; imagine the confusing series of cross-referencing the reader's mind would have to do, store, and comprehend. Stay with two; that's tricky enough.

2. You don't have to give equal emphasis to similarities and differences. Sometimes the similarities are much more significant than any differences, so why dwell much on some insignificant differences? Other times, of course, the differences are so great that any consideration of minor similarities only detracts from the overwhelming significance of the deep differences. You only weaken your case when you bring in weak examples of either similarities or differences. It always makes it look as though you've completely run out of good points and are dragging in anything the cat didn't.

3. Make sure that you compare and contrast only items from the same significant class, significant in that it fits well your purpose of the moment. Don't compare something extremely important with something trivial, even if there is about that trivial item something interestingly similar or different. The result of comparing or contrasting such unlike elements can end up absurd. Handled properly, of course, such absurd comparisons and contrasts can provide some great humor. Just make sure you intended the humor.

Just because a mouse and an elephant are similar in color doesn't warrant a serious piece of comparison and contrast. If you went ahead and made some bizarre statements of how a mouse is "like an elephant," you might develop a very funny article, but we're speaking here only of a serious strategy of comparison and contrast that helps you develop for the reader an understanding of something reasonably significant that he or she didn't have before.

4. Just because comparison and contrast is a popular strategy and easy to use, don't use it all the time. Don't use it on trivial items, trivial similarities and differences. Save it for something of some significance. Don't be guilty of C & C abuse. Use it but don't abuse it.

CLASSIFICATION

Like narration, description, and comparison and contrast, the strategy of classification began as a basic method of thinking analytically about the world. A bit more "scientific" than the three above, it tries to bring order out of chaos. It helps us organize; it helps us think more clearly. When we write, it's a powerful method for exposition.

When we finish our research work, and before we start writing, we usually decide what the overall structure will be. Then we begin to organize our research materials around a strategy of some kind(s). First, we have to impose some order on the mess our research notes may resemble. We look for significant groups of thoughts under which our chaotically assembled notes will most logically fit. Scientists may have existing classification systems into which to fit their work. Librarians have long established classification schemes, like the Dewey Decimal system and the Library of Congress system, into which all their books will fit (or be forced). We writers, however, almost always have to invent our own classification schema for the piece at hand.

Fortunately for our creative souls, we don't have to fit our work into any prearranged classification scheme. We classify only according to our interest or purpose of the moment. Classification is an unusual method of thinking, for the same item may be in one "class" today for this purpose, and in a totally different "class" tomorrow for some new purpose. For our purposes, a "class" is a group of individual items that have the same significant distinguishing features. Mice and elephants, for example, *could* be classified together as gray animals, but that would be a trivial class. They could be better put into the more significant class of *mammals*. Either class is valid; one is significant.

When we try to classify (put into a class) an object, we don't describe the class by describing all the individual objects within it. Rather, we establish the class based on the "idea" or the "concept" behind the class. The idea or concept has to do with the qualities of the items that may be assigned to that class.

Basically, we say, "There are two (or three, or four) kinds of X." Then we go on to explain what characterizes each kind. When we think of the class "human," for instance, we don't think of Mary, John, and Hortense in all their particularities. We consider only the significant qualities the three have in common. It's their humanness that classifies them (puts them into that class). For another article, you might not want to classify at such a high level. Say your article deals with people who use computers for fun versus those who use them exclusively at the office. You'd put John and Mary into the latter "class," because they use computers every day for their work in graphics. Hortense (although still a human) now sits in a "class" with all those people who use computers only for fun and games. Depending on your article's purpose, you might have another class—those who used to play around with computers but now use them strictly for business. Another class might be those who use them at work but have never played a game on one. Another class in your article or book might easily be "those people who have never used a computer for anything whatsoever." With this strategy in hand, you could proceed to organize your research notes, interview notes, etc., under those classes. Some writers like to make their classes into headings and put them up on a bulletin board on 3x5 cards. Then they line up their various note cards under the classes or headings they seem best to fit.

Unless you have thought through your classification scheme very well, you may now find that some of the items don't fit any one of the classes, or you may find that some items lap over into two or more. Called a "cross-ranking error," this problem requires that the classification system be revised. Public opinion pollsters and others who classify things every day watch warily for this error. They know enough to get it straight before beginning their surveys. Suppose, for example, that you've already conducted a phone survey and are now analyzing the completed forms. Your classifications are (1) high school graduates, (2) high school dropouts, (3) black students, (4) Asian students, (5) Catholic students, (6) Protestant students. Now you find that one of those interviewed on the phone was a Protestant black girl who had graduated from high school. Logically, her name must be put under (1), (3), and (6). The trouble is that you wanted all the columns (1) through (6) to total up to the total interviewed. Unfortunately for your statistical sanity, she and the Asian kid who is a high school dropout and who belongs to the Catholic church (or worse, for your purposes, an oriental religion that doesn't appear at all in your breakdown) will appear in more than one class. Cross-ranking must be avoided—and it had best be avoided way back at the beginning of your planning. Classes must be mutually exclusive; an item must not fit comfortably into two classes. One example of this difficulty hits close to home for readers of this book and people interested in "creative nonfiction," "nonfiction novels," "dramatic nonfiction books," and other such relatively new classes of books. They may find that one library has such books squeezed uncomfortably into "Fiction," while another library will have them under "Nonfiction." Very likely, they'll not be listed under "Literature." Someday they will be so classified, I predict, but not for a long time.

You can devise your own logic for classifying whatever you're faced with, but I'll mention one relatively simply classification scheme useful for many purposes—the *dichotomous* classification system. You simply divide the people, items, or ideas, into two piles (classes)—those who do have some characteristic deemed by you as significant to your present purpose; and those who do not. We hear this used every day because it's so useful and so simple. (Watch out, though—it can also be simplistic.) We read frequently of "the haves" and "the have-nots," a dichotomy based on economic status. Presuming that you want to get deeper than that, you take each class and divide it into two subclasses; e.g., the "haves" could be divided into *those who live in North America*, and *those "haves" who do not live in North America*. Depending again on the purpose of your piece, you might again divide those who live in North America into another dichotomous pair, *those "haves" living in North America who are black*, and *those "haves" living in North America who are not black*.

Just to make the point that this dichotomous division can go on and on, you might decide that you need to divide those "black 'haves' who live in North America" into *those who have a college degree* and *those who have no degree*. Now you could go ahead and discuss, for example, the value of a college education in the life of a black person living in North America versus one living in a Third World country (a "have-not" country). You could use the same classification scheme, of course, to discuss the role of the mother in black families living in Chicago versus that of the Nigerian mother in Lagos. It simply enables you to think your way out of chaos into order—and keeps everything coherent for your reader.

Clearly, the first thing you must do when creating any strategy, but especially this one, is to think long and hard about just what the purpose of this particular piece of work may be. All the mental effort toward this will pay off in many ways beyond the decisions about structure and strategy. A clear, crystal clear, understanding of your purpose will inform and guide your thinking throughout. Someone said that a problem accurately defined is half solved. It's a truism to tape to your typewriter.

ILLUSTRATION

Since the reader doesn't always understand completely what we mean when we first broach a subject, we look for a way (a strategy) to make the generalization clearer. One of the most natural strategies we turn to is illustration. Also called "exemplification," illustration shows the reader, by example, how the generalization works. If the example seems imperfect, inexact, or incomplete, we tend naturally to provide another example, another illustration, until we believe that the reader must grasp the point.

I should make clear first a distinction between two closely related terms: *example* and *illustration*. "I get along well with Mary because she, too, loves animals. She's always down at the zoo." (An *example* of how we should understand that Mary loves animals.) "I get along well with John because he loves animals. He's got at his house right now two Siamese cats, two Husky puppies, and some goldfish in the pond out back." (*Illustrations* of the statement that John loves animals.) These specifics are more illustrative—i.e., they throw more illumination on the generalization that John loves animals. The difference between the two terms is of degree.

When we decide to provide the reader some examples or illustrations to clarify the generalization, we search for the most concrete (not abstract) ones. Even philosophers, who deal with abstract principles, try hard to find concrete examples to illustrate for us what the principle or generalization or abstraction means in "down-to-earth" terms.

We use examples and illustrations, first, for their concreteness that provides clarity to a naturally fuzzier generalized statement. Second, we use examples and illustrations because we readers find these stories (that's what they amount to) interesting as well as informative. If, for example, you give examples from your own experience, examples common to most people, specific statistics, times, dates, villages, highways, cars, names, we not only enjoy them, we tend to believe them more readily because they're more familiar than the generalization. They're real, not abstract.

Illustration (exemplification) is a basic and frequently used strategy. Like comparison and contrast, narrative, and description, it pops up all the time in the midst of another strategy or strategies. A close cousin to analogy, illustration is a strategy fundamental to human thought—hence, an excellent strategy for the writer to develop a thought within the reader's brain.

Perfect illustrations or examples come hard. A good example would be one that, when well developed, makes it easy for the reader to see why you selected it to illustrate (make clear) your subject. The writer should not need to explain for the reader why the example illustrates the general subject. Rather than "explain" an example's relevance, if you think matters still fuzzy, add another example, one coming from some new angle, some new perspective. A reader who apprehends how the two examples relate to each other, and then sees how they, indeed, illustrate the subject, is pleased to have made the connection for him- or herself—rather than through your "telling" him or her about it. You've "shown" the reader by the examples.

You can exemplify or illustrate your generalization by an anecdote, a quote, a quotation (from someone historic), a metaphor (especially an analogy), statistical tables, pie charts, bar graphs, paintings, photographs, etc.

One principle to bear in mind is that your example must come from the same class of things as your generalization. If you're talking about teachers, your examples had best be related to teachers, not astronauts. True, teachers and astronauts share several classes in common, e.g., they're both from the class of man; they're both from the class of highly educated people; they also share the class of people who have their heads in the clouds, but you've got to keep the teachers within the narrower classification of "teachers."

Decide before writing which "class" you're working within for this particular piece. If the class is of people who make their main living by instructing other people, draw your examples and illustrations from those who do that.

You could occasionally step outside that class boundary to pick up an example, but you'd be obliged to explain that action. If, for instance, you stepped outside and brought in a rabbi as an example of "teacher," you've changed your strategy to comparison and contrast. You'd write about how a "teacher" in a religious institution compares and contrasts with a "teacher" within an educational institution. That's a valid thing to do, but you must make the reason for that switch clear to your reader. If you know in the beginning that you'll be pulling in a rabbi to make a point and you plan also to bring in a scoutmaster, you might rather define your "class" as "those people who teach other people." If you wanted also to talk about wild animal trainers as teachers, you'd define your class as "those people who teach or train." Define in advance (for yourself, anyway) the boundaries within which you will operate. A scholar will lay this out very clearly at the beginning, so that other scholars can decide at the outset whether they agree with the boundaries he or she has drawn. This will affect how they accept or reject what follows. The creative nonfiction writer had probably better not lay it out so fully for the reader. Just know for yourself, and then stay conscientiously within the class you've defined.

You can also exercise a little strategy (or this would be a tactic) within your strategy. When you have a list of examples and illustrations in mind to clarify your subject, which should come first? I suggest that, right after the generalized statement, you present the best all-around example from your list. That may do the trick by itself, of course, but if you want to reinforce it with further examples or illustrations, drop down your list to one of the less perfect ones and use it as your second example. Then, build your way back up the list until the second-to-best one serves as your final example. Since it's now in the final position, it acquires added emphasis. The result is that you've hit the reader with a great example first off, and then left him or her with one just as powerful because of its final position.

ANALYSIS

This strategy grows out of an appreciation that we can understand something complex better by dividing it into its component parts. Then we can concentrate our attention on each, one at a time. A sky-rocket, for instance, isn't just a loud bang—it's also the material of which it's made (fuse, core, stick) and all the processes that went into it (selection of materials, manufacture, sale, final use; or, ignition, liftoff, highest altitude, speed, explosion, any of a variety of colors, noises, smoke, and so on). A dog isn't just a furry lump; a falling cat doesn't turn all four feet together to make a safe landing, even though it may look that way to the casual eye.

Analysis is a little like filming something in slow motion and a little like catching it in a close-up. Each element that helps make up a thing or an event can be put under a microscope, or looked at through powerful binoculars, to let a reader see all of its parts in detail and in proper proportion to the whole.

Analysis may use one or several of the writing strategies discussed in this section. Quite often, analysis will employ *narration*, telling what things happen in what order, then switch to *cause and effect* to explain why the specific part or action under study is the way it is. It may be a good idea to use *description* to let the reader "see" the part clearly. The writer might *compare* it to something more familiar (a launch vehicle for a satellite with our backyard skyrocket, maybe, or microwaves with radio waves) or *contrast* it with something unlike it in significant ways (though both are thick-skinned and eat leaves, an elephant is *not* a rhinoceros). Writers will frequently *illustrate* what's under discussion with specific examples, the way I've tried to do here, or even with exploded drawings, sketches, or photographs.

Whatever other strategies may be employed, though, the heart of any analysis is the act of dividing something into its parts, telling exactly what each part is and how it works, and how it relates to the other parts and to the whole. Like the photographer's bag of tricks I mentioned a minute ago—slow motion, close-up—and like a scientist's equipment of telescope and microscope, analysis lets us see and understand anything from a subatomic particle to a woman ceremonially pouring tea in Tokyo.

CAUSE AND EFFECT

Narration works on the *what* and the *when*; description works largely on the *who* and the *where*; and analysis of process tries to tell us the *how* of things; but it's the cause and effect strategy that has the nerve to attempt the *why*.

Hard-news journalism bases its approach on the *who, what, where, when*, and *how*, but generally avoids explanation (the *why*). The beat reporter leaves this to the investigative reporter, the columnist, the feature writer, or the editorial writer, people with more time for research and reflection. Figuring out the "why," the cause and effect of anything significant, requires a great deal of clear thinking.

When you adopt cause and effect as a strategy, you must be cautious and reflective. You must be careful not to attribute a "why" to a Y, for example, simply because the Y was preceded by an X. One is drawn easily into this error, especially when Y has always followed X. As in their relationship in the alphabet, X doesn't "cause" Y—it simply precedes it in a sequence established by someone a long time ago. "Sequence" (as with an alphabet) is certainly one way that things or events relate to each other; another, deeper relationship is "causation"—why something happens. Some things always follow each other in a sequence, but that may be merely a chronological coincidence.

In some pieces of writing, you'll work from a "known effect" back to an "unknown cause"; at other times you may work the other way 'round—working from some "known cause" to speculate about or predict future "effects."

In the former case, you may be writing, for example, about the thousands of homeless men and women (an effect) and try to work back to the cause (perhaps a government policy; perhaps a socioeconomic phenomenon we'll always have with us).

In the latter case, you might write about deforestation (a known cause) in northern Africa and how this has resulted in desertification (a known effect) of once-productive land. The desert created has then become a cause of starvation (effect).

As you dig deeper and think about the possible multiple causes and effects; about the paradoxes of effects becoming causes (and vice versa); and the historic (remote or ultimate) causes, you find your article or book coming into full bloom. Whereas you originally wondered how you could ever get enough material to write about, you now find that by following the strategy of cause and effect, you have the possibility of having too much.

To distinguish between relationships that merely seem causational and those that truly are so related, you must investigate to learn whether two conditions obtain:

1. Y does not occur without a preceding X.

2. Whenever X occurs, Y invariably follows it.

When those two conditions are met, you can be pretty certain that you've identified two "things" related by cause and effect. Several confusing factors, though, may haunt your efforts:

1. You may think you have it straight in your mind as to which is cause and which is effect, but then realize that what seemed at first blush "ef-

fect" turns out to be "cause." This paradox of causes and effects working in reverse makes interesting and informative reading, so keep your eyes open for inherent paradoxes.

2. What you've identified as the cause may be only the "immediate" cause. As you think more deeply about your subject, you may find a more "remote" cause that had eluded your earlier thinking.

3. It turns out that the cause that seemed to create "the" effect actually caused multiple effects. Most causes, in fact, create ripple effects. This may provide you more materials to write about, but at some point you must narrow down and select only those effects you can deal with reasonably well, given the length of the piece you intend to write, the research resources available, your present state of development, your audience, and your purpose. The selection may prove difficult and time consuming.

4. An effect that you have initially attributed to one cause may turn out to have multiple causes, or a "complex" cause. This complex, interrelated, interdependent world consists mostly of multiple effects caused by multiple causes. Ask an ecologist who deals every day with unbelievably complex networks of interactive systems and subsystems of intricately interconnected components and subcomponents.

5. You may overlook in your original analysis a tiny cause because it has such a disproportionately huge effect—or many, many effects. A kingdom might be lost because the king's horse is shot out from under him in the heat of battle; his troops retreat because they think the king is dead; the unrescued, de-horsed king is felled by a peasant's pitchfork; and an empire abuilding fails to materialize. Because of that, all kinds of socio-economic-political effects ripple out from a single cause—a dead horse.

Obviously, if you want to write about something that requires a cause and effect strategy, you've got to know the subject extremely well, and you must have your wits about you all the time—everywhere lurk the hobgoblins of loose logic. If you slip up and identify something as "the" cause, and your readers realize that that's only the "immediate" or "proximal," not the remote or ultimate cause, they may give up on you and your further, perhaps excellent, reasoning.

A writer is always advised to keep his or her audience in mind, but it's even more imperative when claiming relationships between certain causes and certain effects. You'll persuade one audience through your litany of startling facts; another audience by the entertaining way you present your reasoning; but you may put off another audience by your "proofs" that are too startling, too dramatic, or too entertaining (and therefore, suspect)—they want calm, cool, reflective logic from the magic loom of your mind.

A final note—there's no final, absolute, ultimate explanation of WHY about anything (except that explained by faith), so don't intimidate yourself by thinking that you shouldn't try to "prove" anything to anyone through a strategy of cause and effect. As difficult and challenging as it may be, just do the best that you can at your present state of development with what's available to you.

ARGUMENTATION AND PERSUASION

Argumentation tries through logical analysis to move an audience to a belief, rarely to an action. It does so through two basic methods: (1) *deduction*, which uses only logical formations to "prove" something, or to arrive at "Truth"; and (2) *induction*, which uses many methods: evidence, definition, comparison and contrast, analogy, authority, cause to effect, effect to cause.

Argumentation's purpose is "truth finding," truth as discoverable through the exercise of reason. Argumentation is based on logic alone, and has rules to follow, rules established by the great Greek and Roman rhetoricians and philosophers.

This book will not dwell on argumentation as strategy, because argumentation depends not on the creative side of mind but the logical side. People are not (and should not be) argued into a position by "creative" argumentation. Because persuasion, on the other hand, depends partly on creative thought, we will look more thoroughly at the act of persuasion.

Persuasion's purpose has not so much to do with truth seeking as with mind changing. Argumentation is based on logic; persuasion on psychology. The persuader tries either to change the persuadee's belief to what the persuader wants, or to reinforce what the persuadee already believes. Persuasion wants to move the persuadee to some kind of action more often than does argumentation.

The persuader also works on the persuadee's logic, but works harder on the persuadee's emotions. That's the basic difference between persuasion and its seemingly similar partner in the general business of persuasion, argumentation. Argumentation, by its rules, must never appeal to emotions to find the truth or to prove an assertion to someone. Persuasion has no rules to prohibit its playing on the emotions. It believes that the whole person should be approached in the process of persuasion, since that's how life works. Life presents itself to both our reason and our emotions. We act out our lives according to how we perceive objective and subjective realities—another way of saying that life presents itself to us and we have to figure it all out according to what our reason and our emotions tell us—in concert.

The persuader will often try first to persuade the persuadee that they share a great deal—that is, the persuader tries to get the persuadee to identify with him or her. This is done by laying out the common ground on which they stand. Not that the persuader lies—he or she just doesn't bother to bring up differences. Or a persuader may bring up differences in order to point out that these aren't really differences—they just *look* like differences and then go back to stressing the real similarity of their opinions about the issue at hand. The persuader may even try to persuade by implying that if they feel so similarly about those other (totally irrelevant, nongermane) issues, why should the persuadee continue to hold the present differences about *this* matter?

Part of this persuasive magic is worked by studying the persuadee's background in advance, knowing that person's (that audience's) likely attitudes, desires, ideals, and levels of knowledge (about the matter at hand and about life in general)—to prepare the most effective strategy.

Persuasion can be promoted by using even individual words or short phrases—loaded words. The effective persuader (and we are all at some point persuaders) knows that certain words connote all kinds of things beyond what they appear on the surface to say. Sometimes the writer/persuader will be overt about the use of slanted, prejudicial words, working deliberately on the emotional impact he or she knows the word will have on this particular person at this particular time. *Her prose is practically poetry,* one reviewer might write. A different writer reviewing the same book might say, instead, *Her prose is romantic, sentimental slush.* Each reviewer is simply trying to persuade his or her readers to share his opinion of the author's prose.

Such slanted words accumulate to give the overall review a tone. We are persuaded (or not persuaded) partly by this general tone. If the tone makes us think that the reviewer has been "carried away" by his or her own emotions, we may well be turned off and not persuaded by the would-be persuader.

The clever (effective) persuader will mix some quietly loaded words with an appeal to the reader's logic. Most persuaders operate on the principle that the whole reader must be addressed if they are to persuade. Only the most intellectual person is persuaded by purely logical argumentation. Most people are persuaded by clearly stated logical ideas combined with quiet appeals to the emotions. Some people, of course, can be moved to a belief by a wild appeal to their emotions. In wartime, for example, appeals to patriotism bypass reason and go straight to the heart (emotions). Men and women in romantic situations persuade best by direct appeals to the heart (emotions). Logic and lust do not good bedfellows make.

Creative nonfiction gets much of its power through its appeal to emotions, so it can make good use of the strategy of persuasion, even though it probably could not very often make good use of formal argumentation. Argumentation intends objectivity untainted by subjectivity; persuasion intends both objectivity and subjectivity in its attempts to present reality (if not Truth).

DEFINITION

A definition's strategic purpose, to explain what something "is," or "means," can be as short as a typical dictionary's entry, or as long as an essay. It could even be as long as a book. Because definition, as a strategy, is so basic yet so flexible, it appears everywhere.

A short, dictionary-like definition may appear in an article to establish for the reader what the "ordinary" meaning of a thing, a word, or a concept is, establishing the ground on which the writer intends to stand—or intends to jump off from. Then the article may take off and define at length what the writer thinks it "really" means. That definition might run for several paragraphs, far beyond a dictionary's explanation, or it may form the entire article, an extended definition (a definition essay).

Tom Wolfe's book *The Right Stuff* could be called an extended definition of that phrase he'd heard so often applied to test pilots—that the great ones, like Chuck Yeager, had "the right stuff" to be effective test pilots. He wrote one of the longest definitions of a phrase one could imagine—over 400 pages, perhaps 150,000 words. Some phrases are like that.

Imagine how many words have been written over the years in attempts to define one little word, "love," and it has yet to be defined adequately. Some concepts are like that; no, all concept are like that. If you can define a concept adequately in a few words, maybe it's not very conceptual after all.

"Structure" and "strategy" come together here in a discussion of definition as strategy. When the structure of a piece that employs definition as a major strategy also uses a strategy of definition, it begins to sound like a circular definition. Fundamental things are like that.

The strategy of definition is apt to use any or all other strategies, which is why I've listed it last. *The Right Stuff*, for example, uses every one of the strategies discussed in this chapter. In his *narration*, Tom Wolfe provides many *descriptions* of people, aircraft, and places. In those descriptions he *compares* all the test pilots to find the similarities that have been used to classify them as potential astronauts, i.e., pilots who do indeed (and in deed) show the right stuff. He also *contrasts* the wives in some detail. He *illustrates* the validity of the pilots' classification by using many examples of their capabilities and personalities through interesting, vivid anecdotes. The entire book *analyzes the process* by which NASA finds, trains, and uses astronauts. The book is replete with *effects* attributed to certain *causes*. Finally, he *persuades* us to his beliefs about the men and the system. All these strategies in the service of one strategy perhaps weakly labeled as *definition*.

It's always hard at first to think of form separate from content, to make what seems a single thing, glass-of-water, into *glass* + *water* and then *choose* what kind of glass is best for this particular water. Readers usually don't notice structure. Writers have to, because readers and editors certainly *do* notice if the writing is interesting and clear or not—and, most often, that's as much a matter of structure and strategy as one of content.

As we writers become more aware of the choices available to us, we can make those choices more effectively, until they become part of our basic repertoire and of that indefinable something that's called *personal style*.

ELEVEN

RESEARCH METHODS

Although I've set aside this section to discuss research in the creative nonfiction writing process, it's not too much different from research done for any good nonfiction writing. Readers today expect creative nonfiction writers, journalists especially, to provide not only a complete and objective treatment: they also expect a subjective treatment, which usually means treating the emotional content of the story. They want the complete picture, a picture that includes fully developed scenes, captured conversations, and even internal monologs (although they don't all agree on this latter technique).

Through those and other techniques discussed in earlier chapters, the creative nonfiction writer deliberately excites the reader emotionally as well as intellectually—in recognition of the fact that our minds always use emotions to add meaning and clarity to straight factual information. This, of course, sets the creative nonfiction writer aside from the journalist who believes, or is instructed, that emotions should not play a role in understanding the news of the outer world.

Creative nonfiction writers still use the basic research method, interviewing, but they also use many more methods. They talk with the people immediately involved in the story to flush out, and later to flesh out, the WHO, WHAT, WHERE, WHEN, WHY, and HOW elements of a typical deadline news story. The traditional reporter barely has time on a daily paper to ferret out all those elements with the accuracy and completeness he desires. Since the creative nonfiction writer normally doesn't write to a tight deadline, he may take weeks, months, even years, to get the story as accurate and complete as possible.

SATURATE AND IMMERSE

This highly involved research effort, sometimes called, appropriately, *saturation reporting* or *immersion research*, necessitates that the writer be willing (and financially able) to stick with a story for weeks, months, or years. The writer has to be willing also to move in on the lives of complete strangers and to dig deep into those lives, warts and all. Gay Talese, speaking on a panel at Yale, "New Journalism—Two Decades In Perspective," told the audience of students and writers, "You've got to do deep and thorough research—you've got to have an affair with your subject."

Mark Kramer said that he spent several years living among or around the men and women he wrote about in *Three Farms*, a book that takes the reader through the lives of people operating farms of different types, sizes, and locales.

The fiction writer can hole up in a garret or cabin and work largely out of his or her memory and imagination, but the creative nonfiction writer can't work out of those sources alone; he or she must conduct research out in the real world, the raucous world, the dirty world. This requirement to work away from the studio or the study turns some writers away from this form of writing. Others, however, love that side of the profession—it's what draws them in. I write this not to discourage you from the profession but to suggest that you keep clearly in mind the requirements: the need to work away from home, family, and friends for long stretches of time; the need sometimes to sleep in strange beds under alien roofs; and the need sometimes to live for long periods with no income other than the publisher's advances on royalties (not always available to the beginner in this field).

Not only must you undertake great amounts of research, you must, absolutely must, be sure that every piece of information you produce is verifiable. On that Yale University panel, sponsored by the Poynter Institute, Talese said, "In creative nonfiction the rules of accuracy must not be violated. All that we write should be verifiable." Everyone on that remarkably talented panel moderated by Shelley Fisher Fishkin (Didion, Dunne, Lapham, Plimpton, Talese), stressed this requirement of accuracy. They may have been reacting, too, to the allegations made against the New Journalists that they ignored accuracy in the pursuit of drama. In those early days (the sixties and early seventies) some self-proclaimed New Journalists (or parajournalists) were enamored more with the joys of self-expression than with journalistic accuracy. Some were not journalists so much as advocates for favorite persons and causes—and because this was all fairly new, they thought they must be New Journalists.

No one labels himself a New Journalist today, partly because of the stigma left over from those early days of no discipline. Today's more mature species, the ones I call Creative Nonfiction Writers (and whom others call literary nonfiction writers), concern themselves greatly with the accuracy and thoroughness of their research. Some of his early critics were surprised (and pleased) with the thoroughness and accuracy of the research conducted by Tom Wolfe in preparing to write *The Right Stuff*. That book presents one of the best models for writers who want to write creatively about well-researched subjects. His readers learn a great deal about NASA's space program and about the astronauts' lives in a book whose style makes it fun to read, even while getting all this information.

Philosophers have always worried about Truth, and many have made a living worrying it around. The Yale panel of writers also kicked the same gong around—that if facts don't exist, why all this worrying about accuracy and objectivity? Philosophers can make a living on nonexisting facts, but a working writer can't base his or her profession on the slippery foundation that facts do not exist. The writer must indulge in double-think: He or she must try to dig out the facts anyway, and must verify them through independent sources; and must keep in mind that "facts" and "Truth" are elusive.

The writer must recognize, too, that the accuracy of any fact has largely to do with who's providing it. Some creative nonfiction writers become so frustrated by that fact about facts, that they come to trust their own feelings more often than surface "facts."

Traditional journalists have only to report the variations or versions of "truth" given them by a variety of sources, and simply enclose the versions of truth in quote marks. They're not required to figure it all out and come to some synthesis of what the truth is—in fact, they're constrained by journalistic traditions (and editors) not to introduce their feelings or understandings at all.

Creative nonfiction writers, however, may well bring themselves into a story, either strongly or subtly, believing it only fair to let the reader gauge for him- or herself the writer's credibility—and thus the accuracy of the facts presented. Creative nonfiction writers believe that to hide themselves, in a sincere attempt at objectivity, gives the reader no reference point. The innocent reader has no choice—he or she must believe the facts, or reject them totally. According to Mailer and others, facts are not "nuanced"—and we need to read of the unspoken forms of communication, the gestures—that is, we need the nuance.

Many creative nonfiction writers feel, too, that if they include character sketches about the people central or peripheral to the story, the reader will be able to gauge the credibility of the facts presented by those people. If a person is merely named, the reader can't be sure what credibility to assign. If the person is also identified by a title, especially by an impressive-sounding title (say, Director), but with no other personal background, the reader may ascribe too little or too much credibility, based solely on name and title. This places considerable responsibility on the writer's shoulders to provide "accurate" and "objective" character sketches. The writer's sketches must be credible, if the reader is to judge fairly that person's readability.

The only way you can ensure that your work will be accurate is to do your research work well. What does it mean, to do it well? First of all, it means not to stint. Dig in. Read. Observe. Interview. Newspaper reporters dig in, read, observe, and interview—but they don't have the time to do all the research that's essential for the kind of "reporting" we're talking about here. The terms *saturation* research or *immersion* research are metaphors which accurately describe what must go on. You must saturate your mind with information—by immersing yourself in the subject as deep as you can go. The result: Your writing yields something beyond what might be expected, whether that means information unexpected, or information expressed in a creative (unexpected) way. It takes time to gather information—as I've said before—weeks, months, years—and that certainly implies saturation and immersion. To write in a style that is appropriately "creative" also requires time. Some of this time may be required by the complexity of the subject, or it may be required by the difficulty of conducting all the necessary interviews. Either there are many, many people to interview, or the interviewees are few but geographically inconvenient, or the person being written about has such a complex life that you find it necessary to keep studying him or her for a lot longer than you might have anticipated. The chances are, of course, that anyone worth spending a lot of research and interview time on for a major article or book will be a very busy, complicated person living a complex life—so this necessity to take a long time comes with the territory. Interviewing is usually a great part of the research effort for this kind of writing, but other sources also provide background.

SOURCES OF INFORMATION

Libraries

Readers of this book undoubtedly know how to conduct research in a library, so I need only remind them of the necessity to dig into all available libraries to find what others have written about the subject or the person being written about. I'll also point out that you should, according to most writers, do your library homework in advance of doing any interviewing. John McPhee is one exception to this—he says that he'd rather begin his interviews as a *tabula rasa*, a clean slate, which I'll take up shortly when we consider the matter of preparing for the interview itself.

While you're in the library, don't forget the possibilities in: *old newspaper files* for previous interviews of your person, interviews with other relevant persons, articles on the subject matter; *periodical files* in the special field, partly for any interviews, profiles, sidebars, etc. about the person or subject, partly for *articles written by the person* you're writing about and *general information* to provide you with background you may lack in the field; *books written* by *your person*, about *your person* or about *the topic of concern*. Don't overlook nonfiction books labeled for "Young Adults." These short, specialized books (usually about 100 pages) can often provide you with enough background to help you interview a specialist on some topic you have no reason to be expert in. These excellent books are frequently not stored on the shelves where you'd likely be searching, so you might have to inquire (without any embarrassment) at the Reference Desk.

Electronic Information Retrieval Services

One of the newest services provided by many libraries is electronic information retrieval. The library's computer can search out information from all across the country in minutes. Libraries and other information sources (data bases) provide, for a fee, all kinds of specialized information you may need for an article or book—and you may not even have to leave your study or dining room table. If you have a good word processor with a "modem" (short for modulator-demodulator) attachment that converts computer output into the proper kind of input for telephone transmission and reception, you may be able to gain access to all kinds of specialized information retrieval services by yourself, without going through a library's mainframe computer.

These special information services spring up daily. The first one to operate, *Knowledge-Index*, claims to provide over four million summaries of articles, books, and reports on thousands of topics: science, medicine, business, computers. This data base gives you information from about ten thousand professional journals, magazines, and government reports, and over four hundred popular magazines. *The Source*, a subsidiary of the Reader's Digest Association, Inc., provides information on financial markets, news, sports, science, etc. It can also give immediate access to the United Press International news service.

CompuServe, owned by H&R Block, Inc., provides information more for consumers than for researchers, but it does offer information from the *Washington Post* and the Associated Press wire service that many researchers need. The *Dow-Jones News/Retrieval* data base has all kinds of business data, instant access to stock market information, and news from the *Wall Street Journal.* The country's largest bibliographic index (*Bibliographic Retrieval Services*) is available to researchers and writers who need information from scientific abstracts, medical journals, business indexes, and major magazines and newspapers. One nice thing about this organization is that it also has a service called BRS/AFTER DARK which enables writers to access all this valuable information less expensively between midnight and 6:00 A.M., when most of its clients (businesses and libraries) are closed.

All these wonderful services for the writer are fairly expensive, especially if you're not organized in your approach to using them. First, you pay a one-time registration fee (usually between $35 and $100), and from then on, pay only for the time you spend on the line—anywhere from $5 to $25 per hour. It sounds high, but if you figure out your own hourly cost of going to a library (perhaps a number of them) and trying to track down some information sources, writing or calling them, and waiting for their mailed responses, etc., the fee suddenly seems reasonable. If you want to avoid spending too many expensive hours on the line, you must do some thinking in advance and limit what you ask the service to re-trieve. The first time I tried using one of these services, I was interested in Eskimo dogsleds. I didn't limit my request intelligently, so the computer printed out reams of article references on everything from Eskimo dental problems to Eskimo religions. Needless to add, I spent some time think-ing through a search request the next time. You can request just biblio-graphic references which you'll then choose from; you can request summaries of articles or books from which you may then order entire ar-ticles to be printed out on your computer or mailed to you. You could, of course, find for yourself all this data base information in some book or article, somewhere (after all, that's where the service got its information), but where to look: which directory, which index, which table of contents, which library, which government office. Telecommunications in the service of writers. A wondrous thing.

If you should be writing about a famous person, search in the person's hometown library for less obvious materials, e.g., diaries, daybooks, jour-nals, field notebooks. These may not have been published but may be on file in the local library, church, or historical society. Presuming you have the family's cooperation, you may find documents like these, photo albums, or even old letters stored in the attics of relatives, friends, and lovers. Such doc-uments may well turn out to be the most important for you, because much of the other information has been available to other writers over the years, making it difficult for you to add anything very new or unexpected.

Interviewing Significant Others

Another important pre-interview research activity is that of inter-viewing people other than your subject. Coworkers or bosses, for exam-ple. Not that you take as Truth what these people say about your main interviewee, but they do give you some early insight into the person, in-formation you may want to probe more deeply in the actual interview. In most cases, you'll find people with a wide spectrum of opinion about the subject, sometimes because of their relationship but sometimes simply because of the human tendency to see things differently. If you, in subse-quent interviews, find yourself not seeing what any of them saw, you had best think some more, research some more, interview more people. It could be that the person is an extremely clever actor who comes off one way in an interview but quite different in a day-to-day working relationship. Or, the person may not handle an interview well but is wonderful to work with. You have to dig, dig, dig.

You may want, also, to interview people who know the person on a more social level—fellow country club members, fellow members of Kiwanis, Rotary, or other fraternal or service organizations. Neighbors, old high school teachers, high school sweethearts, summer camp friends, etc., are all possible sources of information. And, of course, family members. Their information, while always suspect, can be interesting—and will sometimes lead to names of other associates, enemies, etc., who might/should be interviewed.

One group of significant others whom you should consider interviewing are fellow specialists in your subject's specialty. Professors in the field, whether or not they know your person, may know of his or her work in the field—and may have an opinion about it. Or they may know some other specialist for you to interview—providing additional valuable information.

Adopt the insurance salesman's tried-and-true technique: never leave one contact without the names of two more he or she thinks might need insurance. Don't leave one interview without one or more other possible interviewees. Just the fact that you've been referred by a respected colleague will get you by many a secretary. That's part of the insurance salesman's gambit. Another good reason to interview specialists in the subject is that they will teach you something about the field, providing you either with special knowledge that may directly enter your piece, or with material for your next interview making it apparent that you've done some homework—and everyone appreciates the writer/interviewer who's done that.

Personal Observation as a Research Tool

Personal observations serve as valid research information for writers of creative nonfiction. "Research" connotes scientific, rigorous, highly controlled investigation, possibly in a laboratory setting, but the word means many things. Taking it literally, the writer is forever "re-searching," looking again at something, or for something. A newspaper reporter is re-searching as he or she runs around the city tracking down information, usually people to interview, but sometimes other kinds of information from libraries and other data sources.

The writer of creative nonfiction searches and searches for large truths, and for bits and pieces he or she hopes will add up to something larger. This kind of research is valid for the nonfiction writer. He or she searches in the libraries, the information retrieval services, and through interviews with significant others somehow connected with the topic or with the main person to be interviewed, and constantly observes, observes, observes. The writer notes everything he or she comes across, not just the data that's on pages or screens. He or she observes the real world that surrounds the situation.

The creative nonfiction writer observes through his or her senses, not considering them as somehow invalid as research tools. He or she knows that writing good nonfiction, and especially creative nonfiction, will require an appeal here and there to the reader's senses, and thus collects data of this kind just as he or she collects other kinds of more obviously relevant information. The writer may take an actual inventory of his or her senses, pondering the evidence of smell, hearing, and touch in addition to that of sight. This research isn't limited to the true senses; the writer will also make note of any emotions at work in the scene. He or she won't write about "emotions," but will collect instances of what people did that implies, or belies, their emotions and report those actions. The reader will infer the emotion behind the action.

The writer will collect other kinds of information about the "environment" immediately involved: what kind of neighborhood a man's business is in; what the exterior of the building looks like; the outer office; the inner office; his home neighborhood; his house; what kind of car, train, or bus he uses; the state of the weather during any scenes described. If possible, the writer may go to the interviewee's childhood hometown.

One of the most instructive and enjoyable evenings I've experienced was at the New York Public Library when David McCullough talked to a group of two hundred people interested in learning how a biographer goes about researching. This was the second in a series of six evenings when different biographers spoke about their profession. The series was co-sponsored by the library and the Book-of-the-Month Club. The talks came out in a 1986 book edited and introduced by William Zinsser, author and general editor at BOMC. The book, *Extraordinary Lives: The Art and Craft of American Biography*, presents the talks given by biographers Robert Caro, David McCullough, Paul Nagel, Richard Sewall, Ronald Steel, and Jean Strouse. Anyone interested in reading or writing biography should read it.

During his talk, "The Unexpected Harry S. Truman," McCullough talked principally about the research for his then upcoming book about that fascinating haberdasher from Independence, Missouri. He talked a great deal about the personal observations that added so much to his "regular" research findings. If you want to know Harry S. Truman, he suggested, you'd better know Independence, Missouri. One way to know your subject is to get to know the territory, the ground your man walked on. Know the neighbors—whether or not they tell the whole truth and nothing but the truth. Sometimes, McCullough observed, it's not the things you go out researching for, but the little things that pop up serendipitously, that will make a line or a chapter come to life.

A problem with interviewing the neighbors of recently famous people is that many of them have probably been "interviewed out." You have to listen intently for the facts and color they give you, but you have to have one ear cocked for the "schtick" or spiel that comes from having told the same story so many times to reporters, tourists, and biographers. McCullough advised listening carefully for dropped names, names you suddenly realize you've seen (or not seen) in all your reading—and here's someone bringing that anonymous name alive for you. It may even open up a trail to tread for further information that may or may not end up in the biography.

"Getting on the ground," McCullough stressed, is the key to finding the concrete details to lend the ring of truth to your manuscript: the courthouse square, the Victorian homes with the huge old elms and maples out front, the wooded hills outside of town, the old swimming hole where your person may have swung on a tire hung from an old willow. You can't get these details from your library research.

He mentioned the primary research sources to be found at the local library—e.g., local newspapers. Seldom found in major out-of-town libraries, these papers may talk about your person or topic during the very time that's of significance to you. You can't dig up that great material elsewhere, not even through electronic retrieval systems, wonderful as they are. Know the territory; get on native ground. Go; dig. These thoughts are just as relevant for other kinds of creative nonfiction writing as they are for biographical research.

I've been talking a lot about interviewing, but mainly about interviewing people peripheral to your person or topic. Note that I speak often as though I mean only interviewing about a celebrity, a V.I.P.. But what I write is relevant to your research about atomic energy, the agricultural crisis, or the trouble with education. Almost inevitably, you'll need to interview one or more people with information on your topic, so the interview is of central importance. You must develop the skills necessary to make your interviews as effective (and as enjoyable) as possible. Approached in the right frame of mind, interviews can be the most satisfying part of the research effort. Approached with the wrong frame of mind (or with poor preparation) the process can be a terrifying and useless undertaking.

THE PURPOSE OF INTERVIEWING

Almost any feature article for a newspaper, a story for a news magazine, a story for a corporate employee magazine or newsletter, requires that you get out and talk with people involved. The interview is the cornerstone for most nonfiction articles and books because interviews add so much:

1. They add *fresh ideas*, ideas you might never have come up with on your own.

2. They provide *different angles, views, perspectives, insights* on the person or the topic under study.

3. They give you *names of other people* you might interview, people you might never have thought of sitting back home in your study.

4. The interviewee may mention *other authorities* you should read for further background.

5. You may hear of *journals, book titles,* even *specialist conferences* you might attend.

6. Very important—interviews will provide you *words, jargon, specialist language,* and *more detailed knowledge* that will lend authority or credibility to your article or book.

7. AND, they enable you to *people your article or book,* an extremely important element in most creative nonfiction. An article that never gives us *people* tends to turn us off after a while. We identify with people. People, by their nature, vivify writing. They bring to it *life*.

Preparing for the Interview

Anything that will provide you all the above information should be well worth preparing and preparing hard for. I won't say a great deal about these preparations because you should read other books specializing in the art of interviewing, books such as *The Craft of Interviewing* (John Brady); *Creative Interviewing* (Ken Metzler); or *Depth Reporting* (Neal Copple). But here are a few hints:

1. Be more than certain about seemingly trivial items: the interviewee's exact address, floor number, room number; check at least once with someone else the agreed-upon date and hour for the meeting; and confirm these details at least several days in advance. (There's nothing worse than flying to Chicago and finding that you were to have interviewed your person the day before.)

2. Arrive early so you can go into the interview relaxed. Come well-groomed yourself, and have with you well-groomed equipment: tape recorder with fresh batteries, clean tape heads, working pens and pencils, plenty of appropriate tapes and notebooks.

3. Bring prepared "questions" to explore. These questions grow out of your own curiosity, your own intuitive understanding, your library research, your interviews with significant others, and from holes you've discovered in your information wherever obtained. Not that you should have a lengthy list of all possible questions that could be asked. This list is a MUST list—only those questions you realize you must not leave the interview without answers for.

I subscribe to the notion that you should prepare yourself thoroughly for the interview, but John McPhee, an interviewer of great skill, says that he acts on a different premise. He says he'd rather begin his interview as a *tabula rasa*, his mind a clear slate. Someone of his obvious intelligence and knowledge is never a completely clean slate, but he says that he likes to walk into the first interview with only his intelligence and curiosity to guide him. He fears that if he has studied up too much on the topic or the person, he may appear to know more than he does, perhaps unintentionally encouraging the interviewee to hold back some essential information, presuming that McPhee must already know that. McPhee may have a point there; there's a very human tendency to show off just how much the interviewer knows—in a vain attempt to impress the interviewee and perhaps establish a better rapport. Better, McPhee says, to risk sounding a little on the dull side, so that the interviewee will take on a teacher role and provide all kinds of information that might otherwise be held back. The interviewer should, nevertheless, demonstrate that the points are getting through, that he or she is a quick and appreciative learner—not to the point of showing off, but just enough that the teacher-interviewee will continue in the role McPhee has clandestinely assigned him.

Conducting the Interview

Interviews are difficult to do well because the interview is an unnatural act. It's forced; there's a pretense, an artificiality to it. Because of that, both the interviewee AND the interviewer are generally uptight about the interview process. An analog would be the situation when you tell someone that you want to take some *candid* photographs of them. Almost anyone feels obliged to *act* before the camera's insistent eye. They're suddenly not themselves; they're actors on stage. Other people react differently; they freeze up before the camera's implacable eye. Since most of us go through life watching other people in the spotlight, we're embarrassed and self-conscious when the spotlight suddenly puts us center stage. In either case, candid does not describe the result; artificial and superficial do. We must do whatever is necessary to DE-FUSE the situation as soon as possible. We've got to get things into a conversational mode.

Using the Tape Recorder

Another element in the interview process is the business of recording what transpired. Should the writer rely on memory, note taking, or tape recording? Only that rare person with almost photographic (or audiographic) memory should attempt the first. Recording on paper what's said while it's being said is the time-honored method, and many interviewers, especially men and women long experienced at this before the arrival of dependable tape recorders, swear that this is the best. It seems to me that tape recording has so many advantages that it's hardly worth discussing anymore. It's been argued that a tape machine, no matter how small and unobtrusive, makes it more difficult to develop that feeling of a conversation I've said is so important. But consider the alternative:

What's so conversational about one of the two people scribbling away like mad, flipping back through the notebook to find something said earlier, scratching something out, asking for a quote verification, and periodically flipping back to the list of prepared questions? Compare this with two people conversing comfortably about the subject while a tape recorder silently records everything. Certainly, the interviewer may occasionally also write something on a pad, but most of the time he or she retains good eye contact with the interviewee—one of the most important attributes of a conversation. How can you retain good eye contact while scribbling in a notebook? I won't say much more about the value of a tape recorder method of interview recording, but I'll emphasize the obvious: There's no better way to get accurate and complete quotes.

The interview is one of the most complex mental exercises you are apt to be called upon to conduct. Considering how many distinct activities the brain must undertake simultaneously, I liken it to that of an air traffic controller at Chicago's O'Hare Field during the Christmas holidays, with a heavy snowfall during prime landing time. It's not unlike the simultaneous thinking processes going on in the brain of a television technical director producing a live news show with multiple "feeds" coming in live from around the world, slides coming in from a projector, film coming in from a film chain, and three cameras operating, not to mention a live radio feed from Beirut supplemented by a videotape that's just arrived by plane. In the midst of voices coming over the headphones and people handing him or her notes, the director has to instruct and coordinate (in real time) the activities of a half-dozen people—and the living room viewer must not be allowed to sense the chaotic control room scene. Everything must seem under cool, professional control. If that seems too much an exaggeration, consider what goes on in the interview situation. I remind you of this not to frighten you unduly but to point up why you should be prepared—and why a tape recorder may be your best friend.

SIMULTANEOUS ACTIVITIES

You're asking questions from the prepared list.

You're writing down the answers to the prepared list.

You're asking new, unplanned questions that evolve.

You're writing down the answers to the new questions.

AND you're THINKING about all that's being said and all that's going on: What's the idea *behind* that response? What other possible meanings lurk between the lines? Is something being held back? What? How can I get at any of this through a new line of questioning? Should I phrase it evocatively or provocatively?

You're *recapping* the interview (internally and sometimes externally): Am I *getting* it? Like the air traffic controller, have I got the whole picture of the situation upstairs? Am I alert to everything that's going on, or am I too hung up on the prepared Q&A's? What else should I ask now or later in view of what's being said at the moment? Should I stick to my prepared "must" questions, or follow up right now on this fascinating new stuff that's developing right before my eyes, stuff I never dreamed would come up when I was making up my list? Which will finally be of more interest to my readers, answers to the prepared questions or answers to this new and intriguing but tangential material?

You're *monitoring* the interview (externally and internally):

You're periodically monitoring the tape recorder dials and reels.

You're monitoring your subject's answers for any contradictions occurring:

between what the subject said a few minutes and what he or she is now saying;

between what the subject said in some other place and what he or she is now saying.

You're asking yourself? How can I explore that contradiction with new questions or with provocative statements? Do I sense in that apparent contradiction duplicity, or simply a change of mind—remembering that everyone does not have to be consistent forever (and remembering that Emerson called a foolish consistency the hobgoblin of little minds).

And you're listening for any contradictions between the *words* used now versus those used earlier; is the *tone* the same? Is the *body language* consistent or contradictory as the subject gives this apparent contradiction or inconsistency?

You're *observing* the dynamics and the details:

any repetitive gestures (that might vivify a narrative)

any repetitive words or phrases

any characteristic body language by the interviewee

if your own body language betrays your feelings (to yourself and, perhaps involuntarily, to the interviewee)

environmental details that might lend authority or sensory interest to the narrative—or give insight into the person's character or lifestyle: the TEXTURE of the setting—people around, weather outside; "weather" in the room; any extraneous events surrounding the interview but not a part of it (e.g., the sound of workmen hammering outside may affect the thinking and the emotional responses of interviewer and interviewee—and that sound may have different "meanings" to each participant)

interactions, physical and psychological, between you and the person interviewed; between the interviewee and his or her staff, friends, associates, spouse, pets, etc. that may happen within the time of interviewing

the subject's behavior toward outside interruption (e.g., the phone or the intercom) during the interview

exterior environment: his or her office, outer office, lobby, the building's exterior architecture, the neighborhood...

THE TWO BASIC INTERVIEW TYPES

The Shopping List Interview

The so-called "shopping list" interview is the familiar Question and Answer (Q&A). It's a quick-in/quick-out technique, it's fast and easy to do, so some writers like to use it. Some magazines overuse it, in my estimation. It depends solely on the list of planned and written-down questions (sometimes, but not always, given in advance to the interviewee). Because it goes so fast, so efficiently, it tends not to be so effective. Its great disadvantage is that there's no time to develop a good rapport between participants. Without rapport, there's little trust developed in either direction. Without trust, there's little credibility developed. The interview is marked by superficiality and artificiality, pretending to offer the interviewee conversation, but providing a formal list of questions with no, or little, leeway for the free flow of ideas. The result of its formality is that the interviewee will be guarded in his or her responses, and the responses are apt to be as succinct (or at least as short) as the questions. If you're in a hurry, of course, that's to your advantage, but if you want a useful exchange, it has to be a conversation, not an interrogation. That is the great disadvantage to a shopping list interview—it is definitely not a conversation, yet conversation, or the feel of it, is what's needed. This can be achieved only by the so-called *in-depth interview* format.

The In-depth Interview

If the major drawback of the quick-in/quick-out Q&A interview is that it does not resemble a conversation so much as an interrogation, and if the failure to develop a conversational tone prevents the establishment of rapport between the participants, you must use whatever devices you can to get as soon as possible into a conversational mode.

First, you must generate in yourself (if it's not already there) a genuine interest in the person or topic you're interviewing about. If your interest is nonexistent or minimal, it will show. It'll show in your voice, in your eyes, in your body language, and in the framing of your original questions—and certainly in your responses as the interview progresses. If you can bring sincerity and empathy into the interview, you'll be 80 percent there. Sincerity, empathy, and genuine personal interest are the ingredients that promote trust and rapport with the interviewee. It's also wise to realize that if you should be conducting multiple interviews about the same person or topic, word will get around quickly that you are interviewing. If you do poorly, for whatever reason, with the first several interviewees, you'll enter subsequent interviews at a distinct disadvantage. If you have been too pushy, nasty, or insensitive, or if you've spoken ill of the first interviewee to the second one, you might imagine your reception and lack of rapport with interviewee number three. People will open up fully only with someone perceived as accurate, trustworthy, sensitive—human.

The Questioning Process

Before you can get into the meat of an interview, you've got to slip into something comfortable—a conversational mode. At first, it may feel stiff, but if you handle the first few minutes well, this unreal conversation will evolve into a real one. Naturally, a lot depends on the person interviewed and his or her willingness or ability to slide into a genuine conversation with a stranger. I'm talking here only about what you can do from your end to establish as soon as possible this conversational feeling.

Many interviewers have with them a list of warm-up questions, questions they've found through experience will put a person at ease, from which they can fall easily into conversation. I think of them as "fall-back insurance," in case you can't find a more natural way into a conversational mode.

If possible, use a more organic method, i.e., find something in the situation, the setting, the day's news (even the weather) to get the two of you talking in a relaxed way. If, for example, you see on the person's shelves a series of golf trophies, it would be better to ask about those (an organic entry) than to ask a typical warm-up question: "What sports do you like?" or "What do you do to relax when not working?" If you see photographs or paintings of children, comment about them, rather than ask from your list of warm-up questions, "Do you have any children?" Even if the photographed children turn out to be his or her nieces and nephews, you're off on a very human level talking about some children who are obviously significant to the interviewee for some reason. What is that reason?

Listen, really listen, to the responses about the children. If you're lucky you may find in the discussion about them something from which you can logically (and organically) launch the actual interview. The discussion, for example, might bring out that the children are, indeed, the interviewee's children and they were at the time of the photograph living in Yahats, Oregon, because that's where she was born, too, and where she returns still every summer to work on her books. (Ah ha!) "What book are you working on now?" "What is it about Yahats that helps you write?" "Which of your other books did you write there?" "Do you think that many authors have certain places that seem to turn on their creative juices?" "I've read many definitions of creativity, but what is it?" There's no telling where that latter discussion will go, but it may lead to other writers' and friends' names which will provide you further questions—or lead you to them for follow-up interviews.

Go with the flow of the conversation, bringing it back into line with new, cleverly invented questions (or old ones you've been waiting to ask from your prepared list and can now slip into the conversation organically).

Act and *react* as you would in a true conversation. Don't jump on certain answers with an accusatorial tone, unless you are an investigative reporter deliberately trying to provoke the person. If an answer stimulates you, pursue it . . . but perhaps a little later on. If you are perceived as a pouncer, the person will put his or her guard back up, the guard you've been trying so hard to lower.

Keep your opinions to yourself, no matter how difficult it may be for you if you're not of a reticent temperament. True, this makes it an unreal conversation for you, but your readers are more interested in the interviewee's opinions than in yours. Feel the person out to plumb the dimensions of his or her opinions, but don't offer yours too often or too obviously. Just ask evocative questions, the kind that pull out further meaning, not the kind that might make the person wish they'd never offered the opinion in the first place. Your job is to find out for your readers what this person thinks about anything. If you're too confrontational about your questioning, the source will soon dry up, and you'll be forced back into a shopping list mode.

Ask open-ended questions, the type that cannot be answered easily by a simple yes, no, or maybe.

Ask "why." A simple "why?" may be the most productive question you'll ever ask. Even when you think you know the answer, ask it. Don't be afraid to look less than a genius; ask it. The answer may surprise you.

Probe the abstract or vague answer. Sometimes, an abstract or vague answer will be completely innocent of deception; at other times, such an answer may be the obvious head of obfuscation rising up to confound you. The only way to find out, for sure, is to ask for details. You'll want details for your readers' ease of comprehension anyway, but the asking for details may flush out obfuscatory intentions. If that happens, PROBE, PROBE, PROBE.

Don't be afraid of "dumb" questions. Someone has said, and often been quoted, "The only dumb question is the question not asked." We all hesitate to ask something that may expose our innocence or our ignorance. Ignore that self-protecting temptation; ask the question. You're not in the interview to demonstrate how much you know about something; you're there to find interesting and informative materials for your readers. Asking questions will uncover what you're looking for—and sometimes the seemingly dumb question will unearth things you never dreamed of.

Ask simple questions. They are often the most fertile, growing the best answers. Oriana Falacci, one of the best-known interviewers, has often been cited for the simple question she asked an astronaut, the type of question most of us would hesitate to ask someone presumably so brave: "Were you scared?" The straightforward reply was informative, interesting, and surprising. "Yes," he answered, and that led to a relaxed conversation between them from that point on. She may have known very well what he would say; she wanted to hear him say it—and what he had to say about it. Unasked, the question could not have been answered.

Elicit anecdotes. During your preliminary interviews with significant others, you have undoubtedly collected a few anecdotes about your main person, or about the topic of your research, but now is the time to get some of the most useful ones. Ken Metzler, author of *Creative Interviewing*, advises us not to ask directly: "Have you got an interesting anecdote that I can use to delight my readers?" That will often draw a blank, or some long, involved story that you can't use. Instead, just keep your ears open for "little stories" the person tells—those are anecdotes.

Keep alert, too, for the potential for a "little story" in what the person is saying at the moment. If the interviewee has mentioned something general about some kind of behavior, ask whether that's ever happened to him or her. Let your subject spin out the little story—and be quiet for a few seconds after he or she stops. The first story may well trigger another one. Then, if you'll "allow" the person to keep pulling up a whole string of memories, you may get all you need. If, however, he or she doesn't come up with a second one (after you've let a few seconds of silence go by) tell one on yourself. That will not only develop further rapport between you, it may also elicit further ones from the subject him as he or she sort of tops yours.

Unless the interviewee is also a writer, he or she may not understand what an "anecdote" is, and how you may use it, so just ask for examples of anything. Don't even ask for "stories"; that may elicit more than you wanted—more words, anyway. The word "example" connotes brevity, and that's probably what you seek. If you then want more words about the example, just ask "why?" or "how come?" or "how's that?" or "why do you feel that way?" These are all open-ended questions meant to elicit or evoke responses.

If you want to encourage the person to come up with more and better anecdotes, act interested, enthusiastic, enthralled, or fascinated by the "little story" evoked. Anyone likes to be appreciated for what he or she says, so show your appreciation (even if you have to stretch a little). Your subject will be tempted to find better and better stories that will elicit from you further appreciation of his or her talent at storytelling. You may use only one or two, but your reader will benefit from your clever eliciting.

Probe for the human side. When you write about a person, especially an "important" personage, one who seems "above us all," you must find ways to remind your readers that this person is a human being not too terribly different from them. They know that he or she is, in fact, very different, but if they can "identify" with some common element behind the mask, they'll feel they understand the person better.

SOME NEGATIVE ADVICE

1. Don't stick rigidly to your prepared list of questions, but have it ready. Try, instead, to play off the conversation *in progresso*. Appear to be inventing the question on the spot, i.e., don't use the formal words as found on your list. Try to use in your oral wording something just said in the interview. Even when that question was far down on your list, work it in now when it has arisen naturally in conversation.

2. Don't steer the conversation—don't lead the jury. Be careful how you word the question so as not to lead the interviewee (unconsciously, perhaps) to go in a direction you wish he or she would go. An apparent tangent may lead to an even more interesting destination, given a chance.

3. Don't fill in conversational gaps. In ordinary, everyday conversations, we all have a fear of "dead air." We jump into a silence and fill it with anything, *garbage, anything.* The interview is not a normal conversation (try as hard as you may to achieve that), so you should act accordingly. Deliberately leave long pauses unfilled. The possible benefit to your purposes is that the interviewee will jump into the gap and start shovelling desperately to fill it, fearing that the interview will look like it's not going well—and he or she may fill it with material he didn't intend to bring up at all. You may hear things tumbling out that you would never in the world have asked—either through sensitivity or through ignorance. After the person says something genuinely interesting, say "wow" or something else to show that you "got" it and liked it, but don't follow it up with other

words or a further question. Just leave that conversational gap for the interviewee to fill.

4. Don't hesitate to revisit earlier questions and answers. After a few minutes of interview, don't be afraid to return to an earlier answer that you didn't fully understand when given, one that seemed fertile but then the interview went off on some new tack, an answer that NOW, with the benefit of hindsight and further information, seems even more significant than it did then. Ask the question in a new way, perhaps, so that the interviewee won't feel abused by being asked the identical question again. Check for inconsistencies. Revisit any question that obviously struck a sour note at the time. You didn't follow it up then because you didn't want to offend the person, or you wanted time to consider the implications before probing a bit more. The trick is to revisit with different wording each time you recycle—and you may wish to recycle a particular question several times.

Revisiting or recycling is a good technique because:

1. You may get better answers now, after good rapport has developed.

2. You may get altogether different answers. If the inconsistency is great, you may want to probe more right now, or revisit again in a few minutes to see what answer then comes out.

3. You may get something totally new, something not even mentioned in the previous answer(s).

Interviewing for Subjective Reality

Although I didn't label it as such, all the previous discussion about interviewing and other research methods had to do with what is sometimes called "objective reality." The writer conducts his or her research to develop material that will be useful in re-creating for the reader just the way things occurred and looked at the time. The New Journalists, and now the creative nonfiction writers, say that the objective reality is not the only reality. There is also the subjective reality—the emotional life of a person, what goes on in his or her mind. Critics of the kind of writing we're talking about in this book think that as soon as the writer leaves objective reality and begins to dip into the subjective reality of a person's emotions and thoughts, he or she is leaving the world of journalism and entering the world of fiction. Creative nonfiction writers maintain that one can present the reader a more complete, more accurate picture of reality by presenting the objective AND the subjective realities of a situation. Everyone lives in a world made up of both realities, so why not report on them?

How can you possibly know what another person thinks? the critics ask. They forget, of course, that when they interview people, they accept what an interviewee says—presumably because he or she doesn't merely "think" it or "feel" it, but actually "says" it. Why not accept what a person says in an interview about what he or she thinks or feels—and report it? If you do report this subjective reality, you must make it clear to the reader that it is what the interviewed person said about his or her feelings and thoughts.

Some creative nonfiction writers, like Tom Wolfe, invent internal monolog for the interviewed person. Wolfe says he can do it because he has researched and interviewed at length, frequently weeks and months, so that he can accurately capture what that person would be apt to think during some event. Some would say that a person of Wolfe's intelligence, imagination, and willingness to dig deep probably can create a monolog that approximates what the person might think, feel, or say—but in how many other writers would we have that much faith?

John McPhee, interviewed by Norman Sims for his book *The Literary Journalists*, said that we cannot get into another person's head and think for him or her. In McPhee's series of excellent books, he tells us in one way or another how the characters feel about something, but he says he never invents what they say they feel—that always comes from the interview. Like Tom Wolfe, John McPhee practically lives with the people he writes about, so that what he writes about their thoughts and feelings is undoubtedly accurate—not only as to details but as to tone.

Tom Wolfe, in Chapter 2 of *The New Journalism*, wrote this about that phenomenon, he being its leading spokesman:

> The idea was to give the full objective description plus something that readers had always had to go to novels and short stories for: namely, the subjective or emotional life of the characters. That was why it was ironic when both the journalistic and literary old guards began to attack this new journalism as "impressionistic." The most important things one attempted in terms of technique depended upon a depth of information that had never been demanded in newspaper work. Only through the most searching forms of reporting was it possible, in nonfiction, to use whole scenes, extended dialogue, point-of-view, and in-

terior monologue. Eventually I, and others, would be accused of "entering people's minds." . . . But exactly! I figured that was one more doorbell a reporter had to push.

Rather than "impressionistic," which implies by analogy to painting that much of the detail is left out of such writing, creative nonfiction is actually more of a "realistic" painting than is regular news reporting. Regular news reporting leaves out the entire realm of the subjective, leaving an "impression" painted by a pile of facts hastily dabbed on the canvas and information from sometimes rather rapid-fire interviews smeared across to give a semblance of truth. Much is, of necessity, left out by "objective" news reporting, making it, not creative nonfiction, the impressionistic mode of expression.

Gay Talese, in Ronald Weber's *The Reporter As Artist*, said this on writing about what another person is thinking:

> I attempt to absorb the whole scene, the dialogue and mood, the tension, drama, conflict, and then try to write it all from the point of view of the persons I am writing about, even revealing whenever possible what these individuals are *thinking* during those moments that I am describing.

Talese has said, too, that he believes he can more accurately reflect a person's thoughts about something than could that person him- or herself, particularly if that person is not a writer. Talese added that this presumes that he's been studying the person a long time, perhaps months. He's interviewed his subject on many occasions on various topics, and he's asked what the person thought about the particular topic. He feels that a clever writer (like himself) can bring out meanings through words much better than the average person he interviews can—especially if the person is merely quoted in casual conversation. No one speaking extemporaneously uses words so well as a professional writer can with lots of time to compose. Talese concludes that he is fairer and more accurate in his reporting when he uses *indirect quotes* than when he uses the expected *direct* quotes. I'll add that while direct quotes give the "impression" of objectivity and accuracy, if a professional writer revises the interviewee's words into a clearer statement, it may, in the end, represent a more accurate expression of the person's thoughts. Talese reminds us always to do as he does: Attribute any indirect quote to its source. This practice requires the ultimate in careful thinking and wording, else one can either unintentionally distort the person's message or intentionally make the person seem to support some point the writer desires to make. The ethical journalist must always keep this in mind.

Two examples from Gay Talese's *Honor Thy Father* demonstrate how he puts into practice indirect quotes in telling us what a person was *thinking* at the time discussed:

> The men slept in shifts through June and July, constantly on the alert for any intrusion, but nothing happened. The monotony, Bill thought, the monotony is maddening, and he was tempted at times to leave again for California; but each time he resisted, fearful that a disaster would strike moments after his departure.

> The children talked excitedly, and Rosalie sat quietly next to Bill, feeling frustration and guilt. She wished that she had found out ahead of time the main reason why both parents had been invited; if she had, she might have protected Bill from that which made him most vulnerable, his ego.

In the second quote, Talese used two approximate equivalents of thinking: *feeling* and *wished*. Whether using *thinking, feeling,* or *wished,* he was not thinking *for* Bill or Rosalie—he had gotten these thoughts, feelings, and wishes from them in a long series of interviews.

Emotional content enables us to create dramatic, vivid, accurate scenes. A scene that lacks "emotional" content will likely be less than successful as a scene. An article full of scenes without emotional content may not fail, but it would probably not qualify as creative nonfiction.

Be as gracious at the end of an interview as you were in the beginning: You may want to come back for a second interview; you may want to ask further questions by telephone later; OR you may want to interview this same person (or his or her colleagues) for a different article or book at a much later date. To use the common aphorism, "Don't burn your bridges behind you."

A part of being gracious and professional is to inform the interviewee just how things go from there: what happens next; when the article might be published; what happens to the tape; and some inside information about the writing, editing, and publishing process, if the person seems not to be familiar with the process. You probably will not want to send the person drafts for approval, but you may say that you'd like to be able to call back to verify any facts, dates, etc. When the article comes out, send a copy immediately. After all, they've given you their time and expertise—the only thing in it for them now is the article's publication.

I recommend that you gain an appreciation for the central importance of the long, hard research work required by this kind of writing by reading any or all of: *The Right Stuff* (Wolfe), *Common Ground* (J. Anthony Lukas), *House* (Tracy Kidder), or *Those Days* (Richard Critchfield).

PROBLEMS ASSOCIATED WITH RESEARCH

A number of problems, or difficulties, plague the research phase of writing creative nonfiction, difficulties not so persistently present for the hard-news, deadline writer who works against his or her own set of difficulties. If you do not have the time, funds (for airplanes, cabs, trains, hotels, research assistance), or persistence enough to pursue research in great depth, more depth than the traditional reporter does, you'd best seek out a different line of work. Reporters speak of how much legwork they have to do to cover a beat or follow a story. Their legwork resembles that needed for the hundred-yard dash; we're speaking here of the legwork required in the marathon.

Some writers who decide to go into creative nonfiction may change their minds when they see that it necessitates getting out from behind the word processor, off the comfortable chair, and out into the sometimes uncomfortable world outside. They may also change their minds when they discover that they have to follow their people around for weeks or months, almost like a bird dog, immersing themselves in the subject, saturating themselves in data and details.

If you go into this line of writing work, you'll have to work with all your senses operating at peak efficiency all the time. You'll try to sense the world with your antennae erect and alert—you've got to try to take it all in. Without this sensory inventory to draw on, once you're back in the office, your writing will not have the creative edge required for this kind of writing. You have to be willing (happily) to dig into that which smells bad (as well as that which smells wonderful) and listen to that which repels (as well as that with which you agree). All this sensory acquisition will provide the concrete and sensory details you'll need to create for your reader the objective reality of the situation. You'll need, too, to dig deep into the emotional side of those interviewed, finding out their innermost thoughts and feelings, if you're to give your readers that subjective reality which, when combined artfully with the objective reality, will paint for them as honest and accurate a picture of the world as it's possible for you, a fallible human, to paint.

One difficulty associated with staying close to a subject is that you may get too emotionally involved, a problem the deadline writer doesn't generally face so often. After weeks or months of research and interviewing, you may love or hate the person. In either case, your writing may tear your heart out. You know that what you finally write will affect this person's future. Can you stay neutral about the subject to be fair? *Should* you? Should you take a position and then build your case while remaining as objective as you can? Should you withhold anything from your article or book? Should you withhold anything from legal authorities? As a sensitive writer, such questions, quandaries, and dilemmas may hurt you deeply. You may feel guilty about your necessary voyeurism. You'll have ask penetrating questions that probe where the person is extra sensitive. That may be just what needs probing, but your sense of propriety may prevent your probing deep enough. If you think that your personality cannot handle such questions without shattering itself, you'd better look around for other writing jobs.

Much creative nonfiction revolves around events and people, and unless you're writing history, you'll want to be present—on the scene—when the events happen. Since you can't control when an event will occur, and since you can't force your interviewees to adapt to your schedule, you have to work almost always within someone else's framework—certainly within the sometimes unpredictable framework of events. They happen when they happen—not when you wish they would.

If you're profiling a person, his or her "events" or "scenes" may have no predictable schedule at all—they just happen when life wants them to happen. Luck may put you there when the great scene unfolds, the scene that'll make your article or chapter leap to life—or you may have gone to Oregon to research some other facet, and miss it. You can't be everywhere at once, but you know you should be. This is a built-in difficulty—it comes with the territory, Willy.

You can see that this kind of research depends a lot on luck and serendipity—things you can't control, so stay clear if you find that you need predictability in your life. The worst case of this happens when the project evaporates. You've put in weeks or months of effort, perhaps all on speculation, and then circumstances unpredictable when you started out fall apart and you're left with your research languishing in notebooks or computer memory.

A book project evaporated on me just recently. When President Reagan fired my daughter and her soon-to-be-husband from their jobs as air traffic controllers, I thought (even in the midst of all that family heartache) that I had the basis for a book about "our air traffic controllers and where they flew" which I'd publish to commemorate the fifth anniversary of the strike and the firing of those 11,400 controllers. Like most of them, my daughter couldn't find a job in her chosen profession. After a year of bartending and chimney sweeping, her husband was hired, along with forty other men, by the Australian equivalent of our FAA. When all these people and their families went "down under" to work, I proposed to write a book centered on this intrepid group and touching lightly on the other thousands. Since that firing so dramatically distorted the lives of so many young families, I thought it a natural—and I had an "in" that most writers would not have. I went to Australia for preliminary interviewing and researching, came back and proposed the book to a number of publishing houses through my agent. I couldn't understand their general response: "By the time the fifth anniversary comes around, no one will even remember the strike, let alone care what happened to all those controllers." I did some more research anyway, before giving up. When the fifth anniversary came around, I found that, indeed, no one remembered the strike, or if they remembered, they couldn't care less. History had moved on—earthquakes had occurred, floods and fires had come and gone, and we had attacked Libya. History has a way of doing that—moving on to other projects. You have to select those topics or people that'll endure—or research and write more rapidly and get the book out there as soon as feasible. Evaporation is a natural phenomenon that affects writers as well as laboratory scientists.

The last problem I'll mention concerns the research itself—over-researching. If you love the research phase of writing, and many do, you may not know when to stop. If the topic has any substance at all, you could probably do secondary research forever. You might even conduct primary research yourself (multiple national mail surveys of public opinion, for example) and just keep going. At some unpredictable time, you'll cross the point of limited returns. Your article or book can handle only so much information, so you'll have to eliminate much of what you've researched so hard to get. The very human tendency is to include as much research-derived information as possible—after all, look at all the time,

money, and effort I've put into the research phase—it seems so w
not to include this, and this, and, of course, that. Don't do it.

The professional may collect tons of information, but only t(
pile to select the best from. Unfortunately, the pile can get so tall that you
won't be able easily to find the best. Winnowing the wheat from the chaff
gets more difficult as the chaff gets excessive. The other problem of over-
researching comes from the time, effort, and money involved in the researching itself. Where does it fail to pay off? That, combined with the
problems associated with winnowing, makes writing tougher, rather
than easier or better. A piece of work not supported by enough research
will show it; a work suffocating under an avalanche of research-derived
information will show it, and may be so burdened as to be unreadable—
or, at least, unread. A writer unread might just as well have stayed in bed.

Implications of ethical considerations run through all these discus-
sions of research methods typically used in writing creative nonfiction.
The writer must design any research with accuracy in mind; report any
results with accuracy as a cornerstone; conduct and report any interviews
within the ethical standards and guidelines established by the various
writing organizations. The next chapter opens up some of the ethical issues inherent in research and writing.

TWELVE

ETHICAL CONSIDERATIONS

Consideration of ethics intrudes on any serious discussion of facts, accuracy, thoroughness, credibility, creativity, or professionalism in any nonfiction writing, but especially in journalistic writing. Entire books have been written on ethics in journalism. We can only brush the surface lightly here, and we can't get at all into the legal implications of unethical behavior. Many books have been written on that subject, too, so we won't even try to touch on it in this book, fascinating as it is. Ethicists and lawyers sometimes clarify these issues for writers; sometimes they don't. I want here only to provide some tips about how a writer can stay ethical. I'll also mention several recent cases where otherwise excellent writers apparently lost track of the absolute requirement that the writer be honest with the reader.

Traditional journalists have fewer difficulties with ethics when they adhere as closely as possible to the facts. The creative nonfiction writer, however, may run into problems because the craft uses techniques borrowed from the fiction writer, making it almost automatically suspect. Skeptics abound in this world, especially in the world of journalists, who make their living as professional skeptics. This skepticism puts an additional burden on the writer of creative nonfiction, or as Norman Mailer has phrased it, the writer of "applied creative writing."

When we write "personal nonfiction," nonfiction (journalistic and otherwise) in which we deliberately insert ourselves into the story, ethics problems diminish in one sense. Since reader skepticism usually derives from the question of credibility, readers of "personal nonfiction" can assess for themselves the reliability of the writer. Traditional journalists, of

217

course, try hard not to write "personally," fearing it will destroy their objectivity. Their readers have to accept at face value the statements made by this faceless, anonymous writer.

When we write "impersonal nonfiction," we have the inherent problem of credibility. A skeptical attitude may sometimes be justified, because the anonymous nonfiction writer, especially when he or she is using fiction techniques heavily, may get carried away and embroider the facts, vary things to make the report more dramatic, more appealing for the reader. As soon as he or she does that, the reporter may cross ethical boundaries, as vague as they are. It's so easy to wander innocently across those fuzzy borders; creative nonfiction writers have to keep their wits about them and behave scrupulously and ethically. It's too easy to fool the reader using fiction techniques, so we must bend over backward to act professionally, i.e., responsibly.

ETHICAL IMPLICATIONS OF TECHNIQUES

I'll proceed here gradually from a discussion of writing techniques that may seem almost outside of any consideration or worry about ethics to techniques considered ethical by some, borderline ethical by some, and definitely unethical by others. It's quicksand terrain, this matter of ethics in writing, and the greenhorn may be sucked under by sands he thought innocent.

Ethical Implications of Diction

The two points I'll make here would probably never come up as a "professional ethics" question, but I sense an ethics component, a personal matter involving a writer, his or her craft, and the reader.

William Safire, in his *New York Times* column "On Language," first brought to my serious consideration the ethics implications of diction. In the column "Caviar, General?" he referred to a "dilemma," which I translated for myself as "an ethical dilemma." He worried around, in that delightful way he does, the problem every writer faces all the time—if you have in mind the perfect word, *le mot juste*, should you use it in the interest of accuracy, even though you realize it will sail loftily over the heads of most of your readers?

Safire posed the dilemma as: "Do you settle for a more generally understood term, thereby pandering to your audience's ignorance—or do you use the unfamiliar word, thereby failing to communicate, and appearing to be a showoff?" Then he summed it up eloquently: "Is your job to communicate or to educate?"

Safire questioned whether to ever use a word that will fly over the audience's heads, and I enjoyed his answer: "Fly over everybody's head only when your purpose is to teach or to tease." He went on to suggest that we should never do it when our purpose at that moment is to persuade.

Since much of our creative nonfiction writing tries to educate (inform) our audience while persuading them, we should take his suggestion and go ahead and use the occasional high-flying, accurate word, PROVIDED we do so in a context that makes clear the meaning. We can even do it by slipping in nearby a phrase or word that's closely synonymous, thereby making the meaning clear, and educating the audience about the meaning of the word. This technique, handled with a lack of empathy for the reader's sensitivity, can fall into a tone of condescension. Better, I think, to gamble that the context will gradually clarify matters, than to condescend, or even appear to condescend to the reader. A well-educated audience actually enjoys learning a new word or a new use for a familiar word (and they'll go to the trouble of looking it up), but they can smell condescension a paragraph away—and they won't come back for more.

Closely related to such "elitist" writing comes jargonistic or specialists' writing. Christopher Lehman-Haupt brought this business to mind in his book review column in the *New York Times*, when he reviewed John McPhee's *In Suspect Terrain*. He made one extremely interesting point not frequently made. The ethical dilemma here was whether the author of a technically oriented book, in this case largely about geology, should use specialists' terminology, or somehow simplify it for the reader. The review reports McPhee's defense of a particularly arcane exchange between two geologists: *It doesn't matter that you don't understand them. Even they are not sure if they are making sense. Their purpose is to try to.*

Lehman-Haupt says that McPhee is partly correct, but that it's maddening for the reader not to understand the author clearly. He also implied that a writer who uses a great deal of specialists' language runs the risk of appearing to put on a show for the specialists. He does like McPhee's work, however, saying that even when you don't fully comprehend what's being said, it is worth going along for the ride, so good is McPhee's writing.

In summary, the reviewer said, " ... you don't have to understand all the details of the talk, as long as you comprehend the talk's significance." It would become an ethical problem only when the writer hides his or her ignorance behind the jargon or specialists' language, or in any other fashion tries to obscure, distort, confuse, or fabricate facts behind the convenient screen of specialists' words.

In the case of elitist language, as in the case of specialized language, the governing criterion is whether you have been honest with the reader. If you can say to yourself that your use of either kind of language was designed only to clarify facts, establish mood, or create a tone to the reader's overall benefit, go ahead and use the language that best does the job.

Ethical Implications of Irony and Humor

Another writing technique frequently employed by creative nonfiction writers, the use of irony and humor, might also seem to have no ethical implications, but they may come close.

The possibility that irony and humor could have an ethical dimension came to me when reading an article by Richard Bernstein in the *New York Times*. He described the interesting competition for French readers between France's major, and largely establishment-oriented, newspaper *Le Monde*, and the rapidly growing paper previously run by Jean-Paul Sartre, *Liberation*.

Liberation is pulling many readers away from the traditional, very staid, very-serious-to-the-point-of-sombre *Le Monde* by writing "creatively" about serious topics. Its tone is not funny; it's ironic. Bernstein quotes French writer Alain Finkelkraut, as saying: "You can hear the chuckle of the journalist audible behind the headlines."

If *Liberation* only poked fun at the news and at the governmental bureaucracy, it would have stayed a small humor sheet, but its writers are serious journalists under it all. Unlike most French papers, which fill their pages with commentary and analysis, not reportage, *Liberation* has taken to sending reporters to the scene to relate what's happening. (Doesn't sound unusual to Americans, but it is unusual there.) There would be no ethical implications if all they did was go for the laughs alone, while calling themselves a humor or parody sheet, but they put themselves forth as a NEWSpaper, so there is the potential for problems. They behave ethically, however, by taking the news and the facts seriously, even though presenting them in an arresting, if sometimes playful, way. As long as they approach matters this way, there should be no major ethical problems. The French, who are said to have a word for everything, may not have a word for the kind of writing produced by *Liberation*, but I'd probably call it creative nonfiction.

The major concern about using irony or humor, especially in journalism, comes about in the reader's mind. The literal-minded person will miss the irony and ascribe the literal meaning to what is said. Since irony very often gets its strength by stating the exact opposite of what's intended, the opportunity for misinterpretation hovers low. A literal-minded person would not have been too well warned by the title of Jonathan Swift's essay back in 1729 ("A Modest Proposal for Preventing the Children of Poor People from Being a Burden to Their Parents or the Country"), but would he or she have been aware of Swift's irony when he wrote in that essay:

> I shall now therefore humbly propose my own thoughts, which I hope will not be liable to the least objection. I have been assured by a very knowing American of my acquaintance in London, that a young healthy child well nursed is at a year old a most delicious, nourishing, and wholesome food, whether stewed, roasted, baked, or boiled; and I make no doubt that it will equally serve in a fricassee or a ragout.

Ethical Implications of Internal Monologs

The use of internal (interior) monolog by creative nonfiction writers has been, and continues to be, the most hotly debated issue in the battle over how far we should go in applying fiction's techniques to nonfiction. Journalists worry most about the use of internal monolog because it appears to overlap too fully into fiction—thereby lowering its credibility in the mind of a skeptical, thoughtful reader. It is the most "creative" technique used in writing creative nonfiction in that the writer invents, the way the fiction writer invents.

Tom Wolfe and Gay Talese, who have been using this technique longer than most, say that they use it cautiously and responsibly. They maintain that it is not pure invention, as it is in fiction. They always write it only after completely immersing themselves in the mind of the person. They get into the person's mind through: interviewing in great depth; observing how the person interacts with others over a long period; working out of letters the person has written and received; using diaries, journals, and anything else that enables them to believe that they can speculate responsibly about that person's thoughts on a subject ("interior states," according to Tom Wolfe). They are sure in their own minds that what they do is ethical because, as we've mentioned before, they dig so deep writing an internal monolog.

Readers may worry about how much to believe of an internal monolog because of the way it sometimes appears on the page. Like fiction's internal monologs or streams of consciousness, the monolog is in italics (although not always); sentences are often incomplete and interrupted by random, disconnected thoughts; and, especially in Wolfe's case, the punctuation may be eccentric, bizarre, unique, and visually exciting. He and the New Journalists went overboard with the freedom of the sixties, and Wolfe still uses internal monologs with unusual punctuation, but in moderation.

Some creative nonfiction writers will not write an internal monolog, figuring it's too far over the line into fiction territory. John McPhee, for example, never uses it, saying that a writer cannot get into another person's head. To imply through internal monolog that the writer has entered and is reporting intracranial happenings borders on the unethical, according to some creative nonfiction writers and probably to all traditional journalists. In the hands of the inept, or the ept but unscrupulous, it is an easy device behind which to hide unethical writing behavior. The beginning writer had best stay away from internal monologs for fear of unintentionally lapsing into unethical writing.

Ethical Implications of Composites and Fabrications in Pursuit of the Larger Truth

A fiction writer very often creates a character by combining facial features from someone the writer knows, a limp from another, and the deep-cracked voice totally out of his or her own imagination. Creating composite characters is not only acceptable and ethical behavior for the fiction writer, it's expected.

When the journalist or creative nonfiction writer, however, creates a composite character and puts that character forth as real, the writer violates the rules of ethical conduct for nonfiction writers. When a writer creates a composite scene made up of bits and pieces of actual scenes or settings, he or she also violates the ethics of the profession. Again, the fiction writer does this all the time to create a more interesting, more dramatic scene or setting. Creative nonfiction writers sometimes do it with the same motivation—but in their case, it's unethical.

On June 18, 1984, *Wall Street Journal* reporter Joanne Lipman wrote in a front-page article that Alastair Reid, who writes for the factually scrupulous *New Yorker*, had for years been creating composite characters and places, and had been publishing them in that magazine as nonfiction. After the *Wall Street Journal* article broke, the *New York Times, Time,* and all the other major papers, magazines, radio and television broadcasts jumped on Reid and his *New Yorker* editor, the highly respected William Shawn, who spoke up for Reid. They seemed to jump a bit more gleefully than one would expect, probably because the *New Yorker*, more than any other publication, had boasted consistently about its scrupulous and hard-working fact-checking department and the magazine's general devotion to accuracy and truth.

Alastair Reid said to reporters that he had spent his career since the fifties creating composite characters and scenes, but all in a sincere effort to get at "the larger truth." *Time* magazine, on its "Essay" page of July 2, 1984, reported that Reid had said: *A reporter might take liberties with the factual circumstances to make the larger truth clear.* Essayist Roger Rosenblatt went on to write that Reid was wrong in assuming that "larger truth is the province of journalism." He added that "where the larger truth is sought, the answer is where it's always been: in history, poetry, art, nature, education, conversation; in the tunnels of one's own mind."

Reporter Lipman complained that in the December 2, 1961, issue of the *New Yorker*, Reid had written in his piece "Letter from Barcelona" about *a small, flyblown bar by the harbor, a favorite haunt of mine for some years because of its buoyant clientele.* Well, *New Yorker* readers loved that flyblown bar, and he says he received letters from people swearing that they'd tracked it down. Unfortunately, Reid now admits that the bar by the harbor doesn't exist—although he insists that it did at one time, but not when he was writing about it, and the conversations he said went on in it actually went on in some other place—in some cases, just in his own head.

The attitude that gets Reid into trouble was the statement that *whether the bar existed or not was irrelevant to what I was after.* He said that he is always after "the poetic whole," that he's like a poet in his concern for conveying the image rather than the mere facts. Coming to his defense, fellow New Yorker Paul Brodeur said that he himself figures that quotes are accurate so long as they *don't do violence to the intent of what was said.* Reporter Lipman wrote that "Brodeur himself subscribes to a form of creative journalism."

William A. Henry III wrote on Time's "Press" page on July 2, 1984: *To critics, it did not matter that Reid's deviations were largely inconsequential. Any departure from fact is the first step on a slippery slope toward unbelievability. Facts are what people can agree on. Truth can be determined by each reader.*

Messrs. Reid, Shawn, and Brodeur may have been genuinely in pursuit of a greater reality, a larger truth, when they created and published their composite characters and scenes, but when a writer gets comfortable with using that fiction technique on inconsequential matters, couldn't he or she slip easily over into using it on more consequential matters—and thus truly violate professional ethics? The consensus of professional writers seems to be that we should not use composites or fabrications of any kind, even for the most inconsequential matters, staying thereby well within the ethics of the profession.

A reporter for the *Washington Post,* Janet Cooke, wrote a story, "Jimmy's World," that won a Pulitzer Prize. A problem developed, a problem of journalistic ethics, a clear case. Jimmy was not a mere composite; Jimmy was a total fabrication of Janet Cooke's imagination. In its embarrassment, the *Post* gave back the Pulitzer Prize, and Janet Cooke resigned. Her letter of resignation, published in the Post, said that "'Jimmy's World' was in essence a fabrication. I never encountered an eight-year-old heroin addict. The September 28, 1980, article was a serious misrepresentation which I deeply regret. I apologize to my newspaper, my profession, the Pulitzer board, and all seekers of the truth. Today, in facing up to the truth, I have submitted my resignation."

In a Master of Arts thesis, "Ethics in Communication: The Case of Two Journalists" (Graduate School of Communication, Fairfield University, Fairfield, Connecticut), its author, Laures J. Lincoln, wrote:

> Jimmy's world is described as a place where people come anxiously to buy drugs and leave in a happy state. "The kitchen and upstairs bed-

rooms are a human collage. People of all shapes and sizes drift into the dwelling and its various rooms, some jittery, uptight and anxious for a fix, others calm and serene after they finally get off."

The story gives a heartbreaking account of how Jimmy's mother started using drugs. It states that Jimmy's mother was raped repeatedly by her mother's boyfriend and Jimmy was the product of one of those rapes. She began to use heroin to forget her worries over this situation. She quickly accepted the offer of heroin from a woman who used to shoot up with her mother. She said "It was like nothing I ever knew before: you be in another world, you know? No more baby, no more mama ... I couldn't quit thinking about it. After I got off, I didn't have to be thinking about nothing."

The end of the story gives a graphic description of Ron shooting up Jimmy after which Ron says, "Pretty soon, man, you got to learn how to do this for yourself."

Reporter Cooke would not reveal to her editors Jimmy's true identity, saying that Jimmy's mother's boyfriend, Ron, threatened to stab Cooke with a knife if she revealed any of their names. Cooke's memo to her editors describing this threat and the surrounding interview filled thirteen and a half pages with minute details about the people and the house where they shot up.

Because the story was so well written, and contained such believable dialog and concrete details, her editors went along even without corroborative evidence in lieu of the principals' identities. They said they had, at first, no reason to suspect her of fabrication. It was a fascinating, if terrifying, story, and they felt it had to be told.

Farther on in her thesis, Laures Lincoln wrote:

The *Washington Post* assigned Bill Green, Ombudsman, to investigate the Cooke hoax. The *Post* dealt with this situation by getting all the facts, listening to Cooke's tapes from her interviews on the story, and reading her notes. After discovering all the events that led to the incident, they printed them in great detail. The *Post* chose to defend themselves by being very verbal about the fraud that had taken place at their newspaper.

The outcome of Mr. Green's investigation became as big a front-page story as Janet Cooke's "Jimmy's World" was. In fact, Mr. Green's investigation included 18,000 words, mostly severe criticisms of the *Post*. He included about 47 interviews with all the people at the *Post* involved in the incident—except Janet Cooke who didn't wish to be interviewed. Mr. Green wrote several stories which detailed the events of the Janet Cooke affair.

Mr. Green's investigation detailed Cooke's background, her progression at the *Post*, and how "Jimmy's World" was published. The investigation also described the ordeal that editors underwent trying to obtain a confession from Cooke.

The thesis concludes that the Janet Cooke affair had a strong impact on daily newspapers: "The most important effect will be the handling of unnamed sources. Most respondents to a *Journalism Quarterly* article, 'How Newspaper Editors Reacted to Post's Pulitzer Prize Hoax,' felt that unnamed sources would be handled more carefully in the future. Most respondents also said that editors would check academic credentials more closely than they had in the past." (The Pulitzer board, once aroused, had checked Cooke's *curriculum vitae* and found that she had lied there, too.)

The *Washington Post* provides its reporters, writers, and editors a guide to ethics in writing for that paper, "Standards and Ethics," which is very detailed, but grows out of the simple set of principles first laid down by Eugene Meyer when he bought the paper in 1933. These statements for ethical writing could apply well to any nonfiction writing—and perhaps particularly to any efforts toward creative nonfiction:

> The first mission of a newspaper is to tell the truth as nearly as the truth can be ascertained.
>
> The newspaper shall tell *all* the truth, so far as it can learn it, concerning the important affairs of America and the world.
>
> As a disseminator of the news, the paper shall observe the decencies that are obligatory upon a private gentleman.
>
> What it prints shall be fit reading for the young as well as for the old.
>
> The newspaper's duty is to its readers and to the public at large, and not to the private interests of its owner.
>
> In the pursuit of truth, the newspaper shall be prepared to make sacrifice of its material fortunes if such course be necessary for the public good.
>
> The newspaper shall not be the ally of any special interest, but shall be fair and free and wholesome in its outlook on public affairs and public men.
>
> These Principles are reendorsed herewith.

Ethical Implications of the Plain Style

One of the most disquieting pieces I've ever read was one by Hugh Kenner, the well-known and highly respected author of books about modern literature. His article in the *New York Times Book Review* (September 15, 1985), "The Politics of the Plain Style," made me clip it out, highlight line after line, and read it time after time. I'm sure I can't do justice to this wonderfully disturbing article, but I'll try to provide its essence.

I found the piece disturbing because I thought at first Kenner might be saying that all the advice I've given in this book, and particularly in *Getting the Words Right*, might lead my readers into unethical writing—hardly my intent. I do find some comfort, of course, in the fact that such world-renowned writers as John McPhee, George Orwell, Joan Didion, and E. B. White have all counseled us to "write plain." Even Jacques Barzun titled his excellent and practical book on rhetoric *Simple & Direct*—another way of saying "Write in the plain style."

Kenner said that the plain, unadorned style began about two hundred years ago in reaction to the previous "high styles" that were esteemed in proportion to their ornateness. The plain style came with the "arrival" of straight, nonpolemical, nonpolitical journalism in newspapers. He says that "the hidden premise" in this new, plain style was that "a man who doesn't make his language ornate cannot be deceiving us." This is the speech of merchants and artisans who handle things and would thus handle words with equal uprightness and honesty, not like the wits and scholars who handle only ideas—and thus are not to be trusted too highly.

Then comes the terrifying premise of his article: *Handbooks and copy editors now teach journalists how to write plainly, that is, in such a manner that they will be trusted. You get yourself trusted by artifice.*

His point, apparently, is that there's something artificial about writing clearly. Therein lies my concern in relation to this chapter—is it a problem in ethics if you deliberately disguise the fact that you're trying to persuade a reader to your way of thinking by writing with plain words, plain images?

He reinforces this notion by writing: *The plain style feigns a candid observer. Such is its great advantage for persuading. From behind its mask of calm candor, the writer with political intentions can appeal, in seeming disinterest, to people whose pride is their no-nonsense connoisseurship of fact.*

And such is the trickiness of language that he may find he must deceive them to enlighten them. Do shades of fascism hover over the plain style?

It took a few readings of the article to leave behind my first interpretation, that we should not use the plain style because it's potentially deceptive—that it only feigns honesty. Finally, I realized that his real message was for the innocent reader, not the honest writer. I had missed the point on the first several times through, but he had made it clear four paragraphs from the end:

> It is clarifying to reflect that the language of fiction cannot be told from that of fact. Their grammar, syntax, and semantics are identical. So Orwell passed readily to and fro between his two modes, reportage and fiction, which both employ the plain style. The difference is that the fictionality of fiction offers itself for detection. If fiction speaks political truths, it does so by allegory.

> That is tricky, because it transfers responsibility for what is being said from the writer to the reader...

I guess this all boils down to two points for us to remember: When we're writers, use the plain style, but understand its potential power to deceive, and write honestly; and, when we're readers, be aware and way of any style, by any writer. Anthony Brandt's column for *Esquire*, "Truth and Consequences: For a Writer Telling the Public What It Has to Know Is Only Half the Battle" (October 19, 1984), ends with an admonition that could serve us all:

> I've learned to pull in my horns, I've learned discretion. I've learned to doubt myself more. I advise my reader to do the same. Beware. Doubt me, doubt my brethren. That way lies the healthy skepticism that will keep us all, readers and writers alike, relatively honest.

You have an unspoken, unwritten, implicit contract with your reader, a contract to tell the truth—whether you're writing fiction or nonfiction. In fiction, you must stay "true to the story," which is different from nonfiction, where you must be true to the facts as you know them. This section deals with the ethics of creative nonfiction, a genre with unique problems, problems growing out of its use, in some cases, of fiction *techniques*, and in other cases of *fiction itself* within an otherwise factual work.

Fictional Bits Within Nonfiction

It doesn't come up too often, but there are times when a nonfiction writer wants to write a short fictional piece, perhaps a paragraph or so, right in the midst of a straight, nonfiction narrative. He or she may want to lapse into fiction: to protect someone's privacy (or forestall a libel suit); to make the same point better, i.e., more colorfully, more entertainingly, more emotionally, and thus more memorably, by inventing a fictional scene; or to get at the "whole truth," the "larger truth," the "greater reality" by introducing some subjectivity—fiction. Bear in mind, though, that Alastair Reid of the *New Yorker* thought he was doing just that.

We can use pure fiction in the midst of nonfiction PROVIDED we *flag* it. We must alert the reader that we've crossed, or are about to cross, over that fuzzy border into fiction territory. We must, for we have a contract with the reader, and without our beloved reader, we writers would whistle in the wind.

Writers have found several flag signals to alert the reader, some more subtle than others. The more subtle, the more artistic. The more artistic, the more dangerous. A balance must be struck between not wanting to be too obvious, too intrusive about it, and wanting to be sure that the code of ethics is not violated by being so subtle that the reader fails to see where the nonfiction leaves off and the fiction begins.

One subtle yet clear way is to italicize the fiction parts. A writer may "get away with" the fiction, i.e., be within the bounds of ethics, if he or she uses merely the italics to flag the fictional parts, but it would be more professional and ethical if he or she also made some reference, outside the italicized portion, to the "previous speculation," or "that fictional look at the future," or some such supplemental signal.

Sometimes the fiction will be in the form of a short internal monolog. The reader who stops to think about it will, of course, realize that the writer could not have known exactly what the person was thinking, but it's more ethical to use additional flagging or warning devices, such as: "she may have been thinking," "he could well have thought to himself," "perhaps she said to herself that day," or "perhaps he said something to himself like...."

We can use words like *probably, possibly,* or *apparently* to reinforce periodically that we are using speculative writing—fiction. Even though you think you've set it out clear enough earlier on, your implicit contract to deal honestly requires that you remind the reader that you've slipped out of nonfiction territory into the land of fiction.

I've talked so far only about those regular nonfiction articles in which fiction, true fiction, is inserted for whatever motivation into the nonfiction narrative. Creative nonfiction articles and books may do that too, but our concern here is with the use of fiction techniques in regular nonfiction work. The same contract stands—you must be honest with the reader.

We can more easily violate unintentionally our implicit contract in creative nonfiction writing, which in some critics' minds is always right on the edge, if not over the edge, of fiction. Obviously, it's impractical to flag every place where we're being "creative," and not "factual" (because we're always true to the facts while presenting them in a creative way). But we've got to honor our contract and tell the reader what we're up to.

The lead editorial in the *New York Times* (October 5, 1986) gave us a fine example of a major newspaper using a creative nonfiction technique. Try to identify the technique, and consider whether the readers were adequately informed that the *Times* (All the News That's Fit to Print) was playing with fiction.

The President, Imagined

No, says a spokesman, the President won't have a news conference before he leaves to meet Mikhail Gorbachev in Reykjavik. It's a special shame, and not just because Mr. Reagan has averaged only seven a year. Rarely has the public so needed to hear from the President.

Then what's the next best thing? A simulation. It's easy to imagine reassuring Presidential answers to three urgent questions.

Q. Mr. President, you've left much confusion about your policy on lying to the public. Did your Administration lie in order to promote news articles that would rattle Libya's Colonel Quaddafi?

A. Well, it has never been our policy to mislead or lie to the media, ever. If a misguided official might have done so in this matter, I regret it and want now to reaffirm our commitment to truth. We know how freely Communist... (and the answer went on)

Q. Sir, you took an unusually stubborn position on sanctions against South Africa, even after Congress passed them. Now both houses have overridden your veto, will you carry out the law ungrudgingly?

A. Well, I'm not happy about Congress taking over executive branch responsibility for conducting foreign policy. But the law stands higher than... (and the answer went on)

Q. Mr. President, some of your supporters think you made a bad deal for a Soviet spy and fear you'll come back from Reykjavik empty-handed.

A. Well, it's way too early to second-guess a deal because so far, there is no deal. What there is between... (and on)

Thank you, Mr. President.

I have to admit that when I first skimmed (too rapidly, perhaps) that editorial on the morning it arrived, I thought it was truly a typical Q&A exchange with a *New York Times* reporter, or perhaps at a presidential press conference. After a while, it dawned on me that the whole exchange was a cleverly written bit of creative nonfiction intended to make me think it was just that—temporarily. The danger of inserting that bit of fiction into a paper noted for its careful handling of the news is that it will be taken for news fit to print.

Because I was deep into this book manuscript, especially this chapter on ethics, I went back to see whether the editor had lived up to what I had just written here about running up flags for the reader, warning of any such change away from the expected course. Yes, they certainly had tried to warn me right in the head: *The President, Imagined.* Imagined—that was the first flag (although it fluttered by me at first reading). The first 'graph sets me up beautifully—it's straightforward narrative reporting.

The second 'graph hints broadly enough with "A simulation," but I skimmed right by it—we're always reading about "simulations." The editor, still worrying about whether the warning is clear (but without ruining the fun by being too obvious), says that "it's easy to imagine...." Looking back through it, I realized what had been done to me—and I loved it. I thought, however, that the editor hit me too cleverly when the editorial ended with an italicized, Thank you, Mr. President. That looked so familiar, so real, so nonfiction, that I took in the line, the hook and the sinker. Had the editor not flown all those warning flags, I would have had an excellent example of how even the great *New York Times* had slipped up—but it hadn't and I didn't. It did provide an excellent example of responsible, ethical, creative nonfiction—and an example of how a reader, given half a chance, will not read something the way you intended. Ethics require open-eyed caution.

In a book-length work, some writers will put a short (sometimes long) statement up front, even as a foreword, that explains how the research was conducted, and just how much fiction is involved. This enables readers to carry that understanding with them as they work their way through the words. Gay Talese added a five-page section ("Author's Note") at the end of *Honor Thy Father* that explained his relationship with the Bonanno family and how he went about researching and interviewing for that book about the Mafia. Because people are still not used to this creative approach to nonfiction, the statement *must* be made somewhere, and it must, in itself, be an honest and clear statement.

Writers will sometimes, but not always, discuss either succinctly or at length their research methods: if they interviewed by tape, by notes, by memory; how long they were in the field with the subject or the characters; whether they had full access to diaries, journals, daybooks, ships' logs; etc. They may also talk about the writing, especially about the fiction techniques used: how "valid" were any conversations used; on what did they base any internal monologs; whether the central characters read the manuscript and if they approved of it in whole or in part; whether they had the "right of approval"; etc.

In short, our professional ethics demand that we be honest with the reader, honest with the characters involved, honest with ourselves, and that we, in general, lay our cards on the table for all to see. Without that honesty, there may be creativeness, lively writing, many good things—but not honorable Creative Nonfiction.

APPENDIX

APPLICATIONS OF CREATIVE NONFICTION

Throughout the book, I've been using examples from some of our best writers of creative nonfiction to illustrate the use of specific techniques, usually fiction techniques, in nonfiction writing. This appendix illustrates how widely the method of creative nonfiction applies in today's world of writing and publishing. The "method" shows up everywhere today, but my own reading indicates that it most often shows up in the applications that follow. I've illustrated each by a few excerpts from some of our best writers, partly for you to see the techniques as applied, and partly as inspiration for you to try writing in the applications of greatest interest to you. If you want further practice at identifying specific fiction techniques, as a way of summarizing for yourself just what you've learned by reading this book, you can use them for that purpose, too. If you're a teacher, you might ask students to identify the fiction techniques being used in each example. I hope, too, that when you read these short excerpts you'll find and read the full book or article. I've used only the best, so you're in for a reading treat.

I've arranged these applications roughly in the order of their chronologic appearance in the literature. Some historians in past centuries have been creative in their writings, especially those writing biographies of the great. They, particularly the British during their days of empire, traveled all over the world for their pleasure or to serve the empire, and wrote interestingly, and creatively, about their travels and about the places they visited or served in. Some of our finest English

233

writers wrote various kinds of personal histories, including autobiographies, allowing themselves to write more dramatically and vividly than they might have allowed themselves when writing about "more serious" topics.

Henry David Thoreau may not have been the first writer to take himself outside the workaday world to live for a time confronting nature, reflecting on it, and then reflecting on the nature of Man, but he's one of the more familiar ones. Other writers thought more about themselves and their everyday lives, writing "personal essays" or "familiar essays." One of our better known personal or familiar essayists, E. B. White, set high standards for this genre.

The application I've labeled "journalism" presents a broad, almost limitless opportunity for writers of creative nonfiction. I've not been able to include, for example, one variety of journalism, sportswriting, yet that field offers many opportunities. The next application, "science and technology," might have been included under "journalism" in some other classification system, but it seemed worth separating out as a special application, especially since a few years ago writers about science or technology rarely allowed themselves to be "creative." Today, partly under the unintended leadership of such great scientists as Lewis Thomas, M.D., men and women are writing very creatively about science and technology. As a society, we need more fine writers of creative nonfiction to keep us abreast (enjoyably) of what's happening in the rapidly growing world of science and technology.

Writers like Tom Wolfe and Joan Didion have inspired a generation of other fine writers who keep us abreast of another world, that of rapidly changing and fascinatingly diverse popular culture. Sometimes these writers give us our first insights into what's happening to us as a people right now. We see our foibles, our fads, and our lives, sometimes distressingly clear, through their marvelously refractive eyes and quick intelligence. We all like to read about ourselves, thus opening a wide field for good writing about popular culture.

HISTORY & BIOGRAPHY

By the ampersand between the two halves of this title, I have shown symbolically that they are more closely related than an "and" would imply. I'm not the first person to think about their closeness. Emerson worried about it when he said, according to the biographer Jean Strouse, *"There is properly no history, only biography."* In "The Real Reasons," collected in *Extraordinary Lives* (edited by William Zinsser), Strouse says, *Good biographers combine the arts of the novelist, the detective work of the historian, and the insights of the psychologist.*

The great American biographer, Leon Edel, says in his *Writing Lives*:

> The writing of lives is a department of history and is closely related to the discoveries of history. It can claim the same skills. No lives are led outside history or society; they take place in human time. No biography is complete unless it reveals the individual within history, within an ethos and a social complex. In saying this we remember Donne: no man is an island unto himself.

In a later chapter ("Dilemmas"), Edel quotes the founder of the new biography, Lytton Strachey, describing biography as *the most delicate and humane of all the branches of the art of writing.* "Delicate," Edel added, "because the biographer seeks to restore a sense of life to the inert materials that survive an individual's passage on this earth—seeks to recapture some part of what was once tissue and brains, and above all, feeling, and to shape a likeness of the vanished figure."

Edel then gives what amounts to a credo for writers of creative nonfiction:

> The writer of biography must be neat and orderly and logical in describing this elusive flamelike human spirit which delights in defying order and neatness and logic. The biographer may be as imaginative as he pleases—the more imaginative the better—in the way in which he brings together his materials, *but he must not imagine the materials.* He must read himself into the past; but he must also read the past into the present. He must judge the facts, but he must not sit in judgment. He must respect the dead—but he must tell the truth.

In his chapter on "The New Biography," Edel presents four of his principles of biographic writing, and then sums up the chapter with a list of devices the new biographer legitimately steals from the fiction writer, all of which will sound familiar to students of "creative nonfiction."

> . . . And the task and duty of biographical narrative is to sort out themes and patterns, not dates and mundane calendar events which

sort themselves. *This can be accomplished by use of those very devices that have given narrative strength to fiction—flashbacks. retrospective chapters, summary chapters, jumps of the future, forays into the past—that is the way we live and move; art can be derived from this knowledge* [my italics].

Let's read now a few examples of how some historians & biographers apply that credo and those fiction techniques to make their work more interesting, yet just as informative as other historians and biographers we may have read.

Under Prince Henry's stimulus, Lagos, a few miles along the coast from Sagres, became a center for caravel-building. Oak for keels came from Alentejo, bordering on the Algarve. Pine for the hulls grew along Portugal's Atlantic seaboard, where it was protected by law. The cluster pines also produced resin to waterproof the rigging and to calk the seams of the hull. Around Lagos there soon developed flourishing crafts of sail-making and rope-making. While Prince Henry at Sagres did not actually build a modern research institute, he did bring together all the essential ingredients. He collected the books and the charts, the sea captains, pilots, and mariners, the map-makers, instrument-makers, and compass-makers, the shipbuilders and carpenters, and other craftsmen, to plan voyages, to assess the findings, and to prepare expeditions ever farther into the unknown. The work Prince Henry started would never end.

DANIEL J. BOORSTIN
The Discoverers

Whether Pitt [England's secretary of state in 1756] possessed the strategic eye, whether the expeditions he launched were part of a considered combination, may be questioned. Now, as at all times, his policy was a projection on to a vast screen of his own aggressive, dominating personality. In the teeth of disfavour and obstruction he had made his way to the foremost place in Parliament, and now at last fortune, courage, and the confidence of his countrymen had given him a stage on which his gifts could be displayed and his foibles indulged. To call into life and action the depressed and languid spirit of England; to weld all her resources of wealth and manhood into a single instrument of war which should be felt from the Danube to the Mississippi;

to humble the house of Bourbon, to make the Union Jack supreme in every ocean, to conquer, to command, and never to count the cost, whether in blood or gold—this was the spirit of Pitt...

WINSTON S. CHURCHILL
The Age of Revolution
A History of the English Speaking Peoples, Volume 3

If any decade could be called the decade of the consumer, it was the fifties: the money rolled in, the living was easy, appetites expanded, and television nightly tickled greed. Twice in that decade the Bureau of Labor Statistics revised the consumer price index to make it reflect the changes in what the average American bought with his pay—an ever smaller percentage, it turned out, for food. Likewise for clothing. But more and more on housing, more and more for leisure, more and more for doctors and medicines. All essentials were easily met by the rising economy, but luxuries and indulgences, what the economists call "discretionary purchasing power," were themselves becoming an essential to the growing national economy, the growing national market. We at *Colliers* wanted our share of this growing market, but we were being shouldered away from the trough.

THEODORE H. WHITE
"The Fifties: Incubating the Storm," in *In Search of History*

So it could happen badly with him [Ulysses S. Grant] when he was alone and cut off and the evils of life came down about him. Marooned in California, far from his family, tormented by money problems, bored by the pointless routine of a stagnant army post under a dull and unimaginative colonel, he could turn to drink for escape. He could do the same thing back in Missouri as a civilian, working hard for a meager living, all the luck breaking badly, drifting into failure at forty, Sam Grant the ne'er-do-well. Deep in Tennessee, likewise, sidetracked by a jealous and petty-minded superior, the awful stain of Shiloh lying ineradicable on his mind, his career apparently ready to end just as it was being reborn, the story could be the same. There was a flame in him, and there were times when he could not keep the winds from the outer dark from blowing in on him and making it flicker. But it never did go out.

BRUCE CATTON
"Glory Is Out of Date," in *A Stillness at Appomattox*

In the White House Robert Lincoln and John Hay sit gossiping pleasantly, Nicolay away at the Fort Sumter flag-raising. The doors burst open and several voices at once tell them the news. They run downstairs, take a carriage, cannot quite believe what they have heard. Slowly their carriage plows a path through the gathering thousands of people around Tenth Street. Dr. Stone gravely and tenderly tells Robert the worst: there is no hope. He chokes. The tears run down his face. After a time he recovers and does his best during hours of the night at comforting his mother.

At about the same hour and minute of the clock that the President is shot in Ford's Theatre, a giant of a young man rides on a big one-eyed bay horse to the door of the Seward house on Lafayette Square, gets off his horse, rings the doorbell, says he is a messenger from the attending physician and has a package of medicine that must be personally delivered to the sickroom of the Secretary of State. The servant at the door tries to stop the young man, who enters and goes up the stairs, suddenly to turn in a furious rush on Fred Seward, beating him on the head with the pistol, tearing the scalp, fracturing the skull and battering the pistol to pieces.

CARL SANDBURG
Abraham Lincoln—The War Years (1864-1865)

PROFILES/SKETCHES/PERSONAL HISTORIES

No perfect definitions exist to separate cleanly profiles from sketches, but personal histories (autobiographies) are written by the person involved, whereas profiles and sketches are written by someone other than the subject. I separate profiles and sketches on the basis of depth of treatment and purpose. A *profile* tries to give us a short (say 1,000 to 10,000 words) biographical summary of a person. The *sketch* tries only to get at the essence of a person, not his or her life's story. A *personal history*, by my loose definition, is of book length (say 50,000 words or more) and may be written with almost any structure the person wants. Different editors and writers call a sketch a profile or a profile a sketch, so I'm not trying here to make a final statement about which is which. The first excerpt comes from a section of the *New Yorker* called "Profiles." Calvin Trillin and other writers for that magazine write some of the best, most thoroughly researched, and longest profiles of any publication. Calvin Trillin wrote one about Edna Buchanan, who writes for the Miami *Herald*.

Profiles

In the newsroom of the Miami *Herald*, there is some disagreement about which of Edna Buchanan's first paragraphs stands as the classic Edna lead. I line up with the fried-chicken faction. The fried-chicken story was about a rowdy ex-con named Gary Robinson, who late one Sunday night lurched drunkenly into a Church's outlet, shoved his way to the front of the line, and ordered a three-piece box of fried chicken. Persuaded to wait his turn, he reached the counter again five or ten minutes later, only to be told that Church's had run out of fried chicken. The young woman at the counter suggested that he might like chicken nuggets instead. Robinson responded to the suggestion by slugging her in the head. That set off a chain of events that ended with Robinson's being shot dead by a security guard. Edna Buchanan covered the murder for the *Herald*—there are policemen in Miami who say that it wouldn't be a murder without her—and her story began with what the fried-chicken faction still regards as the classic Edna lead: "Gary Robinson died hungry."

New York magazine also runs many profiles and sketches written in a creative way. Tony Schwartz, who covers the media waterfront so diligently and so well, wrote a profile (or is it a sketch?) about Dan Rather in the February 3, 1986 issue, "Dan on the Run":

... The son of a ditchdigger, he wants above all to hold on to what he's got. But he also wants to do it on his own terms. He is determined, for example, to be seen with CBS as a company man and head cheerleader. But he also sees himself as the heir to Ed Murrow, the conscience of a corporation he increasingly doubts has the best interests of the news division at heart. He is zealous about protecting his Evening News turf and his authority as managing editor. But he is also, by nature, deeply reluctant to confront his adversaries and extremely eager to get along. He sees himself as a fierce guardian of traditional journalistic values. But he is also committed to winning a ratings battle in which non-journalistic values such as promotion and pizzazz are more and more a factor.

Sketches

Melvin Maddocks wrote a twice-weekly column for the *Christian Science Monitor*, frequently sketches about leading figures. The two excerpts below show how much a good writer can get across in fewer than a thousand words, and how he gets at the essence of the man. The first comes from "The Flower of Ice Hockey Takes His Last Turn," written upon the retirement of Montreal Canadiens hockey player Guy LaFleur; and the second is from "Remembering the Late, Great Count Basie— The Swinging Never Stopped," a column commemorating the pianist-composer upon his death.

> . . . Though deceptively strong, he appeared less burly than the players around him, like a figure skater who had blundered in among the heavy hitters. But there was a special intentness to LaFleur. Even when he coasted on the ice for a routine face-off, he brought drama, urgency. The eye followed him, as the eye follows an actor on stage who has the gift of presence. The tempo of excitement lifted just because he was there. When the puck was dropped, LaFleur moved for it with a bright-eyed hunger. He is one of those players so drawn to the puck that the puck seems drawn to them.

> . . . Basie had a subtlety to match his power. His humor was irrepressible. A Basie solo in the middle of a piece often took on the character of a family joke played back and forth with bassist Walter Page or guitarist Freddie Green or drummer Jo Jones, to name three old hands. Modest to the point of deference in these dialogues, Basie nonetheless had a way of getting in the final witty topper. Everything he played possessed a kind of joy so central to his being as to be beyond his power to suppress. Even his blues came out happy.

Personal Histories

The following excerpt from the book *D. V.* by Diana Vreeland can't do full justice to this unusual personal history written by an unusually vivacious woman who edited for *Vogue* and *Harper's Bazaar* for many years, and who knew everyone everywhere in the world. This short piece does give much of the flavor of the woman and of the book.

For years Yvonne used the rhinoceros horn on my shoes. A highly emotional French lady, she wouldn't lift a finger to polish all my shoes after each wearing—including the soles. Why, I wouldn't *dream* of wearing shoes with untreated soles. I mean, you go out to dinner and suddenly you lift your foot and the soles aren't impeccable . . . what could be more ordinary?

And footsteps! I can't stand the vulgarity of a woman who makes a noise when she walks. It's all right for soldiers, but when I was growing up the quintessence of breeding in a lady was a quiet footstep. Well, it is to me still. Do you know that I let a brilliant worker go at *Vogue* because of the way she walked—the *clank* of those heels! She went to live in Paris after I talked to her. I said, "I can't stand your footsteps. I can't!" But, of course, what it was with her was anger; it is a form of anger if you can't control the foot. I promise you, the *heavy tread* is a form of anger. You ought to pull up your instep, tense the leg, perhaps wear a little lower heel. Or else just take the trouble to walk a little more carefully. And if you can't do that, you *have* to go to Paris! As Napoleon said, "Go to Paris and become a woman."

Filmmaker and author Ben Logan recalls a totally different lifestyle in his personal history, *The Empty Meadow.* Brought up on a Wisconsin farm, Ben writes below of one of his first teenage encounters with a member of the opposite sex.

She bit her lip and wouldn't look at me or let me turn her face toward me. "Everything goes too fast."

"You mean us? Last time?"

She nodded. "I didn't mean to let you kiss me."

I laughed and squeezed her shoulder. "Why did you then?"

She jerked away from my hand. I thought she was going to slap me. "Oh you're something aren't you? You think boys are so different! You think girls are just starched marshmallows or something! You think you can do anything you want with us just so you don't get us wrinkled up or pull off any buttons!"

From a long way off I could hear myself thinking, God-almighty, what the hell is going on?

She looked at me, waiting. The moon had come up and was on her face. She was prettier than ever. She took a deep breath. The front of the suit raised up and down. I watched that happening, thinking about the anatomy of it and almost forgot what we were talking about.

Clyde Rice's personal history, *A Heaven in the Eye*, won the 1984 Western States Book Award for creative nonfiction. Begun when Rice was seventy-five, the book is a memoir of his life from age sixteen until he was thirty-four. He says that the publisher didn't want to hear about his first sixteen years, and he, himself, felt that no one would want to read about what happened after his thirty-fourth year. The Denver Post wrote of the book: *A triumph . . . The saga of a stubborn non-conformist swimming upstream against the relentless social and economic currents of his time.* This short excerpt has to stand for the entire wild and wonderful book, but it does provide some of its gusto:

> I was invited to a few of the fine homes of the old first families of Portland [Oregon]. Scattered throughout the downtown area, these houses were very grand, but the impression I had about the people I met there was of lap dogs atop embroidered cushions, nor did their young impress me any more favorably. Life, my mother's death had recently reminded me, was rich and priceless and soon gone, but here in their fabulous boxes these people were the quiet antithesis of gusto. The sap of life was lost here. After visiting four or five of these fine houses, I said out loud, not to the mirror but with some self-consciousness, "What you seek you won't find in money or prestige." I added this motto to the things I already knew about myself—for example, that I never watched to catch myself simpering in the acclaim of however many mutts, and that I was going to do the sexual thing with Miss Nordstrom.

TRAVEL AND A SENSE OF PLACE

Although the writers quoted below all write about their travel experiences, they are not, in the usual sense, "travel writers." Travel writers intend to help us at home plan our trips to places they discuss, letting us know important information about transportation, sleeping accommodations, restaurants to seek out (or avoid), passport/visa requirements, and the costs of everything. Their purpose is pragmatic.

The writers collected here have a purpose more poetic than pragmatic. They try their best to give us a vicarious sense of a place—its feel. The best travel writers, too, try to give us a feel for the place, but they don't consider their purpose literary. Perhaps those quoted here do not think themselves "literary," but their nonfiction writing is creative and entertaining as it informs. Their writing sometimes entices us to travel to the place, and then we may turn to the travel writer and the travel consultant for practical guidance. The first group transports us; the latter speaks of transportation.

Some of the earliest examples of creative nonfiction writing are from those well-educated and wealthy people (frequently British) who traveled extensively around the empire and came home to write up their "adventures" to the delight of everyone at the club. Some of these same people wrote their autobiographies in a similarly creative, entertaining style, making them forerunners of today's more widely appreciated creative nonfiction work in many fields. Henry David Thoreau was certainly not the first to write creatively about his travels, but his writing continues to delight:

> While we were thus engaged in the twilight, we heard faintly, from far down the stream, what sounded like two strikes of a wood-chopper's axe, echoing dully through the grim solitude. We are wont to liken many sounds, heard at a distance in the forest, to the strike of an axe, because that is the one we commonly hear there. When we told Joe of this, he exclaimed, "By George, I'll bet that was a moose! They make a noise like that." These sounds affected us strangely, and by their very resemblance to a familiar one, where they probably had so different an origin, enhanced the impression of solitude and wildness.
>
> At starlight we dropped down the stream, which was a dead-water for three miles, or as far as the Moosehorn; Joe telling us that we must be very silent, and he himself making no noise with his paddle, while urging the canoe along with effective impulses. It was a still night, and suitable for this purpose—for if there is wind, the moose will smell you—and Joe was confident that he should get some. The harvest moon had just risen, and its level rays began to light up the forest on our right, while we glided downward in the shade on the same side, against the little breeze that was stirring. The lofty, spiring tops of the spruce and fir were very black against the sky, and more distinct than by day, close bordering this broad avenue on each side; and the beauty of the scene, as the moon rose above the forest, it would not be easy to describe.
>
> HENRY DAVID THOREAU
"The Moose Hunt," in The Maine Woods

It was not a popular train, this Simla Mail. Its odd twisted route was undoubtedly the result of the demands of the imperial postal service, for the British regarded letter writing and mail delivery as one of the distinguishing features of any great civilization. And Indians feel pretty much the same.

"Use the shutters," the ticket collector said, "and don't leave any small articles lying around."

The whistle of the Simla Mail drowned the sounds of music from the bazaar. I was soon asleep. But at midnight I was woken by rain beating against the shutters. The monsoon which had hit the Punjab only the day before had brought another storm, and the train struggled through it. The thick raindrops came down so hard they splattered through the slats and louvers in the shutters, and a fine spray soaked the compartment floor.

The Guard knocked on the door at 5:20 to announce that we had arrived at Kalka.

It was green and cool at Kalka, and after a shave in the Gentlemen's Waiting Room I was ready for the five-hour journey through the hills to Simla. I could have taken the small pottering "Simla Queen" or the express, but the white twenty-seat railcar was already waiting at the platform. I boarded, and snoozed, and woke to see mists lying across the hills and heavy green foliage in the glades beside the line.

PAUL THEROUX
"Making Tracks to Chittagong"
Sunrise with Seamonsters: Travels and Discoveries

For all these reasons, to come to Kathmandu expecting it to resemble a spotless mountain city like Zurich or Geneva would be foolish. Apart from anything else, the largely Hindu community lets a plethora of sacred cows wander unobstructed in the middle of the steadily growing vehicular traffic. By changing blocks, one can transport oneself back and forth over various centuries in a way that is almost unimaginable in a Western city. In the course of a few streets, I encountered a Tibetan wearing a T-shirt that said "The University of Hawaii"; a Nepalese teen-ager who tried to sell me hashish or his sister; and a poster in the window of a travel agency describing a night-club act called "Rags to Riches." The poster read "Rags to Riches roaming around the world now in Kathmandu . . . featuring Jonathan from France on guitar and Philip from Iceland on flute. Cheering you up with folk music, jokes, and skits in a friendly atmosphere." I also overheard a woman in the elegant Chinese restaurant in the Annapurna Hotel say delightedly, "Oh, they have American chop suey!"

JEREMY BERNSTEIN
"The Himalaya Revisited," *New Yorker* (February 3, 1986)

We were moving. We had cast off and were sliding away from shore. The party chatter faltered. The Saone at Lyons is a beautiful river, and I stood and watched it reveal itself as we reached midstream and gently chugged upriver through a green allee, between orderly rows of leafy plane trees that lined the gray stone quays. Beyond the trees were rows of apartment houses—dusty yellow and faded orange, with tall windows flanked by faded blue shutters—in the form style of the middle nineteenth century, and rising beyond the apartments were the delicate towers and spires and belfries of churches. The party chatter began again. We crept under a bridge. A racing scull appeared in the distance. It came skimming closer. And closer. And suddenly darted for shore, to sit there bucking and bouncing in our wake. The women from Michigan smiled and waved. The oarsman hunched his shoulders and looked away. The sky to the west brightened into a sunset blaze. A star came out. Up ahead, on the left, a patch of pale-blue neon shone through the trees: "PAUL BOCUSE." One of the New York women saw it, too.

"Oh, look! We had dinner there last night, And it was the greatest. It was just the greatest ever. And Paul Bocuse himself came over to our table and autographed my menu."

BERTON ROUECHE
"Janine" (a barge journey)
New Yorker (October 24, 1984)

It is as though the British Isles are tilted permanently to one corner—the southeast corner, bottom right, where London stands seething upon the Thames. Everything slithers and tumbles down there, all the talent, all the money, and when I got on the M4 motorway that morning I felt that I was being swept away helter-skelter, willy-nilly across the breadth of England. Around me all the energies of the place seemed to be heading in a single direction—the trucks from Cornwall and South Wales, the tourist buses, the ramshackle No Nuclear estate cars, the stream of expense-account Fords, their salesmen drivers tapping their steering-wheels to the rhythm of Radio One. London! London! shouted the direction signs. London! screamed the blue and white train, streaking eastwards beside the road, and when I turned off to the south and made for Dover, still I felt the presence of the capital tugging away at me, as it tugs commuters from their mock-Tudor villas day after day from the far reaches of Surrey and pastoral Hampshire.

JAN MORRIS
"Not So Far: A European Journey"
Journeys

NATURE AND THE NATURE OF MAN

Many creative nonfiction writers find topics of great interest within nature and the out-of-doors. Some writers tell us about the wonders of nature, ecological systems, and life in the wild without drawing any moral message, except, perhaps, that we should conserve nature. Other writers, whose writing I'll cover second, use nature as a kind of jumping-off place to wax philosophical about "the nature of Man." Like most things, neither category is purely one and not the other. People writing about the wonders of nature will often digress for a moment to make some point about how Man could learn something from Mother Nature, but their main message is not philosophical. The more philosophical writers, on the other hand, may also give us much interesting information about nature along with their main messages about the nature of Man.

The first series of three excerpts gives us three writers' thoughts on meeting up with an exciting part of nature:

> The first time I ever saw a bear in the wild, I was on my way back from fishing in a beaver meadow on state land next to the Flathead National Forest, about ten miles from the town of Bigfork, Montana. I was coming around a bend on an overgrown logging road when I saw up ahead a large black animal see me and duck into some thimbleberry bushes. I knew it was a bear. I didn't move and he didn't move for maybe three minutes. There was no likely tree nearby for me to climb. Then the bear hopped out of the bushes, took a look at me over his shoulder, and galloped like crazy down the trail. As he ran, his hind feet seemed to reach higher than his head. He splashed water up and made the rocks clack as he crossed a little creek, and then he went into the brush on the other side with a racket that sounded like a car crashing through there. For some reason, I picked up a rock. I felt the weight of

the rock in my hand, I smelled the breath from a wild rosebush, I saw the sun on the tops of the mountains, I felt the clothes on my back. I felt like a man—skinny, bipedal, weak, slow, and basically kind of a silly idea. I felt as if I had eyes all over my head. I proceeded, a procession of feelings, down the trail where the bear had run. I saw dark blots on the trail where he had splashed water from the creek. I kept saying, "A bear! I saw a bear!"

IAN FRAZIER
"Bear News," *New Yorker*, (September 9, 1985)

By June the Elk are in alpine meadows. There are deer where there is browse; and these black-tailed deer love the river bottoms. The bear are numerous. I remember one bright August day when August Slather had the oars, holding the middle of the Bogachiel on a long slow drift in flat water as I whipped the river with a fly. As we rounded a bend we saw a large black bear on the next point, a couple of hundred yards distant. Augie gave me a knowing look and pointed the boat directly to the animal. The wind was right and, as fortune would have it, the rear end of the bear was pointed our way. He had flipped a big fish from the water and was leisurely engaged in eating it. When the boat was within three feet of the bear, I reached over and gave it a slap on the back, shouting "What are you doing here?" It was seconds before the message reached the bear's brain. Meanwhile his sympathetic nervous system went into operation. His rear legs stiffened; his back seemed to freeze. Then the danger signal reached consciousness and the animal was off through the dense brush, not once looking behind.

JUSTICE WILLIAM O. DOUGLAS
My Wilderness: The Pacific West

...Black bears rarely eat creatures larger than squirrels. They prefer little ones. They eat wasps' nests with the wasps in them. They eat living yellow jackets. When eating honeycombs, they also eat the bees. In 1976, a tagged Pennsylvania bear was caught stealing from a beehive in New Jersey. It was dart-gunned and extradited—home to Pennsylvania. A bear will sit on its butt beside an anthill, bomb the anthill with a whisking paw, then set the paw on the ground and patiently watch while ants swarm over the paw. The bear licks the paw. A bear will eat a snake or a frog. But all these sources of protein do almost nothing to pack that mattress of fat. Fruit and nuts make the fat. Bears eat so many apples sometimes that they throw up the pulp and retain the cider, which ferments in the stomach no less effectively than it would in a pot

still. The bears become drunk. By the Deerfield River, in Massachusetts, a dozen years ago, two inebriated bears full of hard cider lurched
all over a nearby road, wove about, staggered, lolled, fell, and got up on
the hood of a police car. Massachusetts closed its bear season for the du-
ration of the hangover.

JOHN MCPHEE
"A Textbook Place for Bears," *Table of Contents*

The final three excerpts take up parts of nature less physically exciting
than bears, stressing more the beauty of the wild and its appeal to our
senses. These final examples come from a special subcategory of books
about nature and about the nature of man—books written by people
who have deliberately removed themselves from society to reflect on that
society, on nature, and on themselves.

All of us have special places of great beauty. One of my favorites at
sunset in the winter is looking across a barren hillside with a rim of
birches silhouetted against its color. It has always fascinated me and I
have often wished I could paint that delicate tracery against the redden-
ing sky. Another is a high ridge that commands a view of many miles to
the east. Too see a moonrise there, to watch a certain notch begin to
brighten and finally see the golden rim slip above the dark horizon
never fails to fill me with awe and wonderment.

In a lifetime of seeing beauty in the wilderness, I always feel a lift of
spirit and an afterglow of serenity and content. I also know one must
take time and wait for the glimpse of beauty that always comes, and one
must see each as though it were his last chance.

SIGURD F. OLSON
Reflections from the North Country

For sounds in winter nights, and often in winter days, I heard the
forlorn but melodious note of a hooting owl indefinitely far; such a
sound as the frozen earth would yield if struck with a suitable plec-
trum, the very lingua vernacular of Walden Wood, and quite familiar to
me at last, though I never saw the bird while it was making it; Hoo hoo
hoo, hooer hoo, sounded sonorously, and the first three syllables ac-
cented somewhat like how der do; or sometimes hoo hoo only. One
night in the beginning of winter, before the pond froze over, about nine
o'clock, I was startled by the loud honking of a goose, and, stepping to
the door, heard the sound of their wings like a tempest in the woods as
they flew low over my house. They passed over the pond toward Fair

Haven, seemingly undeterred from settling by my light, their commodore honking all the while with a regular beat.

HENRY DAVID THOREAU
Walden

Had I room in this book, I should like to write a whole chapter on the sense of smell, for all my life long I have had of that sense an individual enjoyment. To my mind, we live too completely by the eye. I like a good smell—the smell of a freshly ploughed field on a warm morning after a night of April rain, the cloverlike aroma of our wild Cape Cod pinks, the morning perfume of lilacs showery with dew, the good reek of hot salt grass and low tide blowing from these meadows on summer afternoons.

What a stench modern civilization breathes, and how have we ever learned to endure that foul blue air? In the Seventeenth Century, the air above a city must have bee much the same air as hung over a large village; to-day the town atmosphere is to be endured only by the new synthetic man.

HENRY BESTON
The Outermost House (1928)

PERSONAL REFLECTIONS

Personal reflections are usually written in the essay form, but I've not called the following "essays" because we all tend to associate that form with those dreadful things we were required to write back in school. Personal reflections cover even more forms than does "essay," so I chose to use the more accommodating phrase.

E. B. White, the modern master of the "personal" or "familiar" essay, said in the foreword to *Essays of E. B. White*: "There are as many kinds of essays as there are human attitudes or poses, as many essay flavors as there are Howard Johnson ice creams."

Novelist Maureen Howard, the editor of *Contemporary American Essays*, wrote in her introduction to that collection: "An essay, though it takes as many shapes as weather or daylight, always has the immediacy of a real voice...." The varied examples below each has a voice that we hear in the reflections:

I have noticed on my trips up to the city that people have recut their clothes to follow the fashion. On my last trip, however, it seemed to me that people had remodeled their ideas, too—taken in their convictions a little at the waist, shortened the sleeves of their resolve, and fitted themselves out in a new intellectual ensemble copied from a smart design out of the very latest page of history. It seemed to me they had strung along with Paris a little too long.

I confess to a disturbed stomach. I feel sick when I find anyone adjusting his mind to the new tyranny which is succeeding abroad. Because of its fundamental stricture, fascism does not seem to me to admit of any compromise or any rationalization, and I resent the patronizing air of persons who find in my plain belief in freedom a sign of immaturity. If it is boyish to believe that a human being should live free, then I'll gladly arrest my development and let the rest of the world grow up.

E. B. WHITE
"Freedom," One Man's Meat

At eighteen, I longed to die for it. When World War II ended in 1945 before I could reach the combat zone, I moped for months about being deprived of the chance to go down in flames under the guns of a Mitsubishi Zero. There was never much doubt that I would go down in flames if given the opportunity, for my competence as a pilot was such that I could barely remember to lower the plane's landing gear before trying to set it down on a runway. I had even visualized my death. It was splendid. Dead, I would be standing perhaps 4,000 feet up in the sky. (Everybody knew that heroes floated in those days.) Erect and dashing, surrounded by beautiful cumulus clouds, I would look just as good as ever, except for being slightly transparent. And I would smile, devil-may-care, at the camera—oh there would be cameras there—and the American flag would unfurl behind me across 500 miles of glorious American sky, and back behind the cumulus clouds the Marine Band would be playing "The Stars and Stripes Forever," but not too fast.

RUSSELL BAKER
"The Flag," So This Is Depravity

…I have pursued my own chronology not so much to record it as to explore it. Remembering a particular house often brings back a predominant mood, a certain weather of the spirit. Sometimes, opening the door of a till-then-forgotten room brought on that involuntary shiver, that awed suspension. These sudden rememberings are gifts to writers, like the taste of the madeleine—for much of writing is simply finding ways of re-creating astonishments in words. But as I began to reel in my itinerant past I found that I was much less interested in recording it than in experiencing the sense it gave me of making tangible a ghostly dimension; for an instance of remembering can, without warning, turn into a present moment, a total possession, a haunting.

ALASTAIR REID
"Hauntings," *New Yorker*, (December 23, 1985)

A very, very long time ago (about three or four years), I took a certain secure and righteous pleasure in saying the things that women are supposed to say. I remember with pain—

"My work won't interfere with marriage. After all, I can always keep my typewriter at home." Or:

I don't want to write about women's stuff. I want to write about foreign policy."

Or:

"Black families were forced into matriarchy, so I see why black women have to step back and let their men go ahead."

Or:

"I know we're helping Chicano groups that are tough on women, but that's their culture."

Or:

"Who would want to join a women's group? I've never been a joiner, have you?" Or (when bragging):

"He says I write like a man."

I suppose it's obvious from the kinds of statements I chose that I was secretly nonconforming. I wasn't married. I was earning a living at a profession I cared about. I had basically—if quietly—opted out of the "feminine" role. But that made it all the more necessary to repeat the conventional wisdom, even to look as conventional as I could manage, if I was to avoid some of the punishments reserved by society for women who don't do as society says. I therefore learned to Uncle Tom with subtlety, logical and humor. Sometimes I believed myself.

If it weren't for the women's movement, I might still be dissembling away. But the ideas of this great sea-change in women's views of ourselves are contagious and irresistible. They hit women like a revelation, as if we had left a dark room and walked into the sun.

GLORIA STEINEM
"Sisterhood," *Outrageous Acts and Everyday Rebellions*

There is a housing project standing now where the house in which we grew up once stood, and one of those stunted city trees is snarling where our doorway used to be. This is on the rehabilitated side of the avenue. The other side of the avenue—for progress takes time—has not been rehabilitated yet and it looks exactly as it looked in the days when we sat with our noses pressed against the windowpane, longing to be allowed to go "across the street." The grocery store which gave us credit is still there, and there can be no doubt that it is still giving credit. The people in the project certainly need it—far more, indeed, than they ever needed the project. The last time I passed by, the Jewish proprietor was still standing among his shelves looking sadder and heavier but scarcely any older. Farther down the block stands the shoe-repair store in which our shoes were repaired until reparation became impossible and in which, then, we bought all our "new" ones. The negro proprietor is still in the window, head down, working at the leather.

These two, I imagine, could tell a long tale if they would (perhaps they would be glad to if they could), having watched so many, for so long, struggling in the fishhooks, the barbed wire, of this avenue.

JAMES BALDWIN
"Fifth Avenue, Uptown," *Nobody Knows My Name*

JOURNALISM

The acceptance of creative nonfiction writing by newspaper organizations continues to accelerate. Traditional newspaper reporters and editors of ten or fifteen years ago would never have believed for a moment the possibility that writing in their publications would be increasingly "creative." The word itself connoted that reporters would make up the news, create facts out of whole cloth, or, at best, would write subjectively about the news, instead of objectively as they had been taught by schools and by their editors. They didn't want to accept the increasing evidence that they would have to write more creatively, i.e., interestingly and dramatically, to compete with magazines and the broadcast media. Magazines, especially the growing number of special-interest magazines, have been giving the public more "exciting," more "attractive," more "dramatic" presentations of the news and its background for years now. Difficult as it may be to accept, there has been a rapid magazining of newspapers in America.

Today, most newspapers have accepted the fact that if newspaper journalism is to survive as a medium against the powerful and more attractive media, it has to take on some of their coloration—a sort of species adaptation for evolution and survival. If the newspaper species takes on too many of its competitors' attributes, of course, it is in danger of losing the primary attribute that has enabled it to survive so far—adherence to objective, accurate reporting of the facts. Newspapers must continuously monitor their adaptive efforts, but there are writers who are leading the way, writers who manage to keep the facts straight while surrounding them with interestingly written narrative that borrows with good sense from certain fiction techniques this book describes. The following journalistic writers, plus others referred to elsewhere, show that such adaptive mechanisms can work, and work splendidly, whether to a deadline or not.

NEW YORK—A healthy 17-year-old heart pumped the gift of life through 34-year-old Bruce Murray Friday, following a four-hour transplant operation that doctors said went without a hitch.

Early Thursday morning, three surgeons at Presbyterian Hospital lifted Murray's flabby, enlarged heart from his chest cavity and replaced it with a normal heart that had been flown from St. Louis inside an ice-filled beer cooler. The operation lasted from 3:45 a.m. to 7:30 a.m.

As Murray's diseased heart sat in a stainless steel bowl at the foot of the operating table, doctors gradually weaned Murray away from a heart-lung machine that had kept him alive throughout much of the operation. The new heart, beating slowly at first, gradually took over the task of pumping blood through Murray's body. And by 5:25 a.m., Dr. Eric Rose emerged from the 19th floor operating room and proclaimed the procedure a success.

JONATHAN BOR
"It Fluttered and Became Bruce Murray's Heart,"
Syracuse (N.Y.) Post-Standard (May 12, 1984),
collected in *Best Newspaper Writing 1985*

DALLAS—The charms of the Republicans commend themselves to tastes that are concededly special and may in some quarters be accounted depraved.

But it takes, thank God, moral fiber sterner than my own not to have surrendered to the sight of them Sunday, herded into the welcoming pen for George Bush, abiding the interval greeting various honored guests with the politeness that bespeaks entire unfamiliarity with its object and then breaking forth at last into glad and affectionate cries of recognition when the chairman introduced White House Counselor Edwin Meese and Secretary of Labor Raymond Donovan.

Both Meese and Donovan are, depending on your point of view, either steeped in infamy or bedaubed with smear. But then, we have no reason to believe that these delegates would have heard of either if he had not been made notorious by the jackal packs of journalism.

MURRAY KEMPTON
"The Discreet Charm of the GOP," *Newsday* (August 21, 1984),
collected in *Best Newspaper Writing 1985*

ST. PETERSBURG, Fla.—Suspense is building at the track. Fans mill around the staging area to get a glimpse of what a woman describes as the "fantastic chest" of her favorite contestant. When the runner's name is finally announced, he gets a long ovation. One man hops around, shouting: "Give me a K! Give me an E! Give me another E! Give me an...."

The cheers are for a greyhound named Keefer. Few dogs ever attract so much attention, but when it comes to Keefer, people here get downright dogmatic. They say he is the smartest or the best-looking or the most affable young racing dog they have ever seen. They even applaud when his victories are replayed on the track's closed-circuit television system.

Keefer's trainer, James Schulthess, is his most outspoken fan. He calls Keefer "the best dog in the world, and maybe the best dog that ever lived."

Such biased views aside, this much is certain: At the tender age of two, the big beige hound from Kansas is one hot dog....

FRANCINE SCHWADEL
Wall Street Journal (April 16, 1986)

[Third paragraph] Craig Stedman, a South Kingstown patrolman, headed down Worden's Pond Road to the Tucker house. The rain was really something. He found Charlie lying nine feet from the porch.

There was a loaded .38-caliber pistol near his left elbow and a nine-pound iron bar against his right arm. He had bad head injuries and a sporadic pulse. Stedman knocked on the door and wrote down the first thing that Lucy Tucker said to him.

"I didn't want to kill him, but he had a gun and said he would kill me and the children. He had a gun and wouldn't stop so I hit him. Oh, God, he wouldn't stop."

Stedman radioed for help and then went back outside to check Tucker again. This time there was no pulse. It was 12:15.

MARK PATINKIN
"I Didn't Want to Kill Him, But He Had a Gun"
Providence, R.I. Evening Bulletin (March 20, 1981)
collected in *How I Wrote the Story*

It used to be easy to put together the qualities that made for a good, honest tavern. That's because there were only two basic kinds: simple neighborhood places with the owner serving the drinks and popping for an occasional round, and dim Formica joints that called themselves cocktail lounges, where a hired hand mixed the drinks and shorted the register.

Now there are bars for every taste, or lack of same. We have the California-inspired fern bars, where you can get a sliver of goat cheese in your martini; sports-theme bars, with youngish customers living for the day a TV crew will record them holding up a finger, shrieking that they're number one; and activities bars, where the owners take the place of suburban moms and dads by organizing outings, softball games, dwarf-tossing competitions, and an occasional wedding.

MIKE ROYKO
"A Clean, Well-Lighted Place," *Esquire* (June 1986)

HELSINKI, 1952—[Second paragraph] Sauna (pronounced sowna) is a Finnish bath, and a great deal more. It is a sacred rite, a form of human sacrifice in which the victim is boiled like a missionary in the cannibal islands, then baked to a turn, then beaten with sticks until he flees into the icy sea, then lathered and honed and kneaded and pummeled by the high priestess of this purgatorial pit.

Nothing relaxes a Finn like this ritual of fire worship, water worship, and soap worship. It is an ancient folk custom dating from forgotten times, and it explains why Finland produces so many great marathon runners. Anybody who can survive a sauna can run twenty-six miles barefoot over broken beer bottles.

RED SMITH
"Good, Clean Fun," *The Red Smith Reader*

SCIENCE AND TECHNOLOGY

Since science and technology are frequently lumped together, despite their great differences, I've kept them lumped here as a category, while separating them in the examples. Both endeavors require excellent writing, especially if they are ever to be made clear to the generally nonscientifically and nontechnologically-trained public. Writing clearly about these subjects even for professional colleagues is difficult enough, but to write clearly for others requires even greater skill. Add to clarity the requirements also to write interestingly and engagingly, and you have a high challenge for any writer.

If you are searching for a writing niche, and you enjoy science or technology, these fields are wide open to good writers. More important, the citizenry desperately needs good writers to inform us clearly about all the sciences and technologies that surround us, affect us, change our lives, determine our futures—perhaps even determine the survival of our species.

An informed electorate lies at the very foundation of democracy—and yet we all feel less and less informed about the progress of science and technology. Some of us feel we're sufficiently informed by television news and documentaries, but those media give us a false sense of security about how well informed we are; we just think we're informed. We need writers to inform us in greater depth, but we also want to "enjoy" our informative reading—and that requires creative nonfiction writers like those which follow.

Science

I contend, furthermore, that we have allowed these chemicals to be used with little or no advance investigation of their effect on soil, water, wildlife, and man himself. Future generations are unlikely to condone our lack of prudent concern for the integrity of the natural world that supports all life.

There is still very limited awareness of the nature of the threat. This is an era of specialists, each of whom sees his own problem and is unaware of or intolerant of the larger frame into which it fits. It is also an era dominated by industry, in which the right to make a dollar at whatever cost is seldom challenged. When the public protests, confronted with some obvious evidence of damaging results of pesticide applications, it is fed little tranquilizing pills of half truth. We urgently need an end to these false assurances, to the sugar coating of unpalatable facts. It is the public that is being asked to assume the risks that the insect controllers calculate. The public must decide whether it wishes to continue on the present road, and it can do so only when in full possession of the facts. In the words of Jean Rostand, "The obligation to endure gives us the right to know."

RACHEL CARSON
"The Obligation to Endure," *Silent Spring* (1962)

They were generalists. Those primitive early cockroaches possessed a simple and very practical anatomical design that remains almost unchanged in the cockroaches of today. Throughout their evolutionary history they have avoided wild morphological experiments like those of their relatives, the mantids and walking sticks, and so many other bizarrely evolved insects. For cockroaches the byword has been: Keep it simple. Consequently today, as always, they can live almost anywhere and eat almost anything.

Unlike most insects, they have mouthparts that enable them to take hard foods, soft foods, and liquids. They will feed on virtually any organic substance. One study, written a century ago and still considered authoritative, lists their food preferences as "Bark, leaves, the pitch of living cycads (fern palms), paper, woolen clothes, sugar, cheese, bread, blacking, oil, lemons, ink, flesh, fish, leather, the dead bodies of other Cockroaches, their own cast skins and empty egg-capsules," adding that "Cucumber, too, they will eat, though it disagrees with them horribly." So much for the cucumber.

DAVID QUAMMEN
"A Republic of Cockroaches"
Natural Acts: A Sidelong View of Science and Nature

It is not just that there is more to do, there is everything to do. Biological science, with medicine bobbing somewhere in its wake, is under way, but only just under way. What lies ahead, or what can lie ahead if the efforts in basic research are continued, is much more than the conquest of human disease or the amplification of agricultural technology or the cultivation of nutrients in the sea. As we learn more about the fundamental processes of living things in general we will learn more about ourselves, including perhaps the ways in which our brains, unmatched by any other neural structures on the planet, achieve the earth's awareness of itself. It may be too much to say that we will become wise through such endeavors, but we can at least come into possession of a level of information upon which a new kind of wisdom might be based. At the moment we are an ignorant species, flummoxed by the puzzles of who we are, where we came from, and what we are for. It is a gamble to bet on science for moving ahead, but it is, in my view, the only game in town.

LEWIS THOMAS, M.D.
"Making Science Work"
Late Night Thoughts on Listening to Mahler's Ninth Symphony

Technology

. . . In Boise, Idaho, amid cattle ranches and potato farms, Pitman started a new semiconductor company with a group of kindred spirits: Juan Benitez, who fled Castro's Cuba at the age of 16 and eventually landed a job in a Kansas City tortilla factory; J. R. Simplot, an eighth-grade dropout who became a billionaire by raising pigs and selling frozen French fried potatoes to McDonald's; and Ward and Joseph Parkinson, twin brothers who had earlier merged their divergent computer and legal careers. Had Albania beaten the United States to the moon, it would not have been a more unlikely story. Tiny Micron Technology, Inc., the company they founded, is producing a 64 dynamic RAM memory chip that is more innovative than comparable chips produced by the powerful companies that dominate the business on both sides of the Pacific. With $20 million in start-up money, Micron had only a fraction of the vast resources of competitors like Intel, Motorola and Hitachi.

A wonder of miniaturization, the Micron chip is the smallest 64K chip on the market. It is only 22,000 square mils, the size of an infant's fingernail and a third smaller than most of its competitors. Yet packed into that minute area, like angels on the head of a pin, are more t in 64,000 memory cells, each of which stores one "bit" of information through the presence or absence of a small electrical charge. . . .

STEPHEN SOLOMON
"The Idaho Chip," *Science Digest* (1983)

One holds the knife as one holds the bow of a cello or a tulip—by the stem. Not palmed or gripped nor grasped, but lightly, with the tips of the fingers. The knife is not for pressing. It is for drawing across the field of skin. Like a slender fish, it waits, at the ready, then, go! It darts, followed by a fine wake of red. The flesh parts, falling away to yellow globules of fat. Even now, after so many times, I still marvel at its power—cold, gleaming, silent. More, I am still struck with a kind of dread that it is I in whose hand the blade travels, that my hand is its vehicle, that yet again this terrible steel-bellied thing and I have conspired for a most unnatural purpose, the laying open of the body of a human being.

A stillness settles in my heart and is carried to my hand. It is the quietude of resolve layered over fear. And it is this resolve that lowers us, my knife and me, deeper and deeper into the person beneath. It is an entry into the body that is nothing like a caress; still, it is among the gentlest of acts....

RICHARD SELZER, M.D.
"The Knife," *Mortal Lessons*

POPULAR CULTURE

Every decade seems to end up, if not begin, with a handle—the "flapper era," the "Vietnam period," the "me generation"—all related to some outstanding event or popular practice. These are not official designations assigned by the government. They are usually invented by some writer about popular culture, someone like Tom Wolfe or Joan Didion who seems to see more clearly and earlier some of our human foibles and behavior patterns. I've written in more detail about this business in earlier chapters about the realities of group life, individual lives, and realism in general.

A writer capable of seeing changes, new directions, new behaviors, new loves, new fads before most of us, can carve out a writing niche for himself or herself. Usually, these writers about popular culture point out our foolishness with humor and affection, but others will sometimes write with snide, nasty, elitist commentary. Unless this latter type write in a masterfully clever way, they usually lose their audience to those who write with affection and understanding. E. B. White, for example, might point (with a slightly embarrassed finger) at the latest fad, but always with good humor, wit, and in a graceful style that makes us love him for pointing out our weakness. This series of examples ends with one by Red Smith, who could always see the minor absurdity where others saw only the major reality.

... I was wearing jeans, a blue shirt, a brown knit tie, a dark-blue sport coat, and Weejuns. We walked into a huge suite of rooms. Lynette Bernay, a wardrobe woman, said, "You're not going to wear jeans on Miami Vice."

"I know that," I said. Did she think I was stupid? "I have another pair of pants up in my room."

"What kind of pants?" she said.

"Brown corduroys," I said.

She shook her head. "Sorry," she said. "No earth tones."

She led me into the complex of rooms where the Miami Vice costumes were kept. I had never seen anything quite like it. The first section I ran into contained ties—more ties together than I had ever witnessed in my life. There were lime-green ties, pink ties, and aqua ties, and light-blue ties, and bright-yellow ties, and ties with birds on them. Beyond the ties were shirts and jackets and pants and dresses—all in the same dizzying array of pastel shades. The clothing stretched on as far as the eye could see. At one end of the room was the shoe department. Eleven rows of long shelves, all displaying men's shoes. White shoes, gray shoes, pink shoes—not the kinds of shoes you would ever wear in the regular world. Lynette Bernay pointed out one pair of shoes to me. "Phil Collins wore these on the show," she said.

BOB GREENE
"Vice Capades" (How a mild-mannered reporter from the Midwest traded in his navy blazer for a sixty-second shot at fame and fortune)
Esquire (July 1986)

Those evenings were high drama. There on a low platform before a large fireplace in the lodge was a white-bearded Old Testament-like prophet in a white jumpsuit asking if anyone wanted to volunteer to work with him. To the amazement of those who wouldn't dare submit themselves to such an ordeal, fully a third of the fifty to a hundred people usually present would raise their hands, eager to sit in what Perls called the "hot seat" and have their psyches laid bare for all to see. Perls distrusted long-term therapy. Sometimes in a matter of minutes, employing a keen theatrical sense and a surgeon's skill, he would cut away every prop that his "victim" habitually used to bolster his or her neurosis, even charm and humor, until nothing was left but the opportunity for an existential leap into a new way of being. At this point, as the victim sat paralyzed on the edge of an abyss, Perls would turn to his audience and, in a thick German accent, utter a classic aside: "Ah, ze impasse." It was stunning. It was just what the people who came to Esalen wanted.

GEORGE LEONARD
"Encounters at the Mind's Edge," *Esquire* (June 1985)

Gene Tulich, seventy-three, a consulting engineer: "I've been commuting to Manhattan since December 1945. When I started, I was coming from Poughkeepsie, a two-hour ride up the Hudson River. I did it because I was a licensed engineer, just back from the war, and New York was where the jobs were. After forty years we still have the unwritten rules of commuting, and they haven't changed much. The main one is: No talking. Especially in the morning. You say hello to the people who sit in the same seats around you every day, then you read your New York Times. If someone new comes on and they're chattering away, you still don't say anything, but you give them, you know, the Look.

"And then there's a rule about the three-seater: the person on the aisle absolutely never slides over to let someone else in; he stands up, and if you want to sit by the window or in the middle, you've got to squeeze by. It's awkward, but once you've staked out your seat, it's your territory. Once, years ago, my wife rode down with me and took up a seat that normally belonged to someone else, and boy, did she get the Look. People will abandon their regular seats only in very unusual circumstances, such as when the person next to them slumps over suddenly, sick or dead, which has happened a few times on trains I've been on. After a few stops the conductor would see a lot of empty seats around this one fellow, and he'd call for an ambulance...."

CHARLES LEERHSEN
"Life on the 6:55," *Esquire* (June 1986)

... A visit was made to the [Madison Square] Garden for the dual purpose of schneering at the other dachshunds and admiring the ladies who are led across the ring by toy breeds. It is a scientific fact that the ladies tethered to the tiny toys are invariably the most magnificent members of the species. No exception was taken in this case; the smallest pooch noted was towing the largest handler, a celestial creature measuring seventeen and a half hands at the withers, deep of chest, with fine, sturdy pasterns.

RED SMITH
"In the Doghouse," in *The Red Smith Reader*

INDEX

263

Boston Globe Hx piece
Blacks who bought suburban homes in 60s
Cyd Nichols –

Brookline?
Lynnette Glover

Milton?

what happened
to Newton's
black neighborhood

at the same time – what
was going on w other
ethnic groups

Why didn't planned
integration catch
on here

What happened
that they got
out & why
didn't more

More helpful books on writing and publishing from Ten Speed Press:

WRITE RIGHT! by Jan Venolia

An indispensable desktop guide, revised and updated for the '90s. Covers basic rules of punctuation and grammar, commonly misused and misspelled words, and essentials of style. "An invaluable tool for executives, secretaries, students...it illustrates the right and wrong ways by easy-to-grasp examples."—*Los Angeles Times*
$5.95, 144 pages

REWRITE RIGHT! by Jan Venolia

How to review, edit, and rewrite any piece to make it clearer and more effective. Special section on non-sexist writing. "With clear writing becoming rare in our society, any helpful style manual is welcome. This is a particularly good one."—*Kliatt Book Reviews*
$6.95, 128 pages

QUOTE UNQUOTE
by Jonathan Williams

A strange and wonderful collection of quotes from the famous to obscure, and the sublime to the ridiculous. "Our most outlandish man of letters' answer to Bartlett's . . . it is unalloyedly delicious."—*Booklist*
$7.95, 144 pages

PUBLISHER'S LUNCH
by Ernest Callenbach

An absolutely original novel about how the publishing industry really works—must reading for all aspiring authors. "The book's pages are filled with practical advice."—*Small Press Magazine*
$7.95 paper or $11.95 cloth, 134 pages

Available from your local bookstore, or order direct from the publisher. Please include $1.25 shipping & handling for the first book, and 50 cents for each additional book. California residents include local sales tax. Write for our free complete catalog of over 400 books and tapes.

TEN SPEED PRESS
Box 7123   Berkeley, Ca 94707